CHILDREN

THEIR TRAINING
AND THEIR HOPE

"Come, ye children,
hearken unto me: I will
teach you the fear of the
Lord."   – *Psalm 34:11.*

"The living, the li[ving]
he shall praise thee, a[s I do]
this day: the father [to the]
children shall make k[nown]
thy truth." – *Isaiah [38:19.]*

By

J. F. RUTHERFORD

AUTHOR OF

SALVATION RELIGION
PROPHECY CREATION
ENEMIES GOVERNMENT
and other books

3,000,000 Edition

PUBLISHERS

WATCHTOWER
BIBLE AND TRACT SOCIETY, INC.
International Bible Students Association
Brooklyn, N. Y., U. S. A.

ALSO

London Cape Town Toronto
Strathfield Berne Copenhagen
and in other countries

DEDICATED
TO THE CREATOR

"THE HEAVEN, EVEN THE HEAVENS, ARE THE LORD'S: BUT THE EARTH HATH HE GIVEN TO THE CHILDREN OF MEN.

"BUT WE WILL BLESS THE LORD FROM THIS TIME FORTH AND FOR EVERMORE. PRAISE THE LORD." — PSALM 115: 16,18.

"The heaven, even the heavens, are the Lord's: but the earth hath he given to the children of men.

"But we will bless the Lord from this time forth and for evermore. Praise the Lord." — Psalm 115:16,18.

CHILDREN

CHAPTER 1
CHILDREN

"Train up a child in the way he should go; and when he is old, he will not depart from it."
— Proverbs 22:6.

THE Aldens and Rogers were neighbors, both descendants of the early settlers of New England. Their forebears had fled from religious persecution that persisted in England and the Continent, and found a place on the American Continent where they might exercise freedom of conscience, freedom of speech, and freedom to worship ALMIGHTY GOD according to the dictates of their own conscience.

Joseph Alden was educated for the law, at which he practiced for a time. Having a strong yearning for the freedom of the wide-open country, he emigrated west, where he became a large landowner. He farmed,

9

and his herds and flocks were numerous. His wife was mentally brilliant, physically strong, and a real helpmate. They builded a home in the West and left the latchstring on the outside, and that home became a place of rest and genuine hospitality. Their eldest son they named John, probably having in mind the meaning of his name.

David Rogers, with his young wife Lois, had located in the neighborhood of the Aldens. Rogers had acquired a tract of land in that vicinity and decided to leave his business in the East and become a farmer in the West, where his children might be reared to a better advantage. His wife Lois was a teacher and was well equipped to train their children. Among their five children was a daughter named Eunice, next to the youngest. Of the five children there were three boys and two girls. It was a well-trained and happy family.

The Alden and Rogers families not only were neighbors but became fast friends. Their children played together and attended school together, and visited frequently at each other's homes. Both families were Christians, as that term is generally understood, but they were not bound by any denominational church ties. The elders of the family had observed so much formalism and hypocrisy in the church denominations that they were glad to rear their children free from such influence. They believed in God

and Christ Jesus, and they had a sincere
desire to bring up their children "in the
nurture and admonition of the Lord".—
Ephesians 6:4.

That obligation they attempted to shoulder and bear faithfully. The parents instructed their children in their respective
homes, and at stated times the two families met together and with their children
participated in a study of the Bible and en-
deavored to instill in the young minds the
fear of God and a devotion to Him. They
frequently, together, joined in the prayer
which Jesus had taught his disciples: 'Thy
kingdom come; thy will be done on earth as
in heaven.' (Matthew 6:10) The children of
the two families were examples for good to
other children who attended the day schools.

John Alden had reached the age of six-
teen years. Eunice Rogers was fourteen
years of age. Both had completed the study
course in the country public school. They
must receive further education. John was
sent away to college. Eunice entered a seminary for young ladies. A four-year course
of study had been planned for each one of
them. Meeting together on a Sunday afternoon just preceding their departure for
their respective places of education John
said to Eunice: "We shall see little of each
other for the next four years, but we shall
not forget each other. I shall endeavor to
make good use of the time to improve my

mind as well as my body, and I know that
you will do likewise. I shall look forward
to seeing you at vacation times"; to all of
which Eunice agreed.

Four Years Later

It was a Sunday afternoon at the Alden
home. The family had met, according to
their custom, for the weekly Bible study
together. It was vacation time and the children were at home. In fact it was a day of
reunion of the two families and a time of
happiness unrestrained. The elders and the
children exhibited the same dignity and so-
lemnity which always marked that home,
yet their faces were beaming with joy and
the speech was pleasing. On this occasion
Joseph Alden presided at the study, in
which all present participated.

Four years had brought a change in all
of them. The parents had grown older, and
the children likewise had changed in ap-
pearance. There was young John Alden,
strong and vigorous, a young man, six feet
in height, and with a muscular rhythm peculiar to athletes; a young man clear of vision, and keen of mind, and with an open
and honest countenance. He was redhead-
ed; which he had inherited from his mother.
He was very respectful and honored his father and mother, and in this he had not
changed from the time of his early youth.

Eunice Rogers was now eighteen and had developed into womanhood of rare beauty. Not only was she beautiful in form, but she was beautiful in her deportment and speech, with dark-brown hair and eyes to match. Clothed in plain and tasteful garments, she was graceful in her every movement, and a delight to those that associated with her. She sat beside her mother during the study. John's eyes frequently turned toward her. Who could condemn him for doing so?

The family study being concluded, John and Eunice went for a long stroll over the wide acres. The time was that beautiful season of the year when the fields were green and the flowers blooming. The air was filled with sweet perfume from the numerous wild roses. The sun shone brightly and the songbirds sung to the glory of the Creator, and apparently they were serenading the young man and the girl who walked by his side. Being just fresh from school, they talked about the commencement exercises and of the diplomas that had been given to the graduates; and that opened the way for discussion of their future activities.

Said John: "True, I am graduated now, but that means but little unless I continue to make progress. The ceremony called 'commencement' is really indicative of the beginning of one's course in life. If one becomes negligent and indifferent he makes no progress and amounts to nothing. If he employs his time and his faculties in the right way he may meet with success and with many attending blessings. Our experience at school is really a means of learning how to study, and from the time of graduation onward one must continue to apply himself diligently to the course he elects to pursue during the remainder of his life. You have asked me, Eunice, what I shall do, what profession I expect to follow, or in what business I shall engage. That matter I will discuss with my father and then decide. The cities have no real attraction for me. What is generally called 'society' appears to me to be entirely empty and means nothing. As to politics, that has become so involved that an honest man must shun it. The fact is, I love these broad fields and the things they contain. The great Creator put them here. They are the handiwork of the Almighty, as our lesson this morning told us. Here we breathe the pure air, eat pure food, indulge in purity of speech, and our friends are sincere. Both of us have grown up in this environment, and I should be loath to leave it. What think you, my childhood companion?"

"Why limit the companionship to childhood?" said Eunice. "True, we have seen little of each other during the past four years, but I dare say that those four years have been well spent, and now we are again together in the land we love, together at least for a time. You mention your father,

John, in such terms of high esteem and your mother with gracious words. That pleases me. They are both noble characters. Many times during my studies of American and English history my mind reverted to the sturdy and faithful men and women who braved the storms of the seas, settled on the cold and bleak shores of New England, and there began the laying of the foundation of a great nation. You know that both my ancestors and yours were among those dear souls. They had respect for law and order, feared and served Almighty God, and loved righteousness. Our parents have inherited these good qualities and have tried to instill them in us. I see them in you, John. May I suggest that you consider well and sincerely before entering the turmoil of the cities. There are many good things to be accomplished in this part of the earth, and you possess the qualifications to accomplish them.

"Is there anything in a name? I think so, if we go to the right source for our information and learning. May I be permitted to suggest, John, that when your parents gave you the name 'John' they must have done so with reverential hearts and with a hope that you would have everything the name implies. As you know, John, your name means 'Jehovah hath been gracious'. Surely the almighty Creator, Jehovah, has been very gracious to you. He has given you a kind, firm and loving father and a devoted mother, and they have reared you properly. He has given you a strong body and a clear mind. He has given you an appreciation of His creation, and this I observe you now appreciate. Otherwise you would not speak as you do of the beauties of this land."

"Eunice, you speak with words of grace. Such become you. I perceive that the silly twaddle so manifest by many girls and boys has not turned your head. You have not departed from your early training. And now permit me to say that your name befits you. Your name 'Eunice' means 'Blessed with victory'. For four years you have been closely associated with those who are given over to the lighter things of life. We both can well bear testimony to the fact that the schools for both men and women instill into the mind of the pupil the theory of evolution of the human race, substituting that tradition proclaimed by such men as Darwin for the sure Word of Almighty God. You have withstood that seductive influence and have disregarded the sneers and reproaches that have fallen upon you and to which all persons who manifest their belief in the inspired Scriptures are subjected. I noted at the study this morning that you still firmly hold to the early teachings we have received from our parents in our homes. You have withstood the influence of the modern educators, who would turn young men and young women away from the early instruction of their parents. Truly, then, you have been and are 'Blessed with victory'.

"I am reminded of even a better and more appropriate meaning of the name Eunice, which it is your good fortune to bear. You will readily recognize the source of my information. What you have said, and what I know of you, well proves that the meaning of the name fits you. You have told me that you were required to attend religious service while at the seminary; that the congregational meetings, and the Sunday morning service in particular, were a dress parade having the earmarks of a social gathering; that the minister seldom mentioned the Bible and never made any attempt to explain it, but talked chiefly of evolution, politics and social problems, quoting liberally from books of worldly writers, and that the entire tendency was to discredit the Bible. Well do I understand and appreciate what you have told me. A like condition exists at all colleges, I believe. Such were the conditions at the college where I have been attending for the past four years. Almost all of the professors, including the ecclesiastical instructors, are higher critics and rely on science and the wisdom of men to lead them to higher things, but I observe that they do not reach great heights."

"Yes, John, often have I propounded to myself the question: Why should a man call himself a minister or a doctor of divinity, claiming to be a servant of God, and never attempting even to instruct the people as to the meaning of the Scriptures? Probably it is because he does not understand the Scriptures himself; but he should not pretend to teach them. The minister at the seminary appeared to be quite popular with almost all who attended his church meetings, and the attendants of his social gatherings spoke many flattering words about him and to him; but I must say that often I have felt so out of place at those so-called 'church services and social gatherings' that I have wanted to run away that I might be alone and meditate upon what our parents have taught us in our homes. From what I have learned it appears that the seminaries and colleges have practically forgotten God, and this includes the ministers and theological teachers. As a result of such teaching almost all of the students have become agnostics or infidels."

"In all those religious services you found no satisfaction, I am sure, Eunice. Your mind has constantly been turned to what you learned at home concerning God, and to that you have held firmly. Now, Eunice, I mention the deeper and better meaning of your name. There was a young man who sat at the feet of the apostle Paul and

learned of him concerning God and Christ
Jesus. Paul was very fond of this young
man and frequently addressed him in loving terms. The mother of that young man
was named Eunice, and Paul referred to
her as a woman of 'unfeigned faith'. You
are just like that. Your faith is real and
genuine, and you have firmly held to that
faith in spite of all the contrary influence
that has been about you. I am glad that my
childhood companion has not forgotten her
early training, and that she has not departed from the instruction received in her early
youth."

To that complimentary speech Eunice did
not reply. The two walked on together and
for some time were silent, evidently medi-
tating upon serious matters. Then, speaking, Eunice said: "John, see yonder great
oak tree, under the boughs of which we so
often played together when we were quite
young. That spot is dear to my heart and
I am sure it is likewise dear to you. There
is a convenient log there where we have
often played together. Let us sit there now
and talk over matters. There is in my mind
a weighty matter that only you can remove.
Let us sit here awhile and renew our ac-
quaintance with this lovely scenery, while
I tell you what I have in mind. We have
been apart from each other for nearly four
years, and in that four years there has been
a constant prayer in my heart concerning

both of us, and which is represented in the word 'Mizpah', the meaning of which we learned when young, and which now we well know: 'The Lord watch between me and thee, when we are absent one from another.' — Genesis 31: 49."

Seated under the spreading boughs of that great oak they engaged in a long conversation. Necessarily it was a private talk and too sacred, no doubt, to be repeated, even if the full text thereof were known. When they arose to resume their walk their faces were serious, but radiant. A solemn covenant had been made between them.

As they walked John interrupted the silent meditations. The birds were filling the air with song, and all nature seemed to be rejoicing. "Eunice, this place seems more beautiful to me on this June day than ever before. I am delighted to be here. Father has suggested that I take some time to recuperate before definitely deciding my future course. Together we have considered several things which I might do. Father thinks it might be well for me to take a post-graduate course and then a course at law. But he often concludes his remarks with something like this: 'I would like that you might be here with me and take charge of these fields and flocks. Some day it must be you to whom I would wish to leave this land. Decide not in haste, my son. You may even wait until the autumn season before making your decision.'

"And now, Eunice, seeing that I shall have many days with no pressing duties to meet I have in mind that which I would like to propose to you. During the past four years our attention has been given chiefly to our duties at school. That done, we now have other important things to consider. I would like to devote some of the time during the months that immediately follow to our studies together. I have come into possession of a number of books, all published by the same publishing society, which claim to be of great aid in the study of the Bible. We have both studied the Bible some, but

COMPANIONS

there is much for us to learn. I know that
the fundamental law of the nation is based
upon the law of Almighty God, as set forth
in the Bible. The early writers in the law
referred to God's law as supreme, and I
am sure that is right. The Bible contains
the statement of God's law, a record of
the prophecies and of the teachings of Jesus and his faithful apostles. In our home
study, which I have so much missed during our stay at school, we learned much,
and I would like to continue our studies.
We are now better equipped to make a personal examination and study, and that with
profit to ourselves. We might take the books
that I mentioned, which will be an aid to
us, at least to locate in the Bible the texts
relating to the subject matter under consideration, and with these books together with
the Bible we can learn much more. Suppose
we spend an hour or more each day in this
study, and I feel sure this will be profitable
for both of us. You would be pleased to join
me in such a study of the Bible?''

"John, since I am to be the mother of
your children, what could be of so great importance to us as a knowledge of the Bible
and how children should be reared? I shall
be more than delighted to join you in that
study. We should be able to learn from the
Word of God our duties as parents and our
obligation toward our children. Well do I
remember the proverb, which I have heard

so often repeated by our parents: 'Train up a child in the way he should go; and when he is old, he will not depart from it.' (Proverbs 22: 6) Another scripture text I recall, which is addressed to parents concerning their children: 'Bring them up in the nurture and admonition of the Lord.' (Ephesians 6: 4) Surely we must gain this proper information before we shall know how to teach our children.''

The two agreed to immediately begin the study of the Bible and to set down in their notebooks the many truths that they learned. What appears in the chapters that follow are in substance the truths that they learned.

CHAPTER 2

THE BIBLE

"Sanctify them through thy truth: thy word is truth."—John 17:17.

IN KEEPING with their agreement the two met and began their study of the Bible. Before beginning John remarked: "We begin this study with open mind, without prejudice and with a sincere desire to learn. I feel that we shall be rewarded for our efforts. There have been on my mind this morning the words written by the apostle of Christ Jesus: 'But we all, with open face beholding as in a glass the glory of the Lord, are changed into the same image from glory to glory, even as by the spirit of the Lord.' (2 Corinthians 3:18) As we look into the Bible we there see reflected the glory of the Lord, because his Word tells

24

of his glory; and thus filling our minds with the precious truths contained in the Bible, we may expect to grow into his likeness, even as the apostle said. And now we shall proceed with our study and set down in our notes what we learn." Citations and quotations herein are from THE BIBLE.

———————

The Lord Jesus had finished his earthly ministry as a man and, addressing his prayer to his Father, Jehovah God, in behalf of his faithful followers, he said: "Sanctify them through thy truth: thy word is truth." (John 17:17) Persons who are sincere and honest desire the truth. Where will the truth be found? In the Bible, as such is the Word of God, which is the truth. Almighty God, Jehovah, inspired holy men of old to write down in the Bible the truths revealed by him for man's benefit: "For not at any time was prophecy brought by the will of man, but men from God spoke, being moved by holy spirit." (2 Peter 1:21, *Diaglott*) "All scripture is given by inspiration of God, and is profitable for doctrine, for reproof, for correction, for instruction in righteousness; that the man of God may be perfect, throughly furnished unto all good works." — 2 Timothy 3:16, 17.

The person who desires the approval of God must be guided aright. The Bible, which contains the Word of God, is true and is the correct guide: "Thy word is a lamp

unto my feet, and a light unto my path."
(Psalm 119:105) The Bible guides sincere
persons to desire and to pray for the most
important things that may result to their
welfare. God has put such prayers into the
mouth of his sincere servants, and one of
these prayers is this: "Shew me thy ways,
O Lord; teach me thy paths. Lead me in
thy truth, and teach me: for thou art the
God of my salvation; on thee do I wait all
the day. Remember, O Lord, thy tender
mercies and thy lovingkindnesses; for they
have been ever of old. Remember not the
sins of my youth, nor my transgressions;
according to thy mercy remember thou me,
for thy goodness' sake, O Lord."—Psalm
25:4-7.

The sure and unfailing promises of God
to such sincere seekers for truth are certain, and God will fulfill those promises;
as it is written: "Good and upright is the
Lord; therefore will he teach sinners in the
way. The meek will he guide in judgment,
and the meek will he teach his way. All the
paths of the Lord are mercy and truth unto
such as keep his covenant and his testimonies." (Psalm 25:8-10) "For the word of
the Lord is right; and all his works are done
in truth." (Psalm 33:4) "For the Lord is
good, his mercy is everlasting; and his truth
endureth to all generations." (Psalm 100:5)
"For thy mercy is great above the heavens;
and thy truth reacheth unto the clouds."

(Psalm 108:4) "Thy righteousness is an everlasting righteousness, and thy law is the truth."— Psalm 119:142.

He who would be wise in things that are right seeks pure knowledge, such as is contained in the Bible: "Wise men lay up knowledge; but the mouth of the foolish is near destruction." (Proverbs 10:14) "Whoso loveth instruction loveth knowledge; but he that hateth reproof is brutish." (Proverbs 12:1) "The heart of the prudent getteth knowledge; and the ear of the wise seeketh knowledge."— Proverbs 18:15.

The person who is wise and pursues a wise and prudent course desires to live forever and enjoy all the blessings which God has provided for those who love him. There is but one way to life, and that way is to receive a knowledge of God and Christ Jesus and then obey the commandments of the Lord and continue to follow in the right way: "And this is life eternal, that they might know thee the only true God, and Jesus Christ, whom thou hast sent." (John 17:3) The person that would please God and live must know that Jehovah is the Almighty God and that Christ Jesus is his great Executive Officer, and he must fear to displease God. Such a person begins to acquire the right kind of knowledge. "The fear of the Lord is the beginning of knowledge; but fools despise wisdom and instruction."—Proverbs 1: 7.

One is foolish to rely upon his own understanding and to ignore the Word of God: "Trust in the Lord with all thine heart; and lean not unto thine own understanding. In all thy ways acknowledge him, and he shall direct thy paths. Be not wise in thine own eyes; fear the Lord, and depart from evil." (Proverbs 3: 5-7) To follow the traditions of men, which are contrary to the Word of God, is to pursue a course of evil.

Authenticity

What is the proof that the Bible contains the authentic record of God's Word? The evidence, which furnishes the conclusive proof, is both circumstantial and direct, and the two kinds of evidence fully corroborate each other. Here the evidence circumstantial and that which is direct will be considered together, and will be found to fully establish the authenticity of the Bible as God's Word.

"The Bible" is the name given to what is written in the sixty-six books bound together and forming one book. It has in reality only one Author, who is God, and its one great purpose is to furnish a guide to man who desires to walk in the way of righteousness and live and to honor his Maker. The "canon" of the Scriptures is the collection or catalogue of the books or writings into one volume, THE BOOK, which sacred writings God has provided; and which is called "The Holy Bible". Such contains the true rule and guide for faithful men. Other writings for which claim has been made as to their genuineness, but which are spurious, are called "the Apocrypha".

The word "canon", from the classic Greek, means "a straight rod or rule". It is a measuring rod. As to the Bible, it means the rule of truth. Concerning this sacred rule the inspired apostle wrote: "And as many as walk according to this *rule,* peace be on them, and mercy, and upon the Israel of God." (Galatians 6:16; see also 2 Corinthians 10:13-16) Without any doubt the spirit of Almighty God directed faithful men to arrange the canon of the Scriptures according to his will. That much could not be said of any other book in existence. All the evidence, when considered together, proves beyond all doubt that the Author of the Holy Scriptures set out in the Bible is Almighty God, whose name is Jehovah, and which name means his purpose toward his creatures.

Moses, as a servant and an amanuensis of God, wrote the five books that appear first in order in the Bible. Moses was selected by Jehovah God as his servant to lead the Israelites out of Egypt. At Mount Sinai God took Moses up into the mountain and there dictated to him the fundamental law, which law was written on stone, and which has been translated and recorded in the Bible.

The Scriptures disclose that God invites man to reason with him (Isaiah 1:18); and the fact that the Creator endowed man with faculties of reason shows that it is proper that man reach a conclusion by process of reasoning in harmony with facts and authority which cannot be disputed. Moses was a learned man, "learned in all the wisdom of the Egyptians." (Acts 7:22) Moses records the fact that God spoke to him and directed him to go into Egypt, saying: "Thus shalt thou say unto the children of Israel, I AM hath sent me unto you." (Exodus 3:14) "I AM" means the Everlasting One, not the One who was, nor the One who will be, but THE ONE WHO IS. The great I AM made known to Moses his name Jehovah, and this was the first time his name was thus revealed.—Exodus 6:2, 3.

The general history of the human kind could well have been known to Moses even before God revealed His great truth to Moses and before Moses was selected to go to Egypt, because of the following circumstances and facts, to wit: Adam was the original man, from whom the race sprang. Adam lived 930 years, and lived 300 years of that time after the birth of Enoch, a man whom God approved. Enoch was the father

of Methuselah, who lived 969 years. Noah
was the third generation from Enoch. He
was a grandson of Methuselah and must
have received much information from his
grandfather. (Genesis 5: 3-32) Noah was
600 years old when the flood came. (Genesis 7: 6) Being devoted to Almighty God,
he would certainly gather all the information he could from his forefathers, and hence
would have a very accurate account of the
race from Adam to Noah's day. That information he would transmit to his sons.

Noah and his sons came out of the ark
together, and Noah lived 350 years thereafter. (Genesis 9: 28, 29) His son Shem lived
502 years after the flood. (Genesis 11: 10, 11)
Two years after Noah's death Abraham was
born, and therefore Shem and Abraham were
on the earth together for a period of 150
years. It is reasonable that Abraham would
learn from Shem the facts concerning the
human race which Shem had received from
his forefathers. Abraham bore the title of
'father of the faithful'; and since knowledge is necessary to faith, Abraham must
have had as the basis of faith the necessary
knowledge from the creation of man until
his day.

Isaac was the beloved son of Abraham
and would no doubt receive faithful instruction from his faithful father. The favorite
son of Isaac was Jacob. (Genesis 28: 5-14)
Jacob had twelve sons, and he bestowed his

HANDING DOWN THE RECORD

greatest affection upon Joseph, evidently by
the Lord's direction. Joseph was a man of
great importance in Egypt and would be
widely known by almost all of the people
of Egypt, and particularly by the Israelites who resided there. Only a few years
after the death of Joseph Moses was born.
When Moses became a man he devoted himself entirely to the Almighty God. It is only
reasonable that Moses was thoroughly fa-
miliar with the history of his forefathers
from the time of Adam to his own time,
when God called him to be the deliverer of
the Israelites. From the human viewpoint,
as shown by the facts and circumstances,
Moses was amply qualified to write the history of mankind from the beginning until
his own day. Intelligent men have a natu-

ral tendency to keep a record of facts and events, and it is but reasonable that Moses had a fund of information duly set down to be passed on to other generations. So much from the human viewpoint.

None of the testimony mentioned here will be accepted by evolutionists or higher critics who have no faith in God. "The fool hath said in his heart, There is no God." (Psalm 14:1) A person does not need to say in words, "There is no God"; but by his own conduct or course of action he discloses his secret thoughts. All visible creation testifies to the indisputable fact that there is a Supreme One who is the Creator, the Almighty God.

The miraculous birth of Jesus, his teachings, his crucifixion and his resurrection out of death are supported by a multitude of witnesses, all of which establish the fact that Jesus was not an ordinary man, but the Son of Almighty God. A host of heavenly angels bore testimony at the time of the birth of the babe Jesus that he is "Christ the Lord". — Luke 2:9-14.

The circumstantial evidence of the miraculous birth of Jesus, and the direct testimony delivered by the man Christ Jesus during the three and more years of his ministry, establishes the authenticity of the Holy Scriptures, or Bible, as the Word of Almighty God. After his resurrection by

the power of Almighty God, Christ Jesus
appeared to his faithful disciples, at which
time he confirmed the words which he had
spoken to them before his death. At the
same time he testified as to the authenticity of what is written in the law and in the
prophecies and in the songs which we call
"Psalms". It was then he said: "These are
the words which I spake unto you, while I
was yet with you, that all things must be
fulfilled, which were written in the law of
Moses, and in the prophets, and in the
psalms, concerning me." — Luke 24: 44.

After his ascension into heaven the Lord
gave to John, his faithful servant, a revelation of the things that must come to pass:
"The Revelation of Jesus Christ, which God
gave unto him, to shew unto his servants
things which must shortly come to pass;
and he sent and signified it by his angel
unto his servant John." — Revelation 1: 1.

Jesus Christ is "The Faithful and True
Witness". (Revelation 1: 5; 3: 14) The testimony of Christ Jesus, therefore, imports
absolute verity. Jehovah, the Almighty God,
sent his Beloved, Jesus, to the earth to tell
the truth, and he told the truth. When standing before the Roman governor, charged with
treason, Jesus testified, to wit: "To this end
was I born, and for this cause came I into
the world, that I should bear witness unto
the truth. Every one that is of the truth
heareth my voice."—John 18: 37.

The testimony of Jesus when he was a man on earth is further proof that the Pentateuch, or the first five books of the Bible, were written by Moses at the dictation of Almighty God. (Malachi 4:4; Matthew 8:4; Mark 1:44; 7:10; 12:26; Luke 5:14; John 3:14; 7:19, 22, 23) After his resurrection out of death, and when Jesus appeared unto his faithful disciples, his testimony to them fully confirmed what he had told them when he was with his disciples: "And beginning at Moses, and all the prophets, he expounded unto them in all the scriptures the things concerning himself."–Luke 24:27.

Not only was Moses the servant of Jehovah and used by Jehovah to write the five books first appearing in the Bible, but he was a prophet of Almighty God and foreshadowed Christ Jesus, the great Prophet. The testimony of Jesus confirms this statement when we note that he said: "Moses . . . wrote of me." The religious leaders amongst the Jews were opposed to Jesus and, addressing them, he said: "Do not think that I will accuse you to the Father: there is one that accuseth you, even Moses, in whom ye trust. For had ye believed Moses, ye would have believed me: for he wrote of me."—John 5:45, 46.

Not only did he say that Moses had written a portion of the Bible and had written of Christ Jesus, but furthermore he testified: "Search the scriptures; for in them ye think ye have eternal life; and they are they which testify of me."—John 5:39.

Moses was a type of Christ Jesus, the great Prophet; which the evidence completely establishes. Addressing his words to the Israelites, the covenant people of God, Moses uttered this prophecy: "The Lord thy God will raise up unto thee a Prophet from the midst of thee, of thy brethren, like unto me; unto him ye shall hearken." (Deuteronomy 18:15) That prophecy is fulfilled in Christ Jesus: "For Moses truly said unto the fathers, A prophet shall the Lord your God raise up unto you of your brethren, like unto me; him shall ye hear in all things, whatsoever he shall say unto you. And it shall come to pass, that every soul, which will not hear that prophet, shall be destroyed from among the people."—Acts 3:22, 23.

Christ Jesus is that great Prophet, who speaks with full authority conferred upon him by his Father, the Almighty God, Jehovah. Repeatedly the testimony given by Jesus shows that his Father, the Almighty God, sent Jesus to the earth and that the testimony of Jesus is in exact accord with the will of his Father. (John 6:38,39) To his learned critics Jesus said: "My doctrine is not mine, but his that sent me." (John 7:16) Jesus always testified to the truth as he was directed by Jehovah.—John 8:28, 29, 42.

The holy spirit, which is the invisible power of Almighty God, moved upon faithful men of old to write what is set forth in the prophecies and which is there written according to the will of Almighty God. This is a guarantee that the prophecies are true. The testimony of Jesus confirms the authenticity of the prophecies. Both the acts and the words of Jesus refer specifically to the prophets; which proves that the prophecies written in times of old, as set out in the Bible, are true. Note some of the things which Jesus did in confirming the words of the prophets recorded in ancient times. (Matthew 4:13-16) Early in his earthly ministry he read from the prophecy of Isaiah 61:1,2, to wit: "The spirit of the Lord God is upon me; because the Lord hath anointed me to preach good tidings unto the meek; he hath sent me to bind up the brokenhearted, to proclaim liberty to the captives, and the opening of the prison to them that are bound; to proclaim the acceptable year of the Lord, and the day of vengeance of our God; to comfort all that mourn." (Isaiah 61:1, 2) "The spirit of the Lord is upon me, because he hath anointed me to preach the gospel to the poor; he hath sent me to heal the brokenhearted, to preach deliverance to the captives, and recovering of sight to the blind,

to set at liberty them that are bruised, to
preach the acceptable year of the Lord."
"And he began to say unto them, This day
is this scripture fulfilled in your ears."
(Luke 4:18, 19, 21) Thus he proved the
authenticity of Isaiah's prophecy.

Jesus in fulfillment of a certain portion
of Isaiah's prophecy healed the sick: "that
it might be fulfilled which was spoken by
Esaias the prophet, saying, Himself took
our infirmities, and bare our sicknesses."
(Matthew 8:17) Thus he directly applies
this prophecy to himself. He repeated the
words of the prophet Malachi and applied
the same to himself: "For this is he of whom
it is written, Behold, I send my messenger
before thy face, which shall prepare thy way
before thee." (Malachi 3:1; Matthew 11:10)
He repeated the prophecy written at Isaiah 42:1-3 and applied the same to himself.
(Matthew 12:17-21) From the prophecy of
Jonah Jesus quoted, fully testifying to the
authenticity of that prophecy. (Matthew 12:
39-41) He referred to the prophecy concerning Solomon and the queen of the south and
then said: "Behold, a greater than Solomon
is here." (Matthew 12:42) Jesus spoke in
parables, "that it might be fulfilled which
was spoken by the prophet," at Psalm
78:2: "I will open my mouth in a parable; I will utter dark sayings of old."—
Matthew 13:31-35.

At Matthew 21: 4, 5 Jesus quoted with approval other prophecies: Zechariah 9: 9 and Isaiah 62: 11. Jesus cited with approval the prophecy of Daniel 9: 27 and Daniel 11: 31. (See Matthew 24: 15.) At the same time he spoke of the conditions in the earth that prevailed in the day of Noah, and told his hearers that a similar state of affairs would again obtain upon earth in "the last days", thus proving the authenticity of the prophecy of Noah and prophesying of "the time of the end". (Matthew 24: 37-39; see also Matthew 27: 9-35) Jesus testified as to the authenticity of the law and of all the holy prophets (Matthew 11: 13), and stated that upon these the two great commandments of God are based. (Matthew 22: 36-40) Having testified to the authenticity of the law and of the prophets, which are set forth in the Holy Scriptures, and having stated that he received these truths from the Almighty God, his Father, Jesus summed up the matter in these authoritative words: "Thy word is truth." — John 17: 17.

For more than three years the twelve apostles of Jesus were personally taught by him. God gave him those apostles, and all except one of them remained faithful. (John 17: 6-10) The testimony is abundant that at Pentecost the faithful apostles received the outpouring of the holy spirit of God in fulfillment of the prophecy uttered by Joel. (Joel 2: 28; Acts 2: 1-21) Inspired and moved by the holy spirit of God, Peter, the apostle, then and there testified that the Lord God had raised Jesus out of death, and then added: "God hath made that same Jesus, whom ye have crucified, both Lord and Christ"; and at the same time cited the prophecy foretelling that great and marvelous act of God. (Acts 2:31-36) Later the apostle Peter wrote concerning the prophets: "Knowing this first, that no prophecy of the scripture is of any private interpretation. For the prophecy came not in old time by the will of man; but holy men of God spake as they were moved by the holy spirit."— 2 Peter 1:20, 21; see also 2 Samuel 23:2.

Paul the apostle, who was made a special ambassador of the Lord Jesus Christ and who was anointed and filled with the holy spirit, under inspiration of the holy spirit testified concerning the authenticity of the Scriptures in these words: "All scripture is given by inspiration of God, and is profitable for doctrine, for reproof, for correction, for instruction in righteousness; that the man of God may be perfect, throughly furnished unto all good works."—2 Timothy 3:16, 17.

Prophecy

The prophecies recorded in the Holy Scriptures are the most conclusive circumstantial evidence of the authenticity of the

Scriptures set forth in the Bible, as human-kind could not foretell with accuracy events coming to pass in the long-distant future. All true prophecy proceeds from the Almighty God, Jehovah. He is perfect in wisdom and knows the end from the beginning: "Known unto God are all his works from the beginning of the world." (Acts 15:18) It was the great Jehovah, the Eternal One, who caused these prophecies to be written according to his will.

The true prophet of God is one who speaks as he is directed by the power of Jehovah to speak. He does not utter man's message, but utters God's message. Christ Jesus is the great Prophet of Jehovah, who speaks with authority from his Father. True prophecy is recorded authoritative words declaring things that must come to pass in future days. It appears that at the time of uttering the prophecies the men who uttered or recorded them did not understand the meaning thereof. But in his own due time God makes known to righteous men the meaning of such prophecies. This is proved by the words of Jesus addressed to his disciples. He had told them what the future years would bring forth, particularly with reference to the end of the world. He instructed them concerning the holy spirit, which God would send after Jesus ascended into heaven, and which he did send upon his faithful servants at

Pentecost. During his last days on earth with his disciples Jesus said to them: "And now I have told you before it come to pass, that, when it is come to pass, ye might believe."—John 14: 29.

That which stands out most prominently in the Bible is its teaching concerning the kingdom of God, and because of its paramount importance Jesus instructed his followers that they should always pray for the coming of that kingdom. (Matthew 6: 9, 10) It is God's kingdom, and necessarily all prophecy concerning that kingdom must proceed from the Almighty God. Christ Jesus is the duly appointed and anointed King of the kingdom of God. All the prophets of God foretell the coming of that kingdom and the King, and point forward to that day as one of greatest importance.

When man was in Eden Jehovah God uttered the first prophecy. (Genesis 3: 14-17) Thereafter he used men who had wholly devoted themselves to God's service to utter prophecy and write it down at his dictation. Under inspiration of the holy spirit God caused Peter to utter the words of prophecy concerning the great King, Christ Jesus, and then to say: "Yea, and all the prophets from Samuel, and those that follow after, as many as have spoken, have likewise foretold of these days." (Acts 3: 24) — Acts 3: 20-26.

Over a period of practically four thousand years men of old who were devoted to God and who prophesied according to God's will foretold the coming of Christ Jesus the Messiah. Not only did they foretell his coming, but they recorded the minute details of the place where he would be born, his ministry, his temptation, his persecution, his suffering, his ignominious death, and his resurrection and exaltation. Such wisdom could proceed only from the Almighty God. The fact that those prophecies were fulfilled exactly as foretold proves the authenticity of the same beyond any question of doubt. (For further discussion of the prophecies see the book *Prophecy*.)

Prophecy of God cannot be understood by men who have no faith in God and in Christ. Such men are blind to the truth. A man who has no faith in God and does not believe God's Word cannot understand the Bible. Such men rely upon their own learning and walk on in the dark. Such men class themselves as higher critics and as evolutionists and base their arguments upon the "science" of evolution. Concerning them God says: 'They are fools.' (Psalm 14: 1) In these latter days the colleges teach evolution concerning man, his creation, and his development, and ignore entirely the Word of God. They are wise in their own conceits, and concerning such the Lord in his Word says: "He taketh the wise in their own craft-

iness; and the counsel of the froward is carried headlong. They meet with darkness in
the daytime, and grope in the noonday as
in the night." (Job 5:13, 14) "The wise men
are ashamed, they are dismayed and taken;
lo, they have rejected the word of the Lord;
and what wisdom is in them?"—Jeremiah
8:9.

_____

"These scriptures, written long ago, certainly and accurately describe the conditions that exist in the colleges today," said
John to Eunice. "There is scarcely a pro-
fessor in the college where I attended that
has any faith whatsoever in God and the
Bible. They teach all the young men and
young women to ignore God and the Bible.
Recently I noticed in the *Literary Digest*
that a poll had been taken of the preach-
ers in the United States and a large ma-
jority of them are evolutionists, deny the
inspiration of the Scriptures, and yet claim
to be ministers of the gospel."

"Certainly, John," said Eunice. "This
proves how wonderfully we have been favored by the Lord in giving us parents who
have taught us from our youth up to have
confidence in God and in the Bible, which
is His Word. Without faith it is impossible
to please God, as it is written in the Scriptures."

"That is true, Eunice, and you are a
woman of true and genuine faith. Seeing

that the professors and other teachers in the schools have ignored the Bible and teach that man is a creature of evolution, I suggest that in our next study we give consideration to the Bible teaching concerning the origin of man and the course that men have taken, and learn just why the present miserable conditions exist amongst the peoples and nations of the earth.''

"Let us do so, John; but may I add one more suggestion before we leave the subject of the Bible as being God's Word. The Bible has withstood the assaults of its enemies for many centuries. This we have learned from profane history. All possible means have been used to destroy the Bible, and all these have failed. And is not that strong circumstantial evidence that God has preserved and kept the Bible for the benefit of the man who desires to know the right way? Certainly the Bible contains the Word of Almighty God, which will endure forever. It is man's only true and safe guide, and he who is wise diligently searches its pages to get an understanding thereof; as the Scriptures themselves point out:

" 'My son, if thou wilt receive my words, and hide my commandments with thee; so that thou incline thine ear unto wisdom, and apply thine heart to understanding; then shalt thou understand the fear of the Lord, and find the knowledge of God. For the Lord giveth wisdom; out of his mouth com-

eth knowledge and understanding. He layeth up sound wisdom for the righteous; he
is a buckler to them that walk uprightly.
He keepeth the paths of judgment, and preserveth the way of his saints. Then shalt
thou understand righteousness, and judgment, and equity; yea, every good path.
When wisdom entereth into thine heart, and
knowledge is pleasant unto thy soul, discretion shall preserve thee, understanding shall
keep thee; to deliver thee from the way of
the evil man, from the man that speaketh
froward things.' (Proverbs 2: 1, 2, 5-12)
'Happy is the man that findeth wisdom,
and the man that getteth understanding.'
(Proverbs 3: 13)"

"Eunice, let me read you this news account which tells of that old religious organization recently destroying 110,000 Bibles, which the British Bible Society had
sent to Spain for distribution amongst the
people. No doubt those Bibles were destroyed to prevent the people from reading them and learning that religion is a
snare, as God has said at Deuteronomy
7: 16. When sincere people learn the truth
contained in the Bible, religious dictators
will no longer be able to hold them within
their confines. This news account reads:

" 'One hundred and ten thousand copies
of the Bible, including Testaments, which
the British and Foreign Bible Society sent
to Spain recently for distribution, were de-

stroyed. Spain, as everybody knows, has had
an unenviable reputation for Bible destruction in years gone by, but this wholesale
pulping of a hundred thousand copies is per-
haps the most glaring example of open hos-
tility to the Book that history records. And
it occurred in 1940! It is exceedingly inter-
esting to note, moreover, that this report,
cabled from London, appeared in the early
morning edition of the New York *Times* of
October 6, but was deleted from the second
and following editions. Who ordered that
it be cut out? What invisible censorship
tried to prevent this highly significant item
of news from reaching the people of this
Protestant country? Can anybody guess?'
—*Signs of the Times,* January 21, 1941.

"That we may give heed to God's Word
and that we may keep some important texts
in mind it seems to be well to here set them
down. This will enable us to appreciate the
truth that God's Word alone is our safe
guide: Psalm 119:160; Proverbs 13:13,14;
John 6:63,68; Psalm 119:9-11; Hebrews
4:12; Psalm 91:4; Deuteronomy 4:2; Proverbs 30:5,6; Revelation 22:18,19; Romans
3:3,4; Mark 7:5-13; Isaiah 46:11; Isaiah
55:10,11; Matthew 24:35; Mark 13:31;
Luke 21:33; 2 Timothy 2:15; John 8:31,
32; Romans 10:17. In frequently reading
these texts we are sure to get a real blessing."

CHAPTER 3

THE CREATURE

"I will praise thee; for I am fearfully and wonderfully made; marvellous are thy works; and that my soul knoweth right well." — Psalm 139:14.

"IF WE are diligent and faithful in our studies of the Bible we shall be pursuing the right course and therefore a wise course. We are learning how to study, and we love to acquire knowledge of that which is good. We have the Bible, which is our perfect guide, and our faith in its Author is strong. We have helps to study the Bible, which have been graciously provided by the Lord. I am glad, Eunice, that you are a woman of genuine faith. I am grateful to the Lord that I have retained the faith that my parents have instilled in me while in my childhood. By the Lord's grace, we shall hold fast this faith and not depart from it.

THE CREATURE   49

"It is written in the Bible: 'Without faith
it is impossible to please [God].' (Hebrews
11: 6) We desire to please God and to have
His approval. The words of the text at
Psalm 139: 14, above set down, were uttered by a man of faith. He was one of the
inspired prophets of Almighty God who
spoke as he was moved by the spirit of God,
and this was his testimony: 'The spirit of
the Lord spake by me, and his word was
in my tongue.' (2 Samuel 23: 2) In the
Psalm he said man is 'fearfully and wonderfully made'. That means that perfect
man was a creature by a superior power.
If those bipeds that pose as professors and
that are teachers of evolution are correct,
then man was evolved from a very small
and insignificant thing. That theory is flatly
contradicted by the Word of Almighty God.
No wonder God says that he will make the
expressed 'wisdom' of such men 'foolish-
ness'. From the information that we have
we well know that the prophet of God uttered the truth, that man is 'fearfully and
wonderfully made'. Our studies in school of
physiology and our observation fully convince us of that fact. Man being a creature,
therefore there must be a Creator."

Who made the man? The Bible answers:
"So God created man in his own image, in
the image of God created he him; male and
female created he them." (Genesis 1: 27)

How did God create man? By his unlimited power, which is invisible to man, and hence by His holy spirit: "Thou sendest forth thy spirit, they are created; and thou renewest the face of the earth." — Psalm 104:30.

He created the man out of the elements of the earth: "And the Lord God formed man of the dust of the ground, and breathed into his nostrils the breath of life; and man became a living soul." (Genesis 2:7) He created the man first, and then the woman. —Genesis 2:18, 21, 22.

The attributes of the Almighty God Jehovah may well be named as these: WISDOM (which is fully proved by the following texts: Proverbs 3:13, 19; Proverbs 2:6, 7; Exodus 31:3; Job 12:9-13; Psalm 104:24; Psalm 136:5); JUSTICE (Psalm 89:14); POWER (Psalm 62:11; 29:4); and LOVE (1 John 4:8). These attributes of God have no limitation. Man was created with a limited degree of wisdom, justice, power and love; hence God created man in his own image and likeness. God has dominion over everything in the universe. God gave man dominion over the lower animals of the earth, but not over his fellow man. (Genesis 1:28) Man is accountable to God for his action.

The religious professors say that man was created with an immortal soul, which is separate and distinct from his organism or body, and that the soul never dies. That doctrine is also entirely false and is completely contradicted by the Word of God. Just here I am reminded of the words written in the Bible: "Let God be true, though every man be false." (Romans 3:4, *Diaglott*) When the words of man contradict the Word of Almighty God we know that the man is false, because God is true and all his works are done in truth.

A specific duty was assigned to man, and he was required by the Lord to be completely obedient to the commandment given. God planted a garden, which he named "Eden", and assigned the man to the duty of caring for that garden. God gave to man the privilege of eating the fruit that grew in that garden, with some exceptions, and which exceptions no doubt were for the purpose of testing man's obedience. "And the Lord God commanded the man, saying, Of every tree of the garden thou mayest freely eat; but of the tree of the knowledge of good and evil, thou shalt not eat of it: for in the day that thou eatest thereof thou shalt surely die."—Genesis 2:16, 17.

The man was disobedient, and God's law must be enforced, and therefore man suffered the penalty. Some persons foolishly charge God with cruelty because he enforced his law by condemning man to death for the offense of "eating an apple". The wrongdoing was not in the apple, but the wrongdoing was in the act of disobeying God's commandment, by eating that which God forbade him to eat. Man therefore with full knowledge sinned, and was justly sentenced to death.

If the religious professors who teach the inherent-immortality soul doctrine are correct their conclusion means that man could not have died, because immortality means that which is not subject to death. It cannot be said that only the body dies and that the soul lives on. It is plainly written in God's Word: 'The soul that sinneth, it shall surely die.' (Ezekiel 18:4) "What man is he that liveth, and shall not see death? shall he deliver his soul from the hand of the grave? Selah."—Psalm 89:48.

What is the distinction between soul and man? There is no difference. Every creature is a soul, and hence a soul is a living, breathing, moving creature. God formed the body and then 'breathed into the nostrils the breath of lives, and man became a living soul'. (Genesis 2:7, *Hebrew*) The body of flesh and the breath, and the blood that courses through the arteries and veins, all together constitute a living creature called "a soul". "The life . . . is in the blood." (Leviticus 17:11) The breath puts in action the lungs and the heart, and the blood is propelled throughout the body and life is sustained; and when man's breath goes out, his heart ceases to act and the man is dead.

It is the soul that is dead. (Ezekiel 18:4, 20) The doctrine of the "immortality of all souls" was invented and taught for the very purpose of deceiving men and reproaching Almighty God, and this was where lying began. The Devil is the author of that lie and the other doctrines springing out of it.

Beginning of Wickedness

A creature once enlightened and who then opposes Almighty God is wicked. God, "whose name alone is Jehovah," is The Creator, The Being, the One who is supreme. He is the only BEING. All intelligent things that exist are creatures. Men frequently use the phrase relative to men and say: 'This is a human being.' But that is entirely out of harmony with the truth. Jehovah God is The Being, the Eternal One, and there is none other. He first created The Logos, his Beloved One, and thereafter used The Logos as his active agent in the creation of all things that are created: 'In the beginning was the Word, and the Word was with the God, and the Word was a god. This was in the beginning with the God. Through it everything was done; and without it not even one thing was done, which has been done.' (John 1:1-3, *Diaglott,* interlinear reading) (John 1:18; Revelation 3:14) The Logos, or Word, is Jesus Christ. (Proverbs 8:22-31) Aside from Almighty God there are no beings, but all are creatures, therefore all are souls. The word "god" means Mighty One. There are many mighty ones called "gods", but there is only one Almighty God, "whose name alone is Jehovah," and who is the Most High: "For thou art great, and doest wondrous things: thou art God alone." (Psalm 86: 10) "One God and Father of all, who is above all, and through all, and in you all." (Ephesians 4: 6) Jehovah is the Self - existing One: "From everlasting to everlasting, thou art God." (Psalm 90: 2) Christ Jesus is a mighty one and therefore a god. Jehovah is The Almighty One and hence greater than Jesus: "For there is one God, and one mediator between God and men, the man Christ Jesus." (1 Timothy 2: 5) Note the scriptures, which we here set down, and which speak of other creatures as "gods": "I have said, Ye are gods; and all of you are children of the Most High."—Psalm 82: 6; John 10: 34-36.

Jesus said of his Father, the Almighty God: "My Father is greater than I." (John 14: 28) Jesus speaks of Jehovah as his Father because the Almighty God is the Life-giver to the Son. Jesus furthermore says: "I and my Father are one." (John 10: 30) Manifestly his words mean that he and his Father are in complete unity or harmony, always acting together, and there are many scriptures that show this, particularly the

declaration of Jesus himself as set forth in
Psalm 40:8.

Among spirit creatures of old there was
one named Lucifer, a mighty one and hence
a god. The name Lucifer means "shining
one, or bright star". The Logos, who is the
Lord Jesus Christ, is called "The Bright
and Morning Star". (Revelation 22:16)
Other spirit creatures are called "stars"
and are mighty ones. (Judges 5:20; Psalm
148:3) Lucifer was entrusted with the obligation and charged with the duty of over-
seeing the creation of the earth. He rebelled
against the Almighty God, and did so willingly and deliberately, and therefore became wicked, and from thenceforth he is
known in the Scriptures by the four names
to wit: *Satan,* which means the opposer of
Almighty God; *Serpent,* meaning deceiv-
er; *Devil,* meaning slanderer; and *Dragon,*
meaning devourer. (Revelation 20:1-3;
12:9) All opposition or rebellion against
Almighty God is sin, and an enlightened
creature who willfully sins is wicked. Lucifer's wickedness was made manifest in the
following manner:

The Almighty God created man and created the earth for man. (Isaiah 45:12, 18)
The man Adam, being perfect, was the highest of earth's creation, and when God laid
the foundation of the earth as the place
of man's habitation there was great joy
amongst the spirit creatures of heaven; as

it is written: "Where wast thou when I laid the foundations of the earth? declare, if thou hast understanding. When the morning stars sang together, and all the sons of God shouted for joy?"—Job 38: 4, 7.

Lucifer was there and beheld the great praise given to the Almighty God by His numerous creatures. Covetousness found a place in the heart of Lucifer; he desired to have the praise that was bestowed upon the Most High. (Jeremiah 51: 13) He set about to oppose Almighty God and to entrap man and bring about his destruction, and for this purpose he used the serpent. Adam and Eve were in Eden and had received God's specific commandment to refrain from disobedience, being informed by the Most High that the eating of a certain fruit would constitute an act of disobedience, punishable with death. (Genesis 2: 17) Lucifer approached Eve and inquired why she did not eat of the fruit that was forbidden. Eve replied: "God hath said, Ye shall not eat of it, neither shall ye touch it, lest ye die." Speaking through the serpent that he might deceive Eve, Lucifer replied to her: "Ye shall not surely die: for God doth know that in the day ye eat thereof, then your eyes shall be opened; and ye shall be as gods, knowing good and evil."—Genesis 3: 1-5.

The woman had a desire to "be as gods", that is, to be as wise as spirit creatures, who possess knowledge superior to that of the human creature. Yielding to that desire, she violated the law of Almighty God, and then Adam joined her in the transgression or sin. That was the beginning of wickedness and also the beginning of religion. It will sound strange to some to say that this was the beginning of religion; but it is the truth. Properly defined, "religion" means the doing of anything contrary to the will of Almighty God. That which induced Eve to take a course contrary to God's commandment was the deception practiced on her by Lucifer, and she yielded because she wanted something that had not been given to her by the Most High. Lucifer and many of the other angelic creatures who became wicked introduced and caused men to practice religion. Following the practice of evil or wicked creatures is a snare, and for that reason Jehovah God said to Israel thereafter that they must keep themselves free from religion, because for them to practice and adopt the religion of the Canaanites, who were under the influence of spirit demons, would be a snare unto them.—Deuteronomy 7:16.

It was Lucifer, now known as Satan that old Serpent, the Devil, that led man into sin, and therefore Lucifer is called "that wicked one". (1 John 2:13,14; 3:12; 5:18, 19) Lucifer was a high and mighty one, and his covetousness led to his degradation and will end in his ultimate destruction. Concerning Lucifer, now the Devil, it is written in the Scriptures: "How art thou fallen from heaven, O Lucifer, son of the morning! how art thou cut down to the ground, which didst weaken the nations! For thou hast said in thine heart, I will ascend into heaven, I will exalt my throne above the stars of God: I will sit also upon the mount of the congregation, in the sides of the north: I will ascend above the heights of the clouds: I will be like the Most High. Yet thou shalt be brought down to hell, to the sides of the pit." (Isaiah 14: 12-15) "Thou hast been in Eden the garden of God; every precious stone was thy covering, the sardius, topaz, and the diamond, the beryl, the onyx, and the jasper, the sapphire, the emerald, and the carbuncle, and gold: the workmanship of thy tabrets and of thy pipes was prepared in thee in the day that thou wast created. Thou art the anointed cherub that covereth; and I have set thee so: thou wast upon the holy mountain of God; thou hast walked up and down in the midst of the stones of fire. Thou wast perfect in thy ways from the day that thou wast created, till iniquity was found in thee." "All they that know thee among the people shall be astonished at thee: thou shalt be a terror, and never shalt thou be any more."—Ezekiel 28: 13-15, 19.

For their disobedience Adam and Eve were sentenced to death, in harmony with God's law or commandment: 'In the day you eat thereof you shall surely die.' They did surely and actually die within that same day that they sinned. A day with the Lord is as a thousand years with man; and within that thousand-year period both of them died. (2 Peter 3:8) Adam and Eve were driven out of the garden of Eden and, as a part of their punishment, required to earn their bread in the sweat of their face and to fight the thistles and thorns. Adam was wicked and died as such, and his end is destruction. (1 Timothy 2:14; Psalm 145:20) At the same time Satan was sentenced to death, but his execution was deferred.

Why was not the judgment of destruction executed against the Devil at the time he was adjudged guilty of death? This has been a much debated question amongst men, but the Scriptures make it quite clear. The Devil, seeing that Adam was not immediately put to death, no doubt reasoned that God could not put him to death and be consistent. Satan would reason, 'If God puts Adam to death, that is an admission that His creation is not perfect. If he does not put him to death, then that means that his word cannot be trusted.' Satan would reason that, however the matter turned out, he would be able to prove that God is not all-powerful, and therefore that He could not put a man on earth who would remain true and faithful to God. In earth and in heaven, then, all creation would look upon God as imperfect, hence not all-powerful, all-wise, and all-just, and therefore all creation would give honor and glory to Satan because Satan had thus exposed God. This conclusion of his is justified from the course he took. Satan then challenged Almighty God, saying in substance that God could not put a man on earth who would remain faithful and true to Him; that Satan could cause all men to curse God: "And Satan answered the Lord, and said, Skin for skin; yea, all that a man hath will he give for his life. But put forth thine hand now, and touch his bone and his flesh, and he will curse thee to thy face."—Job 2:4, 5.

That challenge raised the question as to who is supreme. To accept Satan's challenge and give him an opportunity to prove his challenge, and his failing to prove the same, such would show Satan to be a liar, would establish in the minds of creation that God is supreme, and would furnish them a basis for their faith and obedience. God did accept Satan's challenge and announced to Satan at the time that in due time He would have the testimony delivered throughout the earth that God is all-powerful and that then he would exercise his power in destroying Satan and all his works. This record appears in the Bible, wherein God said to Satan:

'For this cause have I permitted thee to remain; to show thee my power, and that my name may be declared throughout all the earth.' (Exodus 9: 16, *Leeser*) That certainly means that God would permit Satan a free hand to do all he could in opposition to Jehovah and against mankind and that in due time God would prove Satan a liar and himself supreme, and prove this to the satisfaction of all creation that love righteousness. God did not permit Satan to continue his wickedness for Satan's benefit, but he did it to furnish an opportunity to all creation to choose between right and wrong and thus prove their own integrity toward Him, and those proving their integrity would be rewarded by life everlasting, and those who hold to the Devil would with him suffer everlasting destruction. The permission of wickedness in the earth over the centuries past, therefore, has afforded the opportunity to all creatures to prove their integrity toward God; and those failing or refusing to do so, thereby prove themselves entirely unworthy of life everlasting. It is further proved that the soul is not immortal and that a creature cannot be willfully wicked and continue to live on forever. It establishes the rule that only those who render themselves willingly in obedience to Almighty God can have life everlasting.

Inherit Death

When Adam and Eve were perfect and in Eden, and before sin had entered, God gave to them this commandment: "Be fruitful, and multiply, and replenish [fill] the earth." (Genesis 1:28) Nothing was done to carry out that commandment while they were in Eden. Not until after Adam and his wife were sentenced to death and driven from Eden did they make any attempt to carry out that divine commandment. It was the imperfect man and woman, sentenced to death, that began to exercise their God-given power to bring children into the world. Cain was the first one born, and then Abel was born. (Genesis 4:1, 2) The test upon human creatures raised by the Devil's challenge began immediately. Cain yielded to the influence of the Devil and murdered his brother. Abel chose to serve God; and his faith and obedience were counted unto him as righteousness. Thus he received God's approval. (Hebrews 11:4) When Lucifer, before he became the Devil, was made overlord he was given "the power of death", which power he thereafter retained. (Hebrews 2:14) By inducing Cain to be obedient to him, and seeing that Abel was faithful to God, the Devil chose to murder Abel in order to carry out his wicked challenge. The Devil is the one that was responsible for the murder of Abel. The Lord

Jesus thereafter stated authoritatively that Abel was a righteous man and that the Devil was a liar, and a murderer from the beginning. (Matthew 23:35; John 8:44) This statement by the Lord Jesus is further proof of the authenticity of the Genesis record. This Divine Record also proves that the Almighty God permits human creatures to choose for themselves whom they will serve and thus the opportunity is afforded to intelligent creatures to fix their own destiny. Those who prove their integrity toward God are rewarded with life everlasting. The Devil has exercised a powerful influence over humankind throughout all the centuries, and God has left the people free to serve whom they might choose. Therefore it is written in the Scriptures: "Know ye not, that to whom ye yield yourselves servants to obey, his servants ye are to whom ye obey; whether of sin unto death, or of obedience unto righteousness?"—Romans 6:16.

From Abel to the time of the flood was a period of more than 1600 years, and within that time only three men, as shown by the Bible record, chose to serve God. The names of those men are Abel, Enoch and Noah. Noah's sons, as later appeared, went with their father Noah, but the three men above mentioned are specifically named. All the other human creatures, as well as many spirit creatures, within that period of time

CAIN WROTH WITH ABEL

fell under the influence and power of the Devil. No doubt the Devil concluded that he was progressing well in proving his own greatness and superiority over Jehovah God.

Satan seduced many of the angels and led many of them into wickedness; and this shows his attempt to turn all creation against the Most High, Jehovah. The angels that became wicked are designated in the Scriptures as demons, with Satan the Devil as the chief of demons. (Matthew 12:24) These demons at all times have exercised influence and control over human creatures. It is those demons, of which Satan is the chief, that have caused men to practice religion, the purpose being to cause the worship of creatures instead of the Creator and thus to bring about reproach to the name of Almighty God. It is the Word of

God that leads men into the way of salvation, and the following scripture shows that men, influenced by wicked angels, have turned to religion and worshiped the creature rather than the Creator and thus have brought reproach upon Almighty God. "For the wrath of God is revealed from heaven against all ungodliness and unrighteousness of men, who hold the truth in unrighteousness; because that which may be known of God is manifest in them; for God hath shewed it unto them. For the invisible things of him from the creation of the world are clearly seen, being understood by the things that are made, even his eternal power and Godhead; so that they are without excuse; because that, when they knew God, they glorified him not as God, neither were thankful; but became vain in their imaginations, and their foolish heart was darkened: professing themselves to be wise, they became fools, and changed the glory of the uncorruptible God into an image made like to corruptible man, and to birds, and fourfooted beasts, and creeping things. Wherefore God also gave them up to uncleanness through the lusts of their own hearts, to dishonour their own bodies between themselves: who changed the truth of God into a lie, and worshipped and served the creature more than the Creator, who is blessed for ever. Amen."—Romans 1: 18-25.

Yielding to the influence of demons, all men on earth, with only a few exceptions, became wicked, and in Noah's day "God saw that the wickedness of man was great . . . and the earth was filled with violence". The exception was Noah; as it is further written: "Noah was a just man, and perfect in his generations, and Noah walked with God." (Genesis 6:1-12) Thus Noah and those who were with him chose the way of righteousness, while those choosing to serve the Devil and oppose Almighty God are doomed to destruction. (2 Peter 2:12) The Almighty God now would express his wrath against the willfully wicked and at the same time make a great prophetic picture foretelling what would be the end of all the wicked nations and peoples of the earth, including the Devil and other wicked demons. Therefore the Almighty God brought the great flood of waters upon the earth and destroyed all human creatures, save only Noah and the members of his family, who had shown their faith in God and chosen to be obedient to the Almighty God. (Genesis 7:1-23) That flood was a type or prophetic picture showing what God's purpose is concerning the wicked and that he will destroy all such at Armageddon, "the battle of that great day of God Almighty," and these truths he has made clear to those who love him and who are now on the earth.

—1 Corinthians 10:11; Romans 15:4; Revelation 16:13-16; 2 Peter 3:6-12.

Noah and his family were carried over the flood in the ark, which Noah had built at the command of Jehovah God, and which ark was a type or prophetic picture of the organization of Jehovah God under Christ Jesus. Thereafter God gave this commandment to Noah and to his sons: "And you, be ye fruitful, and multiply; bring forth abundantly in the earth, and multiply therein."—Genesis 9:7.

Again the human race increased in the earth, and the Devil was busy to see to it that men were turned away from the Almighty God. To accomplish his wicked purpose the Devil organized men into a religious body. Nimrod, a very wicked man, became the dictator of the organized nation of Babylon and not only ruled the people with an iron hand but caused the people to worship him, and hence it was claimed for Nimrod that he was a god and mighty one in the earth: "A mighty hunter before [that is, greater than] the Lord." (Genesis 10:8, 9) Thereafter every nation fell under the powerful influence of the demons, led by Satan their chief, and practiced demonism, otherwise called "religion", which reproached the name of Almighty God and turned the people into wickedness. The purpose of such on the part of the demons was to turn the human race against God and lead them into destruction.

By nature human creatures desire to look up to and worship some higher power, and the Devil has chosen religion as being the easiest means of deceiving the people and turning them away from God by causing them to worship anything, such as images, and to bow down to such, that they might be turned away from God. The Devil has made the most of it, deceiving the people, and has made them think that they were worshiping God, when in fact they were worshiping the Devil. Therefore "religion" clearly means the doing or practicing of anything that is contrary to the will of God or that which tends to turn men away from Almighty God and the worship of the Most High. At the present time there are hundreds of religions practiced in the earth and many of the practitioners thereof think they are serving the Lord God. Because they are in darkness as to God's purpose they are under the influence and power of the Devil and have been turned away from God. None of them in fact serve the Most High, because they follow the traditions of men and ignore the Word of God, which is the only true guide. To learn of the purpose of Jehovah toward mankind one must have an honest and sincere desire to know the truth and then be diligent in seeking to know the truth, and the only way to learn is to study God's word as set forth in the Bible. Therefore searchers for truth must believe that Jehovah God is the Almighty and that the Bible contains his Word of truth. The man who continues to hold to the doctrine of evolution concerning man will never know the truth, but will continue in darkness concerning God's purpose.

Due to Adam's sin, the result of which has been inherited by his offspring, all human creatures have been born in sin under the condemnation of death. Even an imperfect man, however, can have a sincere desire to know and to serve the Almighty God and, then doing so, he may receive the favor of God. Abel was imperfect at his birth, but he had a sincere heart's desire to serve the great Almighty God, and because of his faith and obedience to God he was counted a righteous man. It is even so with all who entirely devote themselves to Almighty God, exercising faith and obedience. Adam and Eve were under the curse of death when their children were born, and necessarily their children were born imperfect: "Behold, I was shapen in iniquity, and in sin did my mother conceive me." (Psalm 51:5) "Wherefore, as by one man sin entered into the world, and death by sin; and so death passed upon all men, for that all have sinned."—Romans 5:12.

The Scriptures abundantly testify that every human creature has inherited death from Adam and, death being the penalty imposed for sin, therefore every human creature must die and must remain forever dead unless the Almighty God provides a means for man to gain life. The Bible abounds with testimony that God has made and provided the means whereby sinful human creatures may be set free from sin and gain life everlasting. The condition upon which a human creature may obtain life everlasting is set forth in the Bible. For this reason a study of the Bible is of greatest importance to anyone who desires to live.

Where Are the Dead?

When Adam died, where did he go? Being a willful wrongdoer, he was destroyed. He chose to serve the Devil and, being wicked, he suffered destruction, as the judgment of Almighty God provides. (Psalm 145: 20) Did not Adam's soul survive somewhere? No; for the reason that Adam did not possess a soul. Adam was a soul, a man, a breathing creature, and when he died it was the soul that died, and that meant everything concerning Adam. Adam, therefore, went completely out of existence.

The doctrine of the "inherent immortality of all souls" is a lie, the great lie first told by the Devil, "that old Serpent," for-the very purpose of deceiving mankind and bringing reproach upon the Almighty God. That lie of the Devil brought about the death of Adam and millions of others since. Hence Jesus said of the Devil that "he was a murderer from the beginning, and abode not in the truth, because there is no truth in him. When he speaketh a lie, he speaketh of his own: for he is a liar, and the father of it". (John 8: 44) While the Devil possesses the power of death, the Devil himself is not immortal. God has entered his judgment of destruction against the Devil, and in due time the Devil shall be completely destroyed; and in execution of that judgment the Lord Jesus Christ will destroy the Devil; as it is written: "Forasmuch then as the children are partakers of flesh and blood, he also himself likewise took part of the same; that through death he might destroy him that had the power of death, that is, the devil." (Hebrews 2: 14) The angels are not immortal, and those spirit creatures that follow the Devil in rebellion shall suffer destruction.—2 Peter 2: 4; Jude 6.

The religious doctrine that the dead are conscious in "purgatory" or in the "hell of torment", undergoing conscious punishment, is entirely false and is the fruit of the Devil's first lie. "Purgatory" is a demoniacal myth that never had a semblance of existence. As to "eternal torment", there is no such place. "Hell," as that word appears in the Bible, means the grave, or tomb, the condition of death or destruction. There is no consciousness in "purgatory" or in hell, and concerning this the Scriptures plainly testify, to wit: "For the living know that they shall die: but the dead know not any thing, neither have they any more a reward, for the memory of them is forgotten. Whatsoever thy hand findeth to do, do it with thy might; for there is no work, nor device, nor knowledge, nor wisdom, in the grave, whither thou goest." (Ecclesiastes 9:5, 10) "The dead praise not the Lord, neither any that go down into silence." (Psalm 115:17) "What man is he that liveth, and shall not see death? shall he deliver his soul from the hand of the grave? Selah."—Psalm 89:48.

The Scriptures abundantly testify that God has provided a resurrection out of death for those who obey him. If those who have died are alive somewhere, then they could not be resurrected, because "resurrection" means coming out of death and standing up to life. The doctrine of "inherent immortality", therefore, would make God a liar; and we know that God cannot lie. This is further evidence that the doctrine of inherent immortality of men originated with the Devil. The Lord Jesus is always obedient to His Father. God raised Jesus out of death; as it is written in the

Bible: 'Christ is risen from the dead, and become the firstfruits of them that slept [in death]; for since by man [Adam] came death, by man [Christ Jesus] came also the resurrection of the dead; for as in Adam all die, even so all in Christ shall be made alive; but every man in his own order; Christ the firstfruits, and afterwards they that are Christ's at his coming.'—1 Corinthians 15: 20-23.

"Immortality" means that which cannot die. Who, then, is immortal? The infallible Word of God answers: 'God only hath immortality.' (1 Timothy 6: 16) Clearly this establishes the fact that all who receive immortality must receive it from Almighty God and that none have it inherently. When Almighty God raised Jesus out of death he clothed Christ Jesus with immortality and gave to him a name above every name, and therefore Jesus is "alive for evermore". (Philippians 2: 9-11; Revelation 1: 18) The faithful followers of Christ Jesus, who continue faithful even unto death, shall be raised from the dead and made immortal, by the grace and power of Almighty God. (1 Corinthians 15: 42-44) Resurrection to immortality is the crown of life, the great gift of Jehovah God to those faithful followers of Christ Jesus even unto death, according to the promise made by the Lord. "Be thou faithful unto death, and I will give thee the crown of life." (Revelation

2:10, *Am. Rev. Ver.*) The fact that immortality is the great gift of God to faithful creatures who shall be associated with Christ Jesus is proof conclusive that no man has immortality.

The Devil's lie of inherent immortality of all souls is the only means by which the false and wicked doctrine of conscious torment in "purgatory" or hell could possibly be supported. Therefore the Devil is responsible for the false teaching of conscious torment after death, which false teaching is used by religionists to frighten human creatures, causing them to serve men and to defame God's holy name.

The dead are out of existence. The only way for any of the dead to live again is to receive the gift of life from Almighty God, administered to them by and through Christ Jesus: "For the wages of sin is death; but the gift of God is eternal life, through Jesus Christ our Lord."—Romans 6:23.

All who desire to live will give heed to the words of the Lord Jesus Christ, to wit: "And this is life eternal, that they might know thee the only true God, and Jesus Christ, whom thou hast sent." (John 17:3) There is no other way to life save that which God has provided by and through Christ Jesus. To the religious leaders of Israel, who brought about the crucifixion of Jesus, these words of authority are addressed, to wit: "Be it known unto you all, and to all the people of Israel, that by the name of Jesus Christ of Nazareth, whom ye crucified, whom God raised from the dead, even by him doth this man stand here before you whole. This is the stone which was set at nought of you builders, which is become the head of the corner. Neither is there salvation in any other; for there is none other name under heaven given among men, whereby we must be saved.''—Acts 4: 10-12.

"These emphatic scriptures are plain and convincing," said John, "and, Eunice, in our next study, let us look well unto the record which tells of God's purpose to give life to those who obey him. The traditions of men, which mean 'human wisdom', so called, have served as a means of leading millions into darkness. Although the kingdom of God is of such great importance to humankind, seldom, if ever, do we hear anything said about God's kingdom. In our next study let us look carefully into this and set down in our notebooks the important and enlightening points that show how God will grant life to obedient human creatures."

CHAPTER 4

THE HOLY CITY

"Great is the Lord, and greatly to
be praised in the city of our God,
in the mountain of his holiness.
Beautiful for situation, the joy of
the whole earth, is mount Zion,
on the sides of the north, the city
of the great King. God is known
in her palaces for a refuge"
— Psalm 48:1-3.

IN SYMBOLIC phrase a
"city" is an organization that governs.
"The city of our God," as stated in the
foregoing text, is the government of holiness that shall govern the world in righteousness. A "mountain" is also used as a
symbol of God's organization, and in the
foregoing text is called "mount Zion",
which is "beautiful for situation". It is
the city of the New Jerusalem, the Holy
City, and of which Jerusalem, established
by the Lord God in Palestine, was a type.
The Lord Jesus Christ revealed to his servant John the importance, the glory and the
beauty of that holy organization, and concerning which John wrote: "And I saw a
new heaven and a new earth: for the first

76

heaven and the first earth were passed away;
and there was no more sea. And I John saw
the holy city, new Jerusalem, coming down
from God out of heaven, prepared as a bride
adorned for her husband. And I heard a
great voice out of heaven, saying, Behold,
the tabernacle of God is with men, and he
will dwell with them, and they shall be his
people, and God himself shall be with them,
and be their God. And God shall wipe away
all tears from their eyes; and there shall be
no more death, neither sorrow, nor crying,
neither shall there be any more pain: for
the former things are passed away. And he
that sat upon the throne said, Behold, I
make all things new. And he said unto me,
Write; for these words are true and faithful."—Revelation 21: 1-5.

The Almighty God is the builder of the
Holy City, "a city which hath foundations,
whose builder and maker is God." (Hebrews 11: 10) It is the capital organization
of the Most High, and over which Jehovah has made his beloved Son, Christ Jesus,
Head, Lord and King. Every whit thereof
is dedicated to the Holy One, Jehovah, and
to his service and to his glory for ever. That
city or organization is the kingdom of the
Almighty God, for the coming of which Jesus instructed his followers to continuously
pray. (Matthew 6: 10) It is Jehovah's government, through which he will vindicate
the name of Him who ministers the bless-

ings of life, and by which the world shall in due time be ruled in righteousness. It is created a city up in heaven, and comes down "from God out of heaven" to take charge of and rule the earth. The Holy City, or Kingdom, is the most important doctrine set forth in the Bible. Every person who loves righteousness and who desires life will diligently seek to inform himself of that great and glorious city. In this study we shall learn of the manifestation of God's loving-kindness and the revelation of his provision for the vindication of his name, for the government of the world in righteousness, and for the ministration of life to obedient men.

In our last study we learned of the expression of God's wrath against wickedness in the great deluge that destroyed all flesh upon the earth, save Noah and his family. The great flood was dried up and Noah and his sons came forth from the ark, by which means they had been brought over from the old world to the new world beginning. Then Noah and his sons began to carry out the divine mandate to multiply, and at the end of 427 years there were many human creatures on the earth. (Genesis 11: 10-31) Then it was that Almighty God began to make pictures pointing to the building of the Holy City, his capital organization. God took Abraham out of his native land and sent him into a strange land called

"Canaan", and concerning this it is written: "Now the Lord had said unto Abram, Get thee out of thy country, and from thy kindred, and from thy father's house, unto a land that I will shew thee: and I will make of thee a great nation, and I will bless thee, and make thy name great; and thou shalt be a blessing: and I will bless them that bless thee, and curse him that curseth thee; and in thee shall all families of the earth be blessed. So Abram departed, as the Lord had spoken unto him; and Lot went with him: and Abram was seventy and five years old when he departed out of Haran. And Abram took Sarai his wife, and Lot his brother's son, and all their substance that they had gathered, and the souls that they had gotten in Haran: and they went forth to go into the land of Canaan; and into the land of Canaan they came."—Genesis 12: 1-5.

In that great prophetic drama, which God began with Abraham, whom he led into a strange land, Abraham pictured God himself, while Sarah his wife played the part picturing God's organization. In that prophetic drama their son Isaac pictured the beloved Son of God, Christ Jesus. Abraham and his wife did not understand the meaning of the parts they were playing in that great drama, and neither did Isaac, but they all had faith in God and obeyed him. This is also proof that only those who have faith in God and obey him can receive his blessings. A brief record of this drama is written by one of the faithful apostles of the Lord Jesus Christ, wherein this statement is made, to wit: "By faith Abraham, when he was called to go out into a place which he should after receive for an inheritance, obeyed; and he went out, not knowing whither he went. By faith he sojourned in the land of promise, as in a strange country, dwelling in tabernacles with Isaac and Jacob, the heirs with him of the same promise; for he looked for a city which hath foundations, whose builder and maker is God. Through faith also Sara herself received strength to conceive seed, and was delivered of a child when she was past age, because she judged him faithful who had promised. Therefore sprang there even of one, and him as good as dead, so many as the stars of the sky in multitude, and as the sand which is by the sea shore innumerable." (Hebrews 11:8-12) Even though Sarah had passed the age of childbearing and her husband was old, yet they both had faith in God that he would make good his promise. — Genesis 12:1-3; 18:1-11; 21:1-7.

As that prophetic drama progressed God put Abraham to a great test of faith. The son Isaac had grown up, and he was the only son of Abraham and Sarah and, to be sure, they loved him dearly. God then commanded Abraham to build an altar and to offer up Isaac his son thereon as a living sacrifice. Abraham, having great faith in God, obeyed to the point of striking dead his own son and offering him upon the altar of fire. Because of his faith and obedience to that point God sent his angel, who held back the hand of Abraham and prevented him from striking dead his son. This part of the prophetic drama foretold the sacrificial death and resurrection of the beloved Son of Almighty God, Christ Jesus, and pointed to him as the one who should be the Savior of the world. (Genesis 22:1-18) "By faith Abraham, when he was tried, offered up Isaac; and he that had received the promises offered up his only begotten son, of whom it was said, That in Isaac shall thy seed be called; accounting that God was able to raise him up, even from the dead; from whence also he received him in a figure." (Hebrews 11:17-19)—Galatians 4:22-28.

Jacob, the son of Isaac, succeeded as heir to the promise which God had made to Abraham. (Hebrews 11:9) God changed the name of Jacob to that of "Israel", which latter name means "prince of God". (Genesis 32:28, 29, *margin*) Later, under God's direction, the descendants of Jacob, now known as "Israel", were domiciled in Egypt, where they remained for some years and were greatly oppressed by the Egyptian rulers. Hearing their cries for help,

God appointed Moses and sent him to lead the Israelites out of Egypt and deliver them. (Exodus 3:9-22) Here another drama was performed and Moses therein played a part picturing Christ Jesus, the Deliverer of his faithful followers from the wicked world into the kingdom of God's dear Son.

Typical

A "type" is that which represents something greater that is to follow. The Lord God caused to be made and recorded in his Word types or prophetic pictures of things that would come to pass in the development of his holy city, his great kingdom or government. He organized the people of Israel into a nation, with himself as the supreme ruler and with Moses as the mediator and visible representative of the Most High. It was to Moses that the Almighty first revealed himself by the name Jehovah, which name means His purpose toward mankind. (Exodus 6:3-8) In Egypt he made a covenant with the Israelites, and at Mount Sinai confirmed that covenant. He gave to that people his promise that if they would obey him they should be to him a holy nation, a peculiar people, and the recipients of his blessings: "Now therefore, if ye will obey my voice indeed, and keep my covenant, then ye shall be a peculiar treasure unto me above all people: for all the earth is mine. And ye shall be unto me a kingdom of priests, and an holy nation." "These are the words which thou shalt speak unto the children of Israel."—Exodus 19: 5, 6.

His chosen people were then under the leadership of Moses, journeying toward the land of Canaan, the land of promise, where later Jerusalem was made the typical holy city. For the protection of his typical people, the Israelites, and to safeguard them from demon gods and their religious practices, the Almighty God caused Moses to declare unto them His law, to wit: "And God spake all these words, saying, I am the Lord thy God, which have brought thee out of the land of Egypt, out of the house of bondage. Thou shalt have no other gods before me. Thou shalt not make unto thee any graven image, or any likeness of any thing that is in heaven above, or that is in the earth beneath, or that is in the water under the earth; thou shalt not bow down thyself to them, nor serve them; for I the Lord thy God am a jealous God, visiting the iniquity of the fathers upon the children unto the third and fourth generation of them that hate me; and shewing mercy unto thousands of them that love me, and keep my commandments."— Exodus 20: 1-6.

Had the Israelites been faithful to their covenant and obedient to God's law, that nation would have survived. They were overreached by the Devil and other demons and repeatedly fell under the influence of the demons, turned away from the service and worship of Almighty God, and practiced religion or demonism. When they repented and cried unto God for help, Jehovah extended his mercy and favor to them again. Time and again they fell away from God under the influence of demonism or religion. They continued to mingle with the heathen nations that practiced demonism or religion and were ensnared by that practice, as God had plainly warned them they would be: "And they served their idols; which were a snare unto them." (Psalm 106:36) For their disobedience and continuous practice of idolatry God destroyed the Israelites as a nation. Only a remnant of that people remained faithful to God and were blessed by him.

To the Israelites God sent his prophets, who were holy men, entirely devoted to Almighty God, and who obeyed his Word. Under inspiration and commandment of the Almighty God those holy men uttered prophecy or prophecies of God foretelling Jehovah's purpose to set up his holy city or kingdom and foretelling that his Anointed One, the Messiah, would be the Head and Ruler thereof. All things that were written in the prophecies and in the law of God were there recorded specifically for the benefit of those persons who would devote themselves to Almighty God and to his service, and who would be on earth at the time of the setting up of the Kingdom, or the Holy City. The dramas in which the Israelites and others played parts were recorded to enable the faithful servants of God, who should be on earth at the end of the world, to have a better understanding of God's purpose concerning them. Therefore it is written: "Now all these things happened unto them for ensamples [types (*margin*)]; and they are written for our admonition, upon whom the ends of the world are come." (1 Corinthians 10:11) This shows that the nation of Israel was a typical nation or people, used by Jehovah to make pictures or prophetic dramas foretelling greater things to come to pass at the time of the setting up of his kingdom, the Holy City, Zion.

The "end of the world" means the end of Satan's uninterrupted rule. For centuries Satan has exercised ruling power over the world without hindrance. In 1914 Christ Jesus was enthroned by Jehovah. That marks the end of the uninterrupted rule of Satan, which is to be followed soon by Armageddon. It is at the end of that time when the Holy City begins to come down from God out of heaven. It is the time of the coming of the great Messiah to oust Satan and to put in operation the kingdom of righteousness. By his prophets God foretold that at that "time of the end" the boastful, self-constituted "wise men" of the earth would be in total darkness as to the purpose of Almighty God; that they would reject the Bible, and that they could not understand the truth, and would join themselves wholly to the Devil and his organization. By His prophecies He also foretold that those who at that time would take the wise course and give heed to the instruction of the Most High as recorded in the Scriptures, and who would be obedient, such should have the light of truth and should understand the truth. Therefore to those devoted servants of God on earth at this time of the building up of Zion, the Holy City, this prophecy is directed, to wit: "Arise, shine; for thy light is come, and the glory of the Lord is risen upon thee. For, behold, the darkness shall cover the earth, and gross darkness the people; but the Lord shall arise upon thee, and his glory shall be seen upon thee."—Isaiah 60: 1, 2.

By another prophet the Lord God foretells the coming of the great Messiah, the blindness of the wicked, and the understanding of those who should be righteous: "And at that time shall Michael [mighty King] stand up, the great prince which standeth for the children of thy people; and there shall be a time of trouble, such as never was since there was a nation even to that same time: and at that time thy people shall be delivered, every one that shall be found written in the book. . . . And he said, Go

thy way, Daniel; for the words are closed
up and sealed till the time of the end. Many
shall be purified, and made white, and tried;
but the wicked shall do wickedly; and none
of the wicked shall understand; *but the wise
shall understand.*"—Daniel 12: 1, 9, 10.

These prophecies show how marvelously
God has carried out his purpose to the building of his holy city and the enlightenment
of those who have been diligent in obedience
to his commandments and in their service
to God and Christ. Such are permitted to
understand.

A college education does not make a man
"wise", as that word is used in the Bible.
The man who gives his heart to God and
devotes himself wholly to the service of God
and Christ Jesus in obedience to the commandments of the Lord is a wise person,
because he is taking the wise course. He
fears to displease God and always seeks to
please the Most High by obeying his commandments: "The fear of the Lord is the
beginning of wisdom; and the knowledge
of the holy is understanding."— Proverbs
9: 10.

The present is the time when those who
have taken the wise course can understand
and appreciate the purposes of Jehovah.
When studying what is written in the Scriptures covering the period of time from Moses to the coming of the Messiah in great
power and glory, it must be kept in mind

that these things were written in the Bible
for the comfort and hope of those in the
"last days" who have given their hearts unto the Lord and who are faithful and diligent in rendering themselves in obedience to
his commandments. "For whatsoever things
were written aforetime were written for our
learning, that we through patience and comfort of the scriptures might have hope."—
Romans 15: 4.

Moses was a type of the Messiah the King.
Joshua, Barak and other faithful men performed parts in prophetic dramas, in which
they pictured Christ the Messiah. Having
these things in mind, the Scriptures written of old, as well as those written by the
faithful apostles of Jesus Christ, are now
to be understood by those who are devoted
to God, and such are studied with profit
and joy.

The King

The "Messiah" means the Anointed King
of the Holy City, the kingdom or government of the Most High. By his prophets
God foretold and caused to be recorded
that the birthplace of the Messiah would
be Bethlehem (Micah 5: 2) ; and that his
name should be called Jesus, the Prince of
Peace; that the government should rest upon his shoulder, and that he is the Minister
to bestow life upon the obedient ones. (Isaiah 9: 6, 7) In God's due time these prophecies began to be fulfilled with the birth of

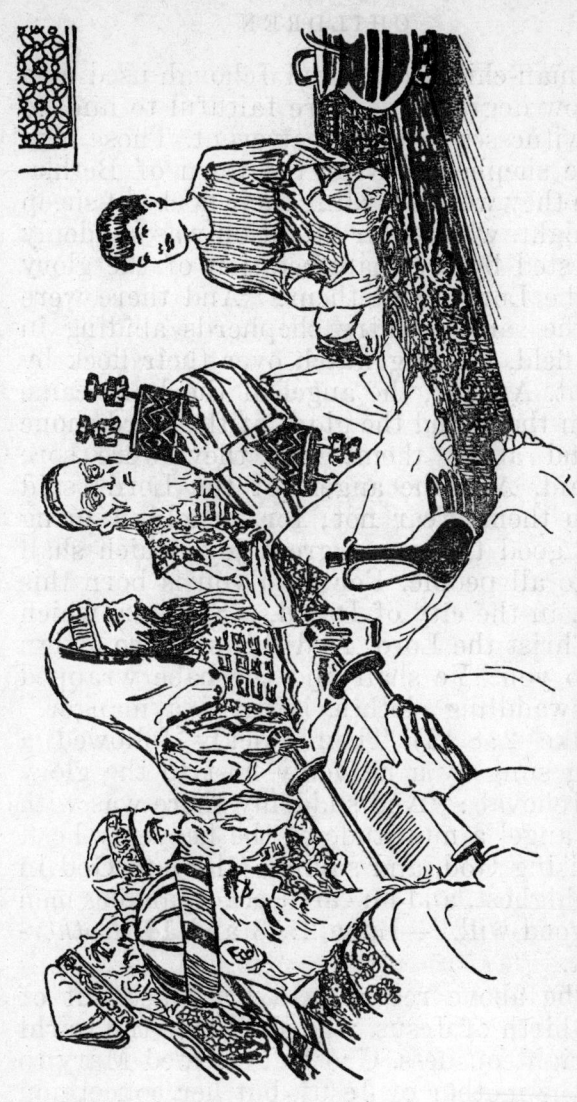

THE CHILD JESUS AT THE TEMPLE

the man-child Jesus, and Jehovah used men
of low degree, who were faithful to him, to
be witnesses to the great event. Those men
were shepherds. Near the town of Bethlehem they were guarding their flocks of sheep
at night, when their attention was suddenly
arrested by the manifestation of the glory
of the Lord about them: "And there were
in the same country shepherds abiding in
the field, keeping watch over their flock by
night. And, lo, the angel of the Lord came
upon them, and the glory of the Lord shone
round about them; and they were sore
afraid. And the angel [of the Lord] said
unto them, Fear not; for, behold, I bring
you good tidings of great joy, which shall
be to all people. For unto you is born this
day, in the city of David, a Saviour, which
is Christ the Lord. And this shall be a sign
unto you: Ye shall find the babe wrapped
in swaddling clothes, lying in a manger."
(Luke 2: 8-12) Then quickly followed a
song sung by a heavenly host to the glory
of Jehovah: "And suddenly there was with
the angel a multitude of the heavenly host,
praising God, and saying, Glory to God in
the highest, and on earth peace, among men
of good-will."—Luke 2: 13 and 14, *Rotherham*.

The above record is a brief account of
the birth of Jesus, who shall rule the world
in righteousness. God had selected Mary to
be the mother of Jesus, but her conception

was not by the power of man, but by the
power of the spirit of the Almighty God.
(Matthew 1: 18-23) God transferred the life
of his mighty Son, the Logos, from spirit to
human that he might be born of a woman,
be a perfect man, and therefore possess the
full qualifications to purchase mankind. By
his prophets God had foretold the same centuries before: "Therefore the Lord himself
shall give you a sign: Behold, a virgin shall
conceive, and bear a son, and shall call his
name Immanuel." (Isaiah 7: 14) The name
Immanuel means "God with us": "And the
Word was made flesh, and dwelt among us,
(and we beheld his glory, the glory as of the
only begotten of the Father,) full of grace
and truth." (John 1: 14) These prophecies
constitute further evidence of the genuineness or authenticity of the Scriptures set
down in the Bible, proving beyond any doubt
that the prophecies came by the command
of Almighty God, and not from any man.

When Jesus was a child of twelve years
of age he sat amongst the learned men of
the Jews, and by his questions and answers
to them concerning the Scriptures those men
were greatly astonished. There he was carrying out the will of his Father, the Almighty
God (Luke 2: 46-49); and from that time
forward Jesus grew into manhood's estate
and greatly increased in wisdom: "And Jesus increased in wisdom and stature, and in
favour with God and man."—Luke 2: 52.

The age of maturity of Jesus, that is, when he possessed the qualification for priesthood, was when he was thirty years of age. He then presented himself before the Lord and commanded John to baptize him in the river of Jordan that he might thus fulfill his Father's commandments, and in that baptism he pictured that God had made a covenant with him and that he had agreed to do God's will, and his baptism was an outward testimony to that effect. The prophetic record is that he had said: "I delight to do thy will, O my God; yea, thy law is within my heart." (Psalm 40:8) "And Jesus, when he was baptized, went up straightway out of the water; and, lo, the heavens were opened unto him, and he saw the spirit of God descending like a dove, and lighting upon him; and, lo, a voice from heaven, saying, This is my beloved son, in whom I am well pleased." (Matthew 3:16, 17) Here the testimony from Jehovah shows that he recognized Jesus as his Beloved One, to whom he had committed the great work and responsibility of being his King.

The Kingdom

Within a short time after his baptism Jesus began to preach and instruct the people, and amongst his first words addressed to the Jews were these: "Repent: for the kingdom of heaven is at hand" (Matthew 4:17); "repent" meaning that they must forsake religion and worship Jehovah. God had anointed Jesus with his spirit to be the King, had begotten or acknowledged him as his beloved Son, and had thus identified Jesus as the Messiah, The Christ, the King of the Holy City or kingdom of God, then and there beginning to be made manifest. It was the anointed King, Christ Jesus, who now was addressing the people, and truly to them he said: "The kingdom of heaven is at hand"; meaning that the Head of God's royal house was then and there present amongst them. Because he is the King and upon his shoulder should rest the government, the kingdom was present and the kingdom was beginning to be made manifest. This is exactly in harmony with his words later uttered in the presence of the Pharisees, to wit: "God's royal majesty is among you" (*Diaglott*); "The kingdom of God is among you." (*Rotherham*) (Luke 17: 21) Four thousand years before that God had foretold that he would set up a government that would be to his honor. Now the development of that government began to appear.

During the three and one-half years that Jesus, the man, walked with his disciples, he taught them and he taught the people who heard him, and in all this time he emphasized above everything else the importance of the Kingdom. This he did because it is the Kingdom, or the Holy City, that shall fully vindicate the name of Jehovah God and prove to all creation that Jehovah is supreme, and by and through the Kingdom the obedient ones of the human race will be delivered from the bondage of Satan and granted life everlasting. When Jesus delivered his great sermon on the mount, there giving specific instruction to his disciples, he put the Kingdom forward as of first importance: "And he opened his mouth, and taught them, saying, Blessed are the poor in spirit; for theirs is the kingdom of heaven." —Matthew 5:2, 3.

Clearly his words here meant that those who have a proper appreciation of themselves and their relationship to the Creator would fully recognize that they are poor and insignificant, and that they would have a desire to know the will of God and to obey him. Such a spirit would be that manifested by those who would be taught and led by the Lord. These are the ones that love to learn, and this is in harmony with God's instruction previously given through the prophet, to wit: "The meek will he guide in judgment, and the meek will he teach his way."—Psalm 25:9.

The worldly-wise men are not poor in spirit, but, on the contrary, think too highly of themselves. They regard their learning and importance above men generally, and themselves too wise to give any heed to the Word of God. The man who appreciates the truth realizes that all he has and that

is worth while and all that he hopes to have
or to be in the future proceeds from Almighty God. He realizes that man's first
duty is to fear God and be obedient to his
law. Being thus poor in spirit, he is in the
way to learn of God's purposes and to advance in all the riches that proceed from
the throne of the Most High.

Then Jesus instructed his followers as to
what constitutes a model prayer, and in that
prayer again he puts forth the Kingdom as
of greatest importance. Mark his words in
this respect: "But when ye pray, use not
vain repetitions, as the heathen do; for they
think that they shall be heard for their much
speaking. After this manner therefore pray
ye: Our Father which art in heaven, Hallowed be thy name. Thy kingdom come. Thy
will be done in earth, as it is in heaven."—
Matthew 6: 7, 9, 10.

Why is that prayer of such great importance? Because it keeps the mind and the
heart of the sincere person fixed upon that
which is of greatest importance and which
will vindicate Jehovah's name and bring
life to the human race. God would have his
creatures keep in mind that he is the Almighty and that through his government of
righteousness the world shall ultimately be
ruled in righteousness and the name of the
Most High shall be magnified above all. The
Kingdom is THE THEOCRACY, that is, the
government of the Almighty God, by and

through which the earth shall be filled with righteous people who shall dwell together forever in peace and joy. Everything else is secondary in importance to the Kingdom, and this Jesus frequently emphasized, and particularly when he used these words to his disciples: "Seek ye first the kingdom of God, and his righteousness."—Matthew 6:33.

By all of his holy prophets God had foretold the coming of his kingdom, or The THEOCRATIC GOVERNMENT. The Almighty God had preached the good news or "gospel" to Abraham long previous to the coming of Jesus, when he said to Abraham: "In thee shall all [the] nations be blessed." Then the scripture adds, it is those who have faith in God and in Christ and his kingdom that shall be blessed. (Galatians 3:8-14) (Genesis 12:3) Jesus made it clear to all who love God and his Word that the final work of his followers on earth at the time of his coming to set up the Kingdom would be to declare the Kingdom, and therefore he said to them: "This gospel of the kingdom shall be preached in all the world for a witness unto all nations; and then shall the end come." (Matthew 24:14) This action was placing the Kingdom above everything else so far as the earth is concerned.

Jesus had finished his work which had been assigned to him by the Most High and then he said to his Father: "I have glori-

JESUS HANGED ON THE TREE · · · · · PAGE 98

JEHOVAH SMITES THE ENEMY

fied thee on the earth: I have finished the
work which thou gavest me to do. And now,
O Father, glorify thou me with thine own
self, with the glory which I had with thee
before the world was. I have manifested thy
name unto the men which thou gavest me
out of the world: thine they were, and thou
gavest them me; and they have kept thy
word."—John 17: 4-6.

This is proof that previously he had been
a spirit in glory with Jehovah God, that he
had been sent to earth to perform a work
which he had done, and that he desired to
return and be with his Father in heaven.
Shortly thereafter he was arrested, charged
with the crime of treason against the earthly rule or government then in control of
Jerusalem. This charge was based upon the
fact that Jesus had repeatedly emphasized
the kingdom of God and had constantly kept
that before the minds of his followers. The
man Jesus, under arrest, was brought before the governor at Jerusalem to be tried,
and there he was convicted and executed for
treason even though he was wholly innocent.
In reply to the charge Jesus said: "My kingdom is not of this world; if my kingdom
were of this world, then would my servants
fight, that I should not be delivered to the
Jews; but now is my kingdom not from
hence." The time had not come for putting the Kingdom in operation in power
and glory, and for that reason, he stated,

his kingdom was not in operation from that time forward. The clear inference must be that there was a further work to be done before he would come in glory and in his power. The Almighty God had another work to be done, as the Scriptures clearly disclose. At that time he was asked by the governor this question: "Art thou a king?" And to which Jesus answered: "I am a king. To this end was I born, and for this cause came I into the world, that I should bear witness unto the truth. Every one that is of the truth heareth my voice."—John 18: 36, 37.

This further establishes the fact that Christ Jesus, the Anointed One of God, was sent to earth and made a King to bear witness to the truth of the majesty and supremacy of Almighty God and of His purpose to set up a kingdom that would completely vindicate the name of the Most High. Within a few hours thereafter Jesus was crucified, being nailed to the tree as though he was a vile sinner. (Galatians 3: 13) Concerning a sinner God's law is: "His body shall not remain all night upon the tree, but thou shalt in any wise bury him that day; (for he that is hanged is accursed of God;) that thy land be not defiled, which the Lord thy God giveth thee for an inheritance."—Deuteronomy 21: 23.

God's law announced through Moses provided that the willful sinner should be hanged on a tree and should be accursed of

God, and thus Jesus' being crucified on a tree (improperly called a "cross") marked him in the eyes of sinful men as a sinner; yet he was without sin. (Deuteronomy 21: 22, 23) Jesus had done no wrong. He was holy, harmless, undefiled, and without sin. (Hebrews 7: 26; 1 Peter 1: 19) Why, then, should the perfect One, the Son of God, be put to death? and why did God permit his beloved Son, who was anointed King, to thus be put to death as though he was a sinner?

The Purchase

As Jehovah God reveals to man the meaning of his Word his devoted servants on the earth more clearly understand God's purpose. They see that the Kingdom, THE THEOCRACY, is that which is of paramount importance in God's purpose and arrangement. They see that everything else is of secondary importance to the great THEOCRACY. At the very beginning of human creation God stated his purpose to bring forth his kingdom that would destroy the wicked one and that would exalt and vindicate Jehovah's great name. (Genesis 3: 15) Then later to Abraham he announced His purpose to set up his capital organization or government that would rule the universe in righteousness and through which all the families of the earth who obey him might receive a blessing. (Genesis 12: 3; 22: 17, 18) It is certain that Abraham did not understand the full meaning of God's promise to him; but that did not alter the matter at all with Abraham. He believed God and willingly obeyed His commandment, and in addition to that Abraham was being used by Jehovah God to make a great prophetic picture. It appears that no man on earth had an understanding of the Kingdom and its real purpose and meaning until after the resurrection of Jesus from the dead. The kingdom of heaven, The THEOCRATIC GOVERNMENT, is the mystery of God. (Ephesians 1:20-23; 5:32) God purposely kept this mystery hid until his own due time to reveal it to his obedient creatures. He first revealed it to his beloved Son and thereafter revealed the meaning of it to those who became the true and faithful followers in the footsteps of his beloved Son, Christ Jesus, and no others have understood the mystery of God. Jesus spoke in parables concerning the mystery, but those who stood by and heard him did not understand the meaning of his words. After the ascension of Jesus into heaven his inspired apostle wrote these words, which are set forth in the Bible: "Even the mystery which hath been hid from ages and from generations, but now is made manifest to his saints." (Colossians 1:26) That great mystery was hidden from all of God's creation and revealed in his own due time to those who should have an opportunity to understand it.

To his beloved Son, the Logos, Christ Jesus, God first revealed his purpose to have a capital organization, that is, the kingdom of heaven, THE THEOCRACY, his great government, his Holy City, the Royal House, all of which names mean the same thing; also the name *Zion* meaning the same; and which Royal House or government should be composed of 144,000 and One, that is to say, Christ Jesus the One, and the 144,000 members of his reigning house. Faithful men from Abel onward understood that God would have a mighty organization and government that would bring blessings to obedient men, but they did not have a knowledge or understanding as to the manner or the time of its coming or how it would operate. It was the apostle under inspiration who said that this mystery is now revealed unto the saints. The word "saints", used in that text at Colossians 1:26, means those persons who are pure of heart and who are righteous in the sight of God. No one can be pure and righteous in the sight of God without faith in God and in Christ and without obedience to God's commandments. That rule entirely excludes the evolutionists from having an understanding of "the mystery of God", because the evolutionists deny God's Word and have no faith in his Word. Thus it is seen that those persons who have faith in God and in his Word and in Christ as the Savior of mankind are greatly favored, and these are they of unfeigned faith.

The Scriptures also clearly show that the Almighty God revealed this great mystery for the first time to his beloved Son, the Logos, and also informed him what would be the requirement of the One who would occupy the exalted position of Head of that great government. Among the requirements announced were full and complete obedience unto the will of the Almighty God, faithfulness even unto death. This is made certain by the words of Jesus, who said: "Therefore doth my Father love me, because I lay down my life, that I might take it again. No man taketh it from me, but I lay it down of myself. I have power to lay it down, and I have power to take it again. This commandment have I received of my Father." —John 10: 17, 18.

These words of Jesus prove that there was a covenant or an agreement between Jehovah the Father and the Son, the Logos, that the Son should lay down his own life in obedience to his Father's will and that the Father would raise the Son out of death in his due time. That covenant Jesus further emphasized by his words which he uttered to his Father after he had finished his earthly ministry, to wit: "I have glorified thee on the earth: I have finished the work which thou gavest me to do. And now,

O Father, glorify thou me with thine own self, with the glory which I had with thee before the world was."—John 17: 4, 5.

Greatest Importance

It is true that the death of the man Jesus provided the ransom price for obedient men, but at this point consideration is given to that which is of far more importance than any human creatures. That which is of the highest importance is the Kingdom, the Holy City; and that should be given first consideration. Note, then, the indisputable argument supporting the conclusion that the Kingdom is that which is of paramount importance to anything and everything pertaining to the human race.

Jesus often spoke in parables, and the parables which he uttered are prophecies, and such prophecies could not be understood until God's due time to understand them, and could be understood then only by those who had devoted themselves to God and to his kingdom. Note these words of Jesus uttered to his disciples in answer to their question as to why he spoke in parables: "And the disciples came, and said unto him, Why speakest thou unto them in parables? He answered and said unto them, Because it is given unto you to know the mysteries of the kingdom of heaven, but to them it is not given. For whosoever hath, to him shall it be given, and he shall have more abundance; but whosoever hath not, from him shall be taken away even that he hath. Therefore speak I to them in parables; because they seeing, see not; and hearing, they hear not, neither do they understand. And in them is fulfilled the prophecy of Esaias, which saith, By hearing ye shall hear, and shall not understand; and seeing ye shall see, and shall not perceive: for this people's heart is waxed gross, and their ears are dull of hearing, and their eyes they have closed; lest at any time they should see with their eyes, and hear with their ears, and should understand with their heart, and should be converted, and I should heal them. But blessed are your eyes, for they see: and your ears, for they hear. For verily I say unto you, That many prophets and righteous men have desired to see those things which ye see, and have not seen them; and to hear those things which ye hear, and have not heard them." (Matthew 13:10-17) He uttered a number of parables relative to the Kingdom, each one of which was a prophecy, which was not understandable until God's due time to reveal the meaning thereof to those who were devoted to him.

When the Logos, now Jesus, learned from his Father that he would have an opportunity to be the Head of God's great capital organization, which organization would prove Satan a liar and fully vindicate Jehovah's name, the heart of Jesus was filled with joy and he straightway took the steps his Father required that he might possess that great prize. This is proved by the prophetic utterances of the Lord Jesus, which later were understood for the first time by those devoted to the Most High. He was emphasizing the importance of the Kingdom to those who heard him when Jesus spoke the parable concerning the treasure hid in the field: "Again, the kingdom of heaven is like unto treasure hid in a field; the which when a man hath found, he hideth, and for joy thereof goeth and selleth all that he hath, and buyeth that field."— Matthew 13:44.

The Treasure

That treasure was hid from all creatures; but it then being made known to the Lord Jesus, his heart was filled with joy and he kept it secret thereafter from all until God's due time to reveal it. At the same time he gave another parable concerning the Kingdom: "Again, the kingdom of heaven is like unto a merchantman, seeking goodly pearls; who, when he had found one pearl of great price, went and sold all that he had, and bought it."—Matthew 13:45, 46.

In these two parables Jesus was making a comparison that would enable his followers, when the time should arrive, to understand the meaning thereof and the importance of the Kingdom as compared with all

things else. The due time for the faithful
disciples to understand was at Pentecost,
and thereafter God revealed, through Christ
Jesus, the understanding to them. Let this
be emphasized at this point, that the purchase here referred to in both of these parables emphasized *the Kingdom* as the *hidden treasure* and the *pearl of great price*.

The English words *buyeth* and *bought,*
used in the above parables, are translated
from the Greek *agorazo,* which means to go
to the market and purchase, as a person buying in the market place that which is sold.
The buying or purchasing mentioned in these
two parables had nothing to do with the purchase of the human race as a whole. While
the blood of Christ Jesus does purchase the
human race, these two prophetic utterances
are limited to that which constitutes the
kingdom of heaven. The buying mentioned
in the parable includes those faithful ones
who are called and chosen of God, and who
prove faithful and who in due time are made
members of the royal house or kingdom of
heaven; but this is a matter separate and distinct from the purchase of the human race
in general. It is written in the Scriptures
that God appointed Jesus his beloved Son
as the heir of all things. "God . . . hath in
these last days spoken unto us by his Son,
whom he hath appointed heir of all things,
by whom also he made the worlds."—Hebrews 1: 1, 2.

His faithful followers, who ultimately become members of "the body of Christ", who are made members of his holy organization, are made joint heirs with Christ Jesus in his kingdom: "The spirit itself beareth witness with our spirit, that we are the children of God: and if children, then heirs; heirs of God, and joint-heirs with Christ; if so be that we suffer with him, that we may be also glorified together."—Romans 8: 16, 17.

How, then, did Jesus become the heir of all things? The answer according to the Scriptures is, by selling all that he had, and with that price he bought the treasure or pearl of great price, the hidden mystery, which is *the kingdom* of heaven, and which treasure is within God's universal organization, and is holy and therefore includes only those who, by God's grace, are made pure and holy and made members of the royal house.

To purchase the kingdom of heaven, the "treasure" or "pearl of great price", Jesus surrendered everything that he had inherited. That he did by laying aside all his heavenly glory and becoming a man, and by then proving his integrity unto God under the most trying conditions, and by remaining faithful and obedient unto God, even to going down to an ignominious death. Jesus, carrying out faithfully his part of the covenant with Almighty God, gave up everything, and the Almighty his Father was entirely faithful in completing His part of the covenant. This is proved by the following inspired words set forth in the Bible, to wit:

"Let this mind be in you, which was also in Christ Jesus: who, being in the form of God, thought it not robbery to be equal with God; but made himself of no reputation, and took upon him the form of a servant, and was made in the likeness of men: and being found in fashion as a man, he humbled himself, and became obedient unto death, even the death of the cross. Wherefore God also hath highly exalted him, and given him a name which is above every name: that at the name of Jesus every knee should bow, of things in heaven, and things in earth, and things under the earth; and that every tongue should confess that Jesus Christ is Lord, to the glory of God the Father."—Philippians 2:5-11.

Men have been inclined to think more highly of themselves than they ought to think, and within such a class many Christians have been included. For a long while the purchase of the human race has been set forth as the most important thing, but when we stop to reason about it we see how far short that comes of the facts. Why should it fill the heart of Jesus with joy and lead him to the giving up of everything he had merely to buy a broken-down, sinful race? That magnifies the importance of humankind far above what it should be. It is far different, however, when we understand that Jesus was giving up everything he had to buy the headship of the Government which should vindicate the name of his Father. In God's economy and lovingkindness he at the same time provided for the purchase of mankind, but this should not be magnified as above or even equal to the purchase of the hidden mystery, the kingdom of God.

The Ransom

By surrendering everything he had the Logos, that is, Jesus, bought the hidden "treasure", the "pearl of great price", himself becoming the Head and Lord of that treasure, to wit, the capital organization of the Most High. He also made a purchase of secondary importance to the Kingdom, and that was the purchase of condemned mankind. In purchasing the Kingdom he gave up his heavenly glory, because it was the will of his Father, and became a man, and then laid down even his life as a man, and thus including everything that he had, that he might be made the vindicator of his Father's name. What was the price required for the purchase of mankind? Certainly not the heavenly glory. The life of a perfect man, that is, a life for a life, was the price required. — Deuteronomy 19:21.

All the creation of God is perfect, and therefore Adam, when created, was a perfect man. "He is the Rock, his work is perfect; for all his ways are judgment: a God of truth and without iniquity, just and right is he." (Deuteronomy 32:4) At the time Adam sinned he was perfect, and from the moment of the pronouncement of God's judgment he was imperfect. For that willful disobedience to the law of God Adam forfeited his life and the right to life. In due time he died, and, all mankind being descendants from the condemned Adam, all are imperfect and all by inheritance are sinners under condemnation and condemned to death. (Romans 5:12) Since it was the perfect man that sinned, nothing less, nothing more, than a perfect human life could purchase the descendants of Adam, because his descendants had proceeded from one who was perfect at the time he was given the authority to bring children into the earth. The life of an angel could not furnish the purchase price, because an angel is greater than a human. All on the earth being descendants of Adam and hence imperfect, no perfect man being in existence, there was no way that man might be redeemed until God should make provision. (Psalm 49:1-7) Therefore all men, after living for a brief space of time, must die and remain dead forever unless provision is made by Jehovah to give them life. Jehovah God has pro-

vided a way for man to get life, and that
way He has pointed out clearly in the Scriptures; and hence it is of greatest importance to mankind that he gain a knowledge
of God's purpose as set forth in the Scriptures.

Jehovah is the fountain of life, that is, the
One from whom all life proceeds. (Psalm
36: 9) "Salvation belongeth unto Jehovah."
(Psalm 3: 8, *Am. Rev. Ver.*) No one could
provide salvation but Jehovah. While the
Logos, that is, Jesus, was purchasing the
Kingdom, with all its rights and powers,
God provided that he should also purchase
mankind. In carrying out God's purpose,
therefore, to purchase the hidden treasure,
the Kingdom, and also to purchase mankind, Jesus laid aside his spirit life and
became a man. Then he willingly laid down
his life and, by the grace of his Father,
Jehovah God, he had the privilege of taking it again because he had that commandment from his Father, as he states. (John
10: 18) To carry out Jehovah's purpose the
man-child Jesus was conceived in perfection
by the power of Almighty God. (Matthew
1: 18-25) He was born of a woman, like
other men, yet without spot or blemish. He
grew to manhood's estate, and then willingly submitted to an ignominious death. Mark
here the Scriptures conclusively proving this
point: "But we see Jesus, who was made a
little lower than the angels, for the suffer-

ing of death, crowned with glory and honour; that he by the grace of God should taste death for every man."—Hebrews 2:9.

The word-for-word rendering of the following text (John 1:14), as set forth in the *Diaglott* concerning the Logos' becoming a man, reads: "And the Word flesh became and tabernacled among us, (and we beheld the glory of him, a glory as of an only-begotten from a father,) full of favor and truth."

The *Authorized Version* of this text reads: "And the Word was made flesh, and dwelt among us, (and we beheld his glory, the glory as of the only begotten of the Father,) full of grace and truth." (John 1:14) "But when the fulness of the time was come, God sent forth his Son, made of a woman, made under the law, to redeem them that were under the law, that we might receive the adoption of sons."—Galatians 4:4, 5.

If the purchase made by the lifeblood of Christ Jesus is limited to the human race in general, why should there be a distinction between the purchase of those who were "under the law", that is to say, the house of Israel, and others of the human race, which were not under the law?

The Israelites were a typical people, and by this people God set up a typical theocracy or kingdom and entered into a covenant with them, through Moses as mediator, that they should be his holy nation or kingdom. To them Jehovah said through Moses: "Now therefore, if ye will obey my voice indeed, and keep my covenant, then ye shall be a peculiar treasure unto me above all people: for all the earth is mine. And ye shall be unto me a kingdom of priests, and an holy nation. These are the words which thou shalt speak unto the children of Israel." "And Moses came, and called for the elders of the people, and laid before their faces all these words which the Lord commanded him. And all the people answered together, and said, All that the Lord hath spoken we will do. And Moses returned the words of the people unto the Lord."—Exodus 19: 5-8.

In this covenant God provided that the Israelites should be a "holy nation" unto him, a "kingdom of priests", a "peculiar treasure". Thus God covenanted with that people for The Kingdom. Israel violated the covenant and were cast away, but, according to the apostle's statement in the above text, Jesus was "made under the law", not only that he might redeem the human race, but that he might "redeem them that were under the law", to wit, the nation of Israel, with whom a covenant had been made for the Kingdom and that they should be a peculiar treasure unto himself. Therefore the man Jesus, in laying down his life as well as in laying aside all his heavenly glory and power, purchased everything pertaining to *the Kingdom* and also purchased the human race in general. This point is here mentioned in order to emphasize the importance of the Kingdom above everything else and that the purchase of the human race in general is secondary to God's kingdom, which was set up typically with Israel and of which the Lord Jesus, by laying down his life, purchased every prospect and everything that had been committed to the nation of Israel.

Later, when the privilege was extended by the Lord Jehovah to Jews and Gentiles alike to devote themselves to him and to Christ, the testimony delivered and recorded shows that this purchase of the Kingdom included the Kingdom class, or those who shall be members of the Kingdom. Concerning this the apostle Peter, under inspiration, authoritatively stated to the faithful followers of Christ Jesus, to wit: "But ye are a chosen generation, a royal priesthood, an holy nation, a peculiar people; that ye should shew forth the praises of him who hath called you out of darkness into his marvellous light: which in time past were not a people, but are now the people of God; which had not obtained mercy, but now have obtained mercy."—1 Peter 2: 9, 10.

Jesus was a perfect man, perfect in his organism, and with full and complete right to life as a perfect man. He did not inherit any of Adam's imperfections, because Jehovah God brought him into the world. The man Jesus, therefore, as it is written, "is holy, harmless, undefiled, [and] separate from sinners." (Hebrews 7:26) The man Jesus, at thirty years of age, was fully qualified as a perfect man to furnish the purchase price for mankind. He immediately presented himself to Jehovah to carry out his agreement or covenant, and he performed his outward immersion as a testimony of that fact. (Luke 3:21-23; Psalm 40:8) He was fully qualified, and was ready and willing, to lay down his life that he might take it again, as he had covenanted with his Father. (John 10:15-18) Jesus died as a man, and, being crucified on the tree as though he was a sinner, he died as a sinner, that sinners might live. Jesus did not forfeit his right to life as a man; hence when he was raised out of death he possessed that right as a valuable thing, which constituted the purchase price, or the ransom price. Jehovah God raised Jesus out of death, not as a man but as a spirit immortal. (Acts 3:26) Jesus was put to death in the flesh and made alive in the spirit and by the power of Jehovah. (1 Peter 3:18, *Am. Rev. Ver.*; 1 Corinthians 15:3-20) Jesus, still possessing the right of human life when raised out of death by his Father and exalted to heaven, there in heaven presented before his Father's judgment seat the value of his perfect human life as the purchase price for mankind then under condemnation of death.

Long before Jesus became a man God caused a prophetic picture to be made foretelling the appearing of Jesus Christ in heaven and there presenting the purchase price or ransom sacrifice, and which prophetic picture, performed on the atonement day, is particularly set forth at the sixteenth chapter of Leviticus. God caused to be erected in the wilderness a tent or tabernacle consisting of two parts, the Holy and the Most Holy, and this was within the confines of a court, the court representing things on earth, and the Holy and Most Holy the spiritual things. Once each year, on the day known as the atonement day, the priests of Israel performed a living picture, which prophetically pointed forward to the sacrifice of Christ Jesus.

On the typical atonement day the picture was made in this manner: A bullock without spot or blemish, which represented the man Jesus, was brought into the court of the tabernacle and slain there, which court of the tabernacle pictured the earth. The blood of the bullock, representing the life-blood of Jesus, which lifeblood was poured out as "an offering for sin" (Isaiah 53:10), was then carried by the typical priest into the Most Holy of the tabernacle and there sprinkled upon the mercy seat. (Leviticus 16:14) The Most Holy of the tabernacle

pictured heaven itself, where Jesus Christ
appeared and presented and offered the asset or valuable thing, his right to human
life, as the purchase price for the offspring
of Adam. (Hebrews 9:3-25) The sacrifice
offered at the tabernacle in the wilderness
once each year on the typical atonement day
foreshadowed or pictured the work of Jesus
in offering himself, that is, his human life,
as the purchase price for man. Concerning
the type, or picture, and the reality, it is
written: "Now when these things were thus
ordained, the priests went always into the
first tabernacle, accomplishing the service
of God. But into the second [the holiest of
all, or Most Holy, picturing heaven] went
the high priest alone once every year, not
without blood, which he offered for himself, and for the errors of the people." "It
was therefore necessary that the patterns
of things in the heavens should be purified
with these; but the heavenly things themselves with better sacrifices than these. For
Christ is not entered into the holy places
made with hands, which are the figures of
the true; but into heaven itself, now to appear in the presence of God for us. Nor yet
that he should offer himself often, as the
high priest entereth into the holy place every year with blood of others; for then must
he often have suffered since the foundation
of the world; but now once in the end of the
world hath he appeared, to put away sin by

the sacrifice of himself.'' (Hebrews 9: 6, 7,
23-26) Thus it is seen that Christ Jesus,
God's great High Priest, the spirit creature, when he appeared in heaven, presented and offered unto Jehovah the asset he
possessed, to wit, his right to human life,
as the purchase price for man, which offering was accepted by Jehovah, and Christ
Jesus became the owner of all of Adam's
offspring that willingly comply with the
rules of Jehovah governing salvation. Thus
God laid the foundation in Christ Jesus for
the salvation of man, and there is no other
possible means of salvation.

The lifeblood of the man Jesus is the ransom price for man. As God declares in his
law: ''The life of the flesh is in the blood:
. . . the blood of it is for the life thereof.''
(Leviticus 17: 11, 14) So the lifeblood of the
man Jesus is the asset, the valuable thing,
by which he ransomed sinful men.

The man Jesus, by the will of God his
Father, turned his perfection and right to
life as such a man into a thing of value with
sufficient purchasing power to purchase or
buy back all the rights which Adam had forfeited for himself and which his offspring
lost by reason of Adam's sin. That does not
mean that Adam was purchased, but that
every right that Adam once possessed was
purchased. When God raised Jesus out of
death a spirit, Jesus still possessed the right
to life as a man, and which constituted an

asset or thing of value, which he paid over
to Jehovah as the price required and thereby became the owner of Adam's offspring
who should in due time avail themselves of
the value of the ransom price. Jesus Christ
then could release from the bondage of sin
and death such of the offspring of Adam as
heard and complied with the rules which
God had provided. That means that the
ransom sacrifice would enure to the benefit
of all of Adam's offspring who believed on
Christ Jesus and who rendered themselves
in obedience to the Lord's commandments.

The man Jesus died, and as a man re-
mains dead; but his right to human life,
continuing to exist and constituting the purchase price, was paid over as the purchase
price. The Lord Jesus was resurrected a
spirit and lives for ever immortal; as he
states: "I am he that liveth, and was dead;
and, behold, I am alive for evermore, Amen;
and have the keys of hell and of death."
—Revelation 1: 18.

By his own blood he purchased mankind,
and to him are granted the right and power
to administer life to obedient men. By the
will of God Adam the perfect man had
received authority from Almighty God to
transmit life, together with the right thereof, to his offspring. (Genesis 1: 28) Jesus,
by his lifeblood, bought that right, and Almighty God has given to Jesus the power
and authority to minister life to all of man-

kind who shall ever live and who therefore must, as a condition precedent, believe on the Lord Jesus Christ and obey him. Therefore it is written in the Scriptures: "For the wages of sin is death; but the gift of God is eternal life through Jesus Christ our Lord." (Romans 6:23) "And this is life eternal, that they might know thee the only true God, and Jesus Christ, whom thou hast sent." (John 17:3) It is only by and through the Lord Jesus Christ that any man can possibly gain life everlasting. There is no other name given under heaven whereby man can be saved.—Acts 4:12.

Life is not the right of an imperfect man. Almighty God is the Fountain of life, and he gives life to those who obey his will. The offense of Adam lost for himself and his offspring the right to life. God's provision is that Christ Jesus, who has bought mankind, may minister life as the free gift to those who obey him: "For if by one man's offence death reigned by one; much more they which receive abundance of grace, and of the gift of righteousness, shall reign in life by one, Jesus Christ. Therefore, as by the offence of one judgment came upon all men to condemnation; even so by the righteousness of one the free gift came upon all men unto justification of life. For as by one man's disobedience many were made sinners, so by the obedience of one shall many be made righteous."—Romans 5:17-19.

A free gift is never effective unless the
one to whom the gift is offered accepts that
gift. It follows, therefore, that anyone who
is not willing to receive the gift of life
through Christ Jesus cannot receive the
benefit of the ransom sacrifice. God's gift
of life is for men who willingly accept it
on the terms given, and those who do accept the gift and render themselves in obedience unto God are made righteous.

To Redeem

Religious teachers would have men believe that all men are immortal and therefore cannot die. Evolutionists would have
men believe that man is evolved from an
insignificant thing and advanced from one
degree to a higher degree until he becomes
perfect. Both theories are entirely wrong,
and both positively disproved by God's
Word. God's provision for man to live is
the only possible provision or means of
obtaining life.

Do the Scriptures show that Jesus died
for all men? He died that all men who will
avail themselves of God's provision for life
might live; but that cannot mean that life
is forced upon any man whether he desires
it or not and whether he obeys God or not.
The one who is a willful and deliberate opposer of God's kingdom cannot receive life
through Jesus Christ. There is no reason to
think that Adam will ever live again, be-

cause he was a wicked man and died as such, and all the wicked shall suffer destruction as God's law provides. (Psalm 145:20) Those persons who deny the existence of God, and who treat the blood of Christ Jesus as a common thing, and who refuse to have any faith in God or in Christ, and who oppose the Kingdom, and who teach the false doctrines contrary to the Word of God, cannot have the benefit of everlasting life. "But there were false prophets also among the people, even as there shall be false teachers among you, who privily shall bring in damnable heresies, even denying the Lord that bought them, and bring upon themselves swift destruction."—2 Peter 2:1.

Way to Life

The kingdom of heaven, the hidden treasure which Jesus purchased by surrendering his all, is the organization of Jehovah created and organized by him and by which the world is to be governed in righteousness. That organization is also designated in the Scriptures as Zion, THE THEOCRACY, the Holy City, and the Royal House of God. Christ Jesus is the duly appointed and anointed King of that heavenly royal house or kingdom. God's provision is that there shall be associated with Christ Jesus in that kingdom 144,000 others, who shall be taken from amongst men and changed from human to spirit, and these are also called kings and priests unto God and unto Christ, and they shall reign with him. (1 Peter 2: 9, 10; Revelation 1: 6; 20: 4, 6) Every member of that kingdom must be spirit, changed from human to spirit in the resurrection and live as spirit creatures in heaven invisible to human eyes. That means that all such must die as human creatures and be resurrected by the Lord as spirit creatures. As it is written in the Scriptures: "It is sown [in death] a natural body; it is raised [to life] a spiritual body. There is a natural body, and there is a spiritual body."—1 Corinthians 15: 44.

Christ Jesus was the first and is the Head and Lord of the Royal House. God has committed to Christ Jesus all power in heaven and in earth, including the power to resurrect from the dead and give life to others, all of which he does as Jehovah's officer and representative. (John 5: 22, 26; 6: 40, 44) God's provision to give life to those who shall become members of his kingdom is by and through Christ Jesus. His disciples were seeking the way to life and Thomas propounded to Jesus the question as to that way, and Jesus answered: "I am the way, and the truth, and the life; no man cometh unto the Father, but by me."—John 14: 6.

Until Christ Jesus had been raised from the dead and had ascended to heaven and paid over the purchase price for mankind, it was impossible for any man to receive life everlasting, and hence impossible for any man to understand how he might receive life everlasting. After Jesus had ascended into heaven, and after the pouring out of the holy spirit at Pentecost, then his disciples understood how God would minister life through Christ Jesus, and then it was that Peter, filled with the holy spirit and inspired to speak, uttered these words concerning the crucifixion and resurrection of Jesus Christ, to wit: "Neither is there salvation in any other; for there is none other name under heaven given among men, whereby we must be saved."—Acts 4: 8-12.

Jehovah God had made a covenant with his beloved Son to make him the King of the kingdom of heaven, the Head of the Holy City, THE THEOCRACY; and now just before the crucifixion of Jesus he announces to his eleven faithful apostles that he made with them a covenant that they should be associated with him in his kingdom: "And you are they who have continued with me in my trials. And I covenant for you, even as my Father has covenanted for me, a kingdom, that you may eat and drink at my table in my kingdom, and sit on thrones, judging the twelve tribes of Israel."—Luke 22: 28-30, *Diaglott*.

The kingdom of heaven being first in importance, it must be first built up before any man could be resurrected to life. The purchase price for mankind had been paid over,

but the Kingdom must first be brought into
operation before the ministration of life.
Those who would be associated with Christ
Jesus in the Kingdom must first be selected, be put to the test, and be inducted into
the Kingdom before others could find and
receive life. Those who are members of the
Kingdom must be redeemed before they
could enter upon the way to life. It is the
lifeblood of Jesus, presented in heaven as
the purchase price, that provides the purchase and redemption for those who shall
be members of the Kingdom and also for
all others who shall comply with God's fixed
rules. What are those fixed rules? "And
this is life eternal, that they might know
thee the only true God, and Jesus Christ,
whom thou hast sent."—John 17: 3.

This is the rule by which every man must
be guided who finds the way to life. He must
learn and know that Almighty God, the Eternal One, is Jehovah and that He is the source
of life. He must learn and know that Christ
Jesus is the beloved Son of the Almighty
God, the Savior of man, the Chief Officer
of Almighty God, the great Judge, and the
One who ministers life unto those who obey
God and Christ. This means that the person must have faith in God and in Christ.
"Faith cometh by hearing, and hearing by
the word of God." (Romans 10: 17) In order for one to have faith he must have some
knowledge, which knowledge must proceed

from a truthful source, and then he must rely upon that information or knowledge so received. Faith, therefore, may be properly defined in this manner: A knowledge and appreciation of God's Word, which is the truth, and a confident reliance upon that Word. The Bible, which contains the Word of God, must therefore be the guide of every one who has and exercises faith that leads to life. "Without faith it is impossible to please [God]." (Hebrews 11:6) The Scriptures define faith in these words: "Now faith is the substance [ground, or, confidence (*margin*)] of things hoped for, the evidence of things not seen."—Hebrews 11:1.

The faith that pleases God is faith in him and in his Word as the only true guide. The traditions of men could not possibly be any ground or basis for faith in God and in Christ. The theories or traditions of men are false guides that lead one into complete darkness, the end of which is everlasting destruction. Religion, demonism and evolution all spring from Satan and all plunge men who follow such theories into complete darkness and destruction. To safeguard men who are looking for the Kingdom and for life everlasting God specifically warns them against religion, demonism or false theories, all of which constitute a snare to man.—Deuteronomy 7:16.

The "gospel" means "good news" received by man from the Lord. It is good news to learn that God has provided for man a way to life and reveals to man how he can obtain life everlasting. And who has brought this good news or gospel to the knowledge of man? Certainly no evolutionist or religionist has brought it to man. The Scriptures answer: "God, who hath saved us, and called us with an holy calling, not according to our works, but according to his own purpose and grace, which was given us in Christ Jesus before the world began; but is now made manifest by the appearing of our Saviour Jesus Christ, who hath abolished death, and hath brought life and immortality to light through the gospel."—2 Timothy 1: 8-10.

By this scripture it is seen that Christ Jesus has brought life and immortality to light, and this proves that Satan's doctrine of inherent immortality of all souls is an absolute falsehood. Almighty God preached this good news to Abraham, but Abraham could not understand how salvation would come; but, regardless of this, he had complete faith in the truthfulness of God's promise and God counted him righteous because of his faith. (Galatians 3: 8, 9) In God's due time Abraham will live and will understand and will rejoice forever. Before that, however, the Kingdom must be fully organized and in operation.—Hebrews 11: 39, 40.

The coming of Christ Jesus in power and glory marks the beginning of his reign as

King. (Matthew 25: 31) When Jesus ascended into heaven he received commandment from his Father to wait until God's due time for Jesus to begin his reign. (Psalm 110: 1; Hebrews 10: 12, 13) In the meantime God proceeds to select from amongst human creatures those who will be associated with Christ Jesus in his kingdom. That selection the Lord does according to fixed rules governing those who have faith. Concerning this selection Jesus said: "No man can come to me, except the Father which hath sent me draw him; and I will raise him up at the last day. It is written in the prophets, And they shall be all taught of God. Every man therefore that hath heard, and hath learned of the Father, cometh unto me."— John 6: 44, 45.

Those who receive knowledge of God and Christ the Redeemer, and who exercise faith, such God draws unto Christ Jesus. Such persons are seeking the way to life. The disciples of Jesus were the first to conform to the rules leading them to be members of the Kingdom, and since then all who have become true followers of Christ Jesus were required to take the same course. To all such Jesus says: "Then said Jesus unto his disciples, If any man will come after me, let him deny himself, and take up his cross, and follow me." (Matthew 16: 24) To deny oneself, within the meaning of this scripture, is to put aside one's own selfish will and agree to do the will of the Lord. Such is consecration, even as Jesus said: "Then said I, Lo, I come; in the volume of the book it is written of me, I delight to do thy will, O my God; yea, thy law is within my heart." (Psalm 40: 7, 8; Hebrews 10: 5-9) Having made a consecration, then one must "take up his cross" and follow Christ Jesus. The "cross" here does not mean a tree or a piece of wood; but the word *cross,* as here used, means the reproaches that have fallen upon the Lord Jesus; and man must willingly bear these reproaches if he would be a follower of Christ Jesus. Concerning such it is written: "For even hereunto were ye called; because Christ also suffered for us, leaving us an example, that ye should follow his steps."—1 Peter 2: 21.

Justification

Since all men are by inheritance sinners, and hence imperfect, how could God accept such as a follower of Christ Jesus, the Perfect One? Because of the man's faith in God and in Christ as his Redeemer, and by his agreeing to do the will of God concerning His purpose, and by devoting himself to God, Jehovah God counts that person as a righteous man, as perfect or righteous. It is by reason of the man's faith and obedience that he is counted righteous by the Lord: "Even the righteousness of God, which is by faith of Jesus Christ, unto all and upon all them that believe; for there is no difference: for all have sinned, and come short of the glory of God; being justified freely by his grace, through the redemption that is in Christ Jesus." (Romans 3:22-24) "Therefore being justified by faith, we have peace with God through our Lord Jesus Christ; by whom also we have access by faith into this grace wherein we stand, and rejoice in hope of the glory of God." (Romans 5:1, 2) This proves beyond any question of doubt that the benefit of the ransom sacrifice enures only to those who have and exercise faith in God and in Christ and who render themselves in obedience to God's will.

It is the will of God that all those who are made members of the Kingdom shall die as human creatures and be resurrected and live in the spirit with Christ Jesus. Such faithful ones die as the Lord Jesus died and, being faithful unto death, have a part in his resurrection, which is the chief resurrection. Those selected to become prospective members of the Kingdom are therefore justified by faith, counted as dead with Christ Jesus, and begotten to life as spirit creatures. Note the Scriptures on this point: "Know ye not, that so many of us as were baptized into Jesus Christ were baptized into his death? Therefore we are buried with him by baptism into death; that like as Christ was raised up from the dead by the glory of the Father, even so we also should walk in newness of life. For if we have been planted together in the likeness of his death, we shall be also in the likeness of his resurrection: knowing this, that our old man is crucified with him, that the body of sin might be destroyed, that henceforth we should not serve sin. For he that is dead is freed from sin. Now if we be dead with Christ, we believe that we shall also live with him."—Romans 6:3-8.

"Beget" or "begetting" means the acknowledgment by the Father that the child is his son. God gives this assurance to the obedient ones by and through his Word: "Of his own will begat he us with the word of truth, that we should be a kind of firstfruits of his creatures." (James 1:18) One begotten of God is counted as a new creature in Christ, on his way to life in the Kingdom, which life he shall receive if he continues faithful unto the end: "Therefore if any man be in Christ, he is a new creature; old things are passed away; behold, all things are become new. And all things are of God, who hath reconciled us to himself by Jesus Christ, and hath given to us the ministry of reconciliation." (2 Corinthians 5:17, 18) "For ye are dead, and your life is hid with Christ in God. When Christ, who is our life, shall appear, then shall ye also appear with him in glory."— Colossians 3:3, 4.

Such begotten ones are called or taken into the covenant for the Kingdom, and if they continue faithful unto the end of their earthly journey they have the assurance of being in the Kingdom.

Those consecrated persons who are justified and begotten by the spirit of Almighty God he calls or invites to the "high calling", that is, to the "holy calling", to the heavenly calling, to a place with Christ Jesus in his kingdom: "Who hath saved us, and called us with an holy calling, not according to our works, but according to his own purpose and grace, which was given us in Christ Jesus before the world began." (2 Timothy 1: 9) From that time onward such begotten ones are admonished to deport themselves in a proper manner as new creatures.—1 Thessalonians 2: 12.

Are the evolutionists and teachers of the traditions of men, generally called "religionists", are such persons called to the kingdom of God? The Scriptures answer: "For ye see your calling, brethren, how that not many wise men after the flesh, not many mighty, not many noble, are called: but God hath chosen the foolish things of the world to confound the wise; and God hath chosen the weak things of the world to confound the things which are mighty; and base things of the world, and things which are despised, hath God chosen, yea, and things which are not, to bring to nought

things that are; that no flesh should glory
in his presence."—1 Corinthians 1:26-29.

Those called to the heavenly calling are
selected to become members of the glorified
body of Christ: "Whereunto he called you
by our gospel, to the obtaining of the glory
of our Lord Jesus Christ." (2 Thessalonians
2:14) One who has become a follower of
Christ Jesus is called to follow in the footsteps of the Lord Jesus Christ: "For even
hereunto were ye called; because Christ also
suffered for us, leaving us an example, that
ye should follow his steps." (1 Peter 2:21)
One being thus called to the Kingdom must
continue to fight the good fight of faith
against everything that seeks to destroy his
faith, and thus he must continue faithful
unto the end: "Fight the good fight of faith,
lay hold on eternal life, whereunto thou art
also called, and hast professed a good profession before many witnesses."—1 Timothy 6:12.

The Church

"The church" is another name applied
to the kingdom of which Christ Jesus is
the Head, Lord and Chief; and the 144,000,
found faithful unto death, are members of
that body. Hence the church is composed of
144,000 and One. (Revelation 7:1-8; 14:1-3)
The word *church* has been much misused
amongst men. Jesus propounded to his disciples this question: "Whom say ye that I

am?'' The manifest purpose of that question was to afford an opportunity for his disciples to make known whether or not they recognized Jesus as the Messiah or Christ, whom God had promised to send: "And Simon Peter answered and said, Thou art the Christ, the Son of the living God. And Jesus answered and said unto him, Blessed art thou, Simon Bar-jona; for flesh and blood hath not revealed it unto thee, but my Father which is in heaven. And I say also unto thee, That thou art Peter; and upon this rock I will build my church; and the gates of hell shall not prevail against it.''—Matthew 16: 16-18.

A religious organization of great power and influence in the world has for centuries taught the people that Jesus said that he would build his church upon Peter; but it is clear that Jesus said nothing of the kind. Peter answered the question, saying to Jesus: "Thou art the Christ." To that answer Jesus replied: 'My Father, which is in heaven, has revealed this unto you. You did not get it from anyone else.' And then Jesus added: "Upon this rock I will build my church; and the gates of hell [death, destruction] shall not prevail against it." This must be true because Christ and the members of his body are the only ones granted immortality.

"Rock" or "Stone" is one of the titles applied to Jesus Christ the King and to his kingdom. (See Daniel 2:26-45.) Jehovah God is called the "great Rock", and the Lord Jesus is "the express image" of his Father, Jehovah. (Deuteronomy 32:4) All those who are called to the Kingdom and who follow faithfully in the footsteps of Jesus are counted as living stones of the Kingdom, and of which class Christ Jesus is the Chief Corner Stone. Such was the understanding of Peter, who heard the words of Jesus, and therefore Peter testified and recorded this fact, which proves beyond any doubt that the church is the body of Christ, that Christ is the Chief Corner Stone, and that the members are builded upon him the foundation: "As newborn babes, long for the spiritual milk which is without guile, that ye may grow thereby unto salvation; if ye have tasted that the Lord is gracious; unto whom coming, a living stone, rejected indeed of men, but with God elect, precious, ye also, as living stones, are built up a spiritual house, to be a holy priesthood, to offer up spiritual sacrifices, acceptable to God through Jesus Christ. Because it is contained in scripture, Behold, I lay in Zion a chief corner stone, elect, precious; and he that believeth on him shall not be put to shame. For you therefore that believe is the preciousness: but for such as disbelieve, The stone which the builders rejected, the same was made the head of the corner; and, A stone of stumbling, and a rock of offence;

for they stumble at the word, being disobedient: whereunto also they were appointed. But ye are an elect race, a royal priesthood, a holy nation, a people for God's own possession, that ye may show forth the excellencies of him who called you out of darkness into his marvellous light: who in time past were no people, but now are the people of God: who had not obtained mercy, but now have obtained mercy."—1 Peter 2:2-10, *A.R.V.*

The claim made by religious organizations that Peter is the foundation of the church and was the first pope is false and is entirely unsupported by any scripture in the Bible. The manifest purpose of such a false doctrine being advanced by Satan and his emissaries is to cause men to violate God's law by worshiping a creature.—Exodus 20:1-5.

Further testimony of the Scriptures fully supports the conclusion that the church is the kingdom over which Christ Jesus is Head and Lord. God made Jesus the Foundation and Lord and Head of the church: "And hath put all things under his feet, and gave him to be the head over all things to the church, which is his body, the fulness of him that filleth all in all."—Ephesians 1:17-23.

The church is the creation or building of God, and means the same thing as the capital organization, or Kingdom. It is the com-

posite body of The Christ, Jesus Christ the
Head and the 144,000 who are the members
of the body, and this arrangement in creation is according to the will of God. "But
now hath God set the members every one of
them in the body, as it hath pleased him."
(1 Corinthians 12: 18) The church of God
is one body, not divers bodies. Jesus Christ,
the beginning of creation, is the Head of
that one body: "And he is before all things,
and by him all things consist. And he is the
head of the body, the church: who is the
beginning, the firstborn from the dead; that
in all things he might have the pre-emi-
nence."— Colossians 1: 17, 18.

Redemption

All those who shall become members of
the body of Christ, being the offspring of
imperfect man, were born sinners. All these
Christ Jesus bought with his own precious
blood. These, when justified, called and begotten of the spirit, and continuing faithful unto the end, constitute 'the church of
God, which he has purchased with the blood
of his own'. (Acts 20: 28, *Emphatic Diaglott*) The ransom sacrifice, and the purchase price, operates first for the benefit of
those who by faith and the grace of God are
called to be members of the Kingdom. Such
are bought with a price, to wit, the blood of
Christ Jesus: "For ye are bought with a
price: therefore glorify God in your body,

and in your spirit, which are God's." (1 Corinthians 6: 20) Such belong to the Lord,
and such creatures must and do faithfully
obey the Lord Jesus Christ and God, rather
than men: "Ye are bought with a price; be
not ye the servants of men." (1 Corinthians
7: 23)—Also Romans 3: 22-24; 1 Corinthians
1: 30; Colossians 1: 14.

The scripture text at Ephesians 1: 5-14 is
addressed to those who are called to be members of the Kingdom and who therefore have
and exercise faith in God and in his King
and are diligent to obey the will of God:
"Having predestinated us unto the adoption
of children by Jesus Christ to himself, according to the good pleasure of his will, . . .
in whom we have redemption through his
blood, the forgiveness of sins, according to
the riches of his grace; . . . having made
known unto us the mystery [the hidden mystery, the Kingdom] of his will, according to
his good pleasure which he hath purposed
in himself."—Ephesians 1: 5-9.

These are sealed or receive "the earnest",
or hand payment, that is, the promise that
they shall be of the Kingdom: "Which is
the earnest of our inheritance, until the redemption of the purchased possession, unto
the praise of his glory." (Ephesians 1: 14)
That which is purchased is the same as mentioned by the apostle Peter in these words,
'a people for God's purpose' (1 Peter 2: 9,
Diaglott), and the language in the two fore-

going texts is limited to that company. These have the full assurance from God of their redemption until the time of the deliverance of the "purchased possession". At the coming of the Kingdom and the destruction of Satan's organization these of the "purchased possession" will experience complete deliverance.

Faithful

Not everyone who is called to have a part in the Kingdom finally enters into the kingdom of glory. If one who is in line for the Kingdom becomes unfaithful he is put out and someone else assigned to that place. (Matthew 13:41) Full obedience and faithfulness to the end is required of all who enter into the Kingdom. Each and every one of the Kingdom company is put to a severe test to prove that he really loves God and Christ. For that reason Jesus says: "If ye love me, keep my commandments. He that loveth me not keepeth not my sayings: and the word which ye hear is not mine, but the Father's which sent me." — John 14:15, 24.

Jesus Christ, the Perfect One, was put to the most severe test and proved himself faithful under the test, and God made him "the Author of eternal salvation" to all them that obey him, and to none other: "Though he were a Son, yet learned he obedience by the things which he suffered; and being made perfect, he became the author of eternal salvation unto all them that obey him."—Hebrews 5:8, 9.

Jesus was made perfect in obedience and faithfulness under that severe test. All the members of the Kingdom must have a like test. (1 Peter 2:21; Hebrews 12:1-10) Suffering the reproach from Satan and his agents, who put reproaches upon the name of God and Christ, is a test of faithfulness to those who are in line for the Kingdom. These are thus permitted to suffer such reproaches and persecution in order that they may prove their integrity toward God. To those who are called and on the way to the Kingdom Jesus says: "Be thou faithful unto death, and I will give thee the crown of life." (Revelation 2:10, *Am. Rev. Ver.*) They must be faithful to the end.

Resurrection

Christ Jesus was the first one raised from the dead to life, to glory and to immortality. The followers in the footsteps of Christ Jesus are those who "seek for glory and honour and immortality". (Romans 2:7) Those who are faithful unto death are resurrected out of death and given eternal life, glory and immortality with Christ Jesus. The resurrection of Christ Jesus is a guarantee to his faithful followers of their privilege of sharing in that resurrection. The Christ, that is, Jesus Christ and the 144,000 members of his royal house, constitute one body, and all share in the first resurrection. All these die as human creatures and are raised to life as spirit creatures. The entire body, Christ Jesus and the 144,000 members, are first in the flesh and at the resurrection become spirit: "But now is Christ risen from the dead, and become the firstfruits of them that slept. . . . There are also celestial bodies, and bodies terrestrial: but the glory of the celestial is one, and the glory of the terrestrial is another. . . . So also is the resurrection of the dead. It [the composite body of Christ] is sown in corruption; it [the composite body of Christ] is raised in incorruption; it [the composite body of Christ] is sown in dishonour; it [the composite body of Christ] is raised in glory; it [the composite body of Christ] is sown in weakness; it [the composite body of Christ] is raised in power; it [the composite body of Christ] is sown a natural body; it [the composite body of Christ] is raised a spiritual body. There is a natural body, and there is a spiritual body."—1 Corinthians 15: 12-58.

Reign

Jehovah's promise concerning the Kingdom is that those who constitute that royal house shall be unto him 'an holy nation, a royal [reigning] priesthood'. (Exodus 19: 5, 6; 1 Peter 2: 9, 10) Such are the ones that have part in the first or chief resurrection, and concerning them it is written: "Therefore I endure all things for the elect's sakes, that they may also obtain the salvation which is in Christ Jesus with eternal glory. It is a faithful saying: For if we be dead with him, we shall also live with him: if we suffer, we shall also reign with him: if we deny him, he also will deny us."—2 Timothy 2:10-12.

The faithful apostles of Jesus Christ died and must remain dead until the coming of the Lord Jesus in power and glory, at which time they are resurrected and receive the crown of life, or immortality: "Henceforth there is laid up for me a crown of righteousness, which the Lord, the righteous judge, shall give me at that day: and not to me only, but unto all them also that love his appearing."—2 Timothy 4:8.

All faithful Christians who died faithful before the second coming of the Lord Jesus Christ are the ones who share in the first or chief resurrection, and all those on earth at his coming and who are faithful at that time and continue faithful until the end, are called "the remnant", and these receive at their "change", or resurrection, life and immortality. (1 Thessalonians 4:14-18; 1 Corinthians 15:51-53) All those who share in "the first resurrection" become kings and priests unto God and reign with Christ Jesus.—Revelation 1:6; 20:4, 6.

The spirit body, the Christ, the Holy Nation, is the Holy City, created and organized

in heaven and which in God's due time comes
down from God out of heaven and as Jehovah God's organization rules the world in
righteousness. That glorious Holy City vindicates the great and holy name of Almighty
God and shall be forever to his glory, serving him and carrying out his purpose according to his holy will. Christ Jesus is the
King, Lord and Head of that Holy City,
and upon his shoulders rests the holy government; and he, as the administrator of
life, gives life to those who receive it, and
hence he is called The Everlasting Father.
(Isaiah 9: 6, 7) During his reign every vestige of the wicked is destroyed and those
who receive life everlasting from the Lord
shall be for ever to the praise of Almighty
God.

"Sheep"

Those who willingly obey the Lord he designates under the symbol of "sheep", and
those who disobey or oppose him and his
kingdom he designates under the symbol of
"goats". (Matthew 25: 32) Note, therefore,
that Jesus says concerning the ransom or
purchase price that buys mankind: "I am
the good shepherd: the good shepherd giveth his life for *the sheep*. I am the good shepherd, and know my sheep, and am known
of mine. As the Father knoweth me, even
so know I the Father: and I lay down my
life for the sheep."—John 10: 11, 14, 15.

Note also that Jesus does not say that he lays down his life for the goats. A man receives a designation as a "sheep", who is obedient unto the Lord, or the designation as a "goat" that is opposed to the Lord; and therefore the man makes his own choice as to whether he will be a "sheep" or a "goat". If he chooses to believe on the Lord and renders himself in obedience unto God and Christ he chooses to receive the benefit of the ransom sacrifice, that is, the purchase price; but if he refuses to believe and to obey the Lord he does not receive the benefit of the ransom sacrifice.

Only those who are obedient to the Lord, that is to say, the "sheep", receive the benefit of the ransom sacrifice, and those called to the Kingdom are the first ones to receive the same. Only those who continue faithful to the end continue to be sheep. Such constitute only a "little flock" as compared with the numerous persons in the earth. These faithful ones must give themselves and all they have to the service of the Lord. They cannot divide their devotion between the Lord and any earthly thing. To that faithful little company Jesus says: "Fear not, little flock; for it is your Father's good pleasure to give you the kingdom."—Luke 12:32.

"John, could you give a brief summary of this study, that we might better keep the points in mind?"

"I shall try to do so, Eunice. The Scriptures reveal the stupendous and glorious purpose of Jehovah, the Almighty God. Long centuries ago God purposed the building of the Holy City, which is his capital organization and of which he has made Christ Jesus the Head and King. That Holy City is THE THEOCRACY, also called Zion, which God has chosen for his special purpose: 'For the Lord hath chosen Zion; he hath desired it for his habitation.' (Psalm 132:13) No wonder it is beautiful for situation, since it is the habitation of the Most High: 'Great is the Lord, and greatly to be praised in the city of our God, in the mountain of his holiness. Beautiful for situation, the joy of the whole earth, is mount Zion, on the sides of the north, the city of the great King. God is known in her palaces for a refuge.'—Psalm 48:1-3.

"In Zion is the throne of the King, Christ Jesus: 'Yet have I set my king upon my holy hill of Zion.' (Psalm 2:6) There is where Jehovah God shines before all who love and obey him: 'Out of Zion, the perfection of beauty, God hath shined.'—Psalm 50:2.

"Note that the Holy City, Zion, The THE-OCRATIC GOVERNMENT, is also called 'the temple of God'. (2 Corinthians 6:16; Le-

viticus 26: 12) Jehovah is the builder thereof, and he builds it to his glory: 'When the
Lord shall build up Zion, he shall appear
in his glory.'—Psalm 102: 16.

"His appearing in his glory necessarily
must be when God begins to reveal to his
people the meaning of his prophecy, thereby disclosing to them his purpose. Then notice this prophecy concerning the Lord Jesus coming to the temple: 'Behold, I will
send my messenger, and he shall prepare
the way before me: and the Lord, whom ye
seek, shall suddenly come to his temple, even
the messenger of the covenant, whom ye delight in: behold, he shall come, saith the
Lord of hosts. But who may abide the day
of his coming? and who shall stand when
he appeareth? for he is like a refiner's fire,
and like fullers' soap: and he shall sit as a
refiner and purifier of silver; and he shall
purify the sons of Levi, and purge them as
gold and silver, that they may offer unto
the Lord an offering in righteousness.'—
Malachi 3: 1-3.

"Eunice, I have read these books that we
have here, and the book called *Salvation* sub-
mits the proof that the Lord Jesus Christ
came to the temple in the year 1918. On
page 160 this appears: 'In the year 1914 the
Lord Jesus was enthroned as king of the
world. (Matthew 24: 3-14) Three and one-
half years thereafter Christ Jesus the King
appeared at the temple of Jehovah and gath-

ered unto himself his faithful followers and
commissioned them and sent them forth to
"preach this gospel of the kingdom"; and
thus is marked the beginning of the Lord's
judgment of the nations, and concerning
which it is written: "And before him shall
be gathered all nations; and he shall separate them one from another, as a shepherd
divideth his sheep from the goats; and he
shall set the sheep on his right hand, but
the goats on the left."—Matthew 25:32, 33.

" 'This identifies specifically two classes
of persons. One class, being extremely selfish and who oppress others and persecute
those who serve God, are designated under
the symbol of "goats". The other class, being kind to God's people, and who love
righteousness, are designated as "sheep".
These latter ones are good and do good unto
those who serve Jehovah as his witnesses.
Such persons of good-will are the "other
sheep" of the Lord.'

"Surely that proves why so many persons are now against the Bible and why
a comparatively small number of persons
are fleeing from religious organizations and
seeking the Lord and his kingdom."

"John, we have learned what we know
about the Scriptures since 1918. If the Lord
Jesus builded up Zion, his temple, at that
time, what about those who have turned to
the Lord since that time?"

"Such, Eunice, are also called 'sheep' if they serve the Lord. We have just seen that the temple, or Kingdom company, is called the 'little flock' of sheep. Note the words of Jesus after speaking of the 'little flock': 'And other sheep I have, which are not of this fold: them also I must bring, and they shall hear my voice; and there shall be one fold, and one shepherd.'—John 10: 16.

"The Kingdom is made up, as we have seen, of a fixed number, that is, 144,000, with Christ Jesus as the Chief One, the Head. These 'other sheep' we must learn about in another study."

"We have been greatly blessed, my dear John, by having received instruction from our parents in our youth concerning the Bible, and now we begin to have an understanding of it, evidently because it is God's due time for us to understand. Thanks be unto our God!"

"Yes, Eunice, your sincere faith has been a great blessing to you all the way. We are very grateful to our God and Lord, our Savior. Let us look a little further into the Scriptures concerning THE THEOCRACY.

Begins to Function

"A few notes should be made here, Eunice, I believe, concerning the Kingdom and when it begins to function as such; and as we continue this study I will write some of these down."

Jesus emphasized the importance of his coming in power and great glory to reign as King. His apostles had received the anointing of the holy spirit and wrote under inspiration concerning God's purpose, and they emphasized the importance of the coming of the Lord and his kingdom. Particularly the apostle Paul stressed the importance of His coming. The appearing of the Lord Jesus in glory and power takes place when his kingdom begins to function. To Timothy Paul wrote: "I charge thee therefore before God, and the Lord Jesus Christ, who shall judge the quick and the dead at his appearing and his kingdom."—2 Timothy 4:1.

The resurrection of faithful Paul and other faithful followers of Christ Jesus could not take place, according to the Scriptures, until the day of the coming of Christ Jesus and his kingdom. (2 Timothy 4:8) When Jesus ascended into heaven Jehovah said to him: "The LORD said unto my Lord, Sit thou at my right hand, until I make thine enemies thy footstool."—Psalm 110:1.

Christ Jesus must wait until his Father's due time for him to begin his reign, and concerning that due time it is written: "The LORD [Jehovah] shall send the rod of thy strength out of Zion: rule thou in the midst of thine enemies." (Psalm 110:2) That proves that the Kingdom begins to function while the enemies, Satan and the other

demons and their agents, are still exercising power over the nations of the earth.

In reply to a question propounded by his disciples concerning his coming and his kingdom and the end of the world, Jesus said: "For nation shall rise against nation, and kingdom against kingdom: and there shall be famines, and pestilences, and earthquakes, in divers places. All these are the beginning of sorrows."—Matthew 24: 7, 8.

The sorrows here mentioned are sorrows which Satan brings upon the peoples of the earth because he knows that his time is short before the final end of his power. This prophecy of Jesus began to be fulfilled in the year 1914, at the beginning of the World War, and that sorrow and distress, with increasing power and fury, is yet upon the earth and must continue until the final climax at Armageddon, which is "the battle of that great day of God Almighty" against Satan and all his forces. In this connection note that it is written in Revelation concerning the Lord Jesus Christ: "Thou hast taken to thee thy great power, and hast reigned. And the nations were angry, and thy wrath is come."—Revelation 11: 17, 18.

When the Lord brings to pass the facts or circumstances fitting exactly his prophetic utterance written long before, we may know that such is the time for the beginning of the fulfillment of that prophecy.

The prophecy of the Lord Jesus concerning the end of the world and the coming of his kingdom began to have fulfillment in 1914, and that fixed the time of his coming and the beginning of his reign as King. As shown by the scriptures we have just seen, he begins his reign while the enemy is yet in power and operating. The twelfth chapter of Revelation tells of a "war in heaven" in which Christ Jesus and his angels fought against Satan and his angels, and that the enemy Satan was cast down to the earth. In the twelfth verse of that chapter it is written: "Woe to the inhabiters of the earth, and of the sea! for the devil is come down unto you, having great wrath, because he knoweth that he hath but a short time." (Revelation 12:12) All the facts show that the woes beginning in 1914 have continued to increase upon the earth, and at the present time the distress and woes are greater than ever before known, and this indicates that Armageddon is very near.—Revelation 16:13-16.

The earthly ministry of Christ Jesus was for three and one-half years, and then he ascended into heaven. Corresponding to that same three and one-half years: Christ began his reign in 1914; three and a half years later he appeared at the temple of God and began to gather to himself those faithfully devoted to him and to his kingdom. That was in 1918 that he came to his temple.

That marks the beginning of the assembly
or gathering to himself of the members of
the Holy City. _____

"At this point, John, may we give some
consideration to Revelation 21:1-8, which
tells of the Holy City coming down from
God out of heaven?"

"Eunice, these two books entitled *Light*
discuss the entire book of Revelation. We
will take a little space here to set down
some of the points concerning the Holy
City. The Revelation is that which Jehovah God gave to his beloved Son concerning the Holy City, and Jesus sent his angel
to transmit that information to his faithful
servant, then a prisoner on the isle of Patmos: 'The Revelation of Jesus Christ, which
God gave unto him, to shew unto his servants things which must shortly come to pass;
and he sent and signified it by his angel unto
his servant John.'—Revelation 1:1.

"Literally 'Revelation' means 'unveiling'.
It is the uncovering of that which is coming to pass within a short time. Jehovah
God committed to Christ Jesus those truths,
which in due time must be made understandable by those who are devoted to Jehovah
and his King. The book of Revelation is
written chiefly in symbols, as it is stated:
'He sent and sign-ified it' to John and recorded the same. Otherwise stated, it was
written in signs or symbols. John the apos-

tle stood in the place as representative of all the faithful followers of Christ Jesus who were on earth in 1918 and thereafter. These are mentioned in the Scriptures as 'the remnant' of the seed of promise.—Revelation 12: 17.

"John the apostle was given a vision of the Holy City, meaning the heavenly organization •of Jehovah God, of which Christ Jesus is Lord and King. It is the New Jerusalem, which means the organization of everlasting peace. 'Of the peace of his government there shall be no end.' (Isa. 9: 7) The Holy City comes down from God, who created it. It is described in symbols as beautiful 'as a bride adorned for her husband'. He heard a voice from heaven saying: 'Behold, the tabernacle [dwelling place] of God is with men.' This language applies specifically to the faithful followers of Christ Jesus on the earth from and after 1918, when the Lord came to his temple. From that time forward the Kingdom functions; and here in symbolic phrase is recorded what it shall accomplish: 'And God shall wipe away all tears from their eyes; and there shall be no more death, neither sorrow, nor crying, neither shall there be any more pain: for the former things are passed away. And he that sat upon the throne said, Behold, I make all things new. And he said unto me, Write; for these words are true and faithful.'—Revelation 21: 4, 5.

"That glorious kingdom will first destroy all wickedness in the earth, which wickedness has caused so much sorrow, crying and death. There will then be a clean earth under the reign of Christ: 'For he must reign till he hath put all enemies under his feet. The last enemy that shall be destroyed is death.' (1 Corinthians 15:25, 26) The kingdom of God, THE THEOCRACY, will remove from the universe all things that cause sorrow, suffering and death, and will give life and peace to all that obey the laws of that kingdom. Furthermore, the Kingdom will completely vindicate Jehovah's holy name. The Kingdom, THE THEOCRACY, therefore, is the greatest thing, next to Jehovah, that exists. Every person now on the earth who hopes to live must flee to the Kingdom and through its administration, by Christ Jesus, receive life everlasting, which is the gracious gift of Almighty God.

"Concerning his vision of the Holy City John the apostle wrote: 'And I saw a new heaven and a new earth: for the first heaven and the first earth were passed away; and there was no more sea.' (Revelation 21:1) The word 'heaven' symbolically means the rule that is invisible to human eyes. 'Earth' is a symbol of the visible ruling powers over the people. 'Sea' is a symbol of and is properly defined as the peoples of the earth that are ungodly, and therefore alienated from God, which peoples nourish, bear up and support the visible ruling power acting under Satan. With the destruction of Satan and his organization, which includes all the wicked ones, there will be no more symbolic sea. The apostle Peter wrote: 'Nevertheless we, according to his promise, look for new heavens and a new earth, wherein dwelleth righteousness.' (2 Peter 3: 13) The promise of which he speaks is the promise which God made to Abraham, to set up a Holy City, the New Jerusalem, which is the new heaven. Concerning the new earth we shall learn as we progress in these studies.''

CHAPTER 5

PRINCES

"Behold, a king shall reign in righteousness, and princes shall rule in justice."
– Isaiah 32:1, *Leeser.*

THE foregoing scripture text describes the government that is exactly the opposite of the governments that now rule this earth. All the nations of the earth are now in distress and in perplexity, and men's hearts are failing them because of what they sense is further coming upon the earth in the way of wickedness. In his great prophecy relating to the end of the world and the coming of his kingdom Jesus told specifically of the sorrowful and dreadful conditions that now afflict the earth. (Luke 21: 25, 26) It is under the rule of the new heaven and new earth that the King shall reign in righteousness and the princes shall rule in justice. Sincere persons are eager to know about that righteous government. It means peace and life to those who flee to it and obey its laws.

The Almighty God appointed Lucifer to the place of overlord or overseer of the earth, and God did not take that position away from him when Lucifer rebelled and became Satan. Christ Jesus, as Jehovah's officer, will take away from the Devil every vestige of authority. The term "the end of the world" means the end of Satan's uninterrupted reign or rule, and which time began in 1914 and which will be completed at Armageddon, the battle of the great day of God Almighty.

When the man Christ Jesus began his earthly ministry, the Devil offered to turn over to Jesus the kingdoms of the world if Jesus would bow down to and worship the Devil. That offer Jesus refused and said to the Devil: "Get thee hence, Satan; for it is written, Thou shalt worship the Lord thy God, and him only shalt thou serve." (Matthew 4:3-11) This is further proof that Satan was then the invisible governor or overlord of the earth. Later Jesus referred to Satan as "the prince of this world".—John 12:31; 14:30; 16:11.

"It seems strange, John," said Eunice, "that so many persons deny the existence of the Devil at the present time. At our

seminary I heard several of our teachers
say: 'There is no Devil.' In these texts which
we have just read Jesus emphatically testified to the existence of the Devil, and there
are many other scriptures showing the same
thing. Note at 2 Corinthians it is written:
'But if our gospel be hid, it is hid to them
that are lost: in whom the god of this world
hath blinded the minds of them which believe not, lest the light of the glorious gospel
of Christ, who is the image of God, should
shine unto them.' (2 Corinthians 4: 3, 4)
There Satan is called the god, or mighty
one, of this wicked world."

"Yes, Eunice, that scripture also says
that Satan has blinded those persons who
believe not. Persons who deny the existence
of Satan the Devil are blinded to the truth
because they have no faith. Again I thank
God, my dear, that you are a woman of unfeigned faith. Now let us proceed with *our
study.*"

Away back in Eden the Almighty God
announced his purpose to build up a kingdom that would crush Satan in due time.
A "woman" is a symbol of Jehovah's organization, and the seed of his "woman"
or organization is Christ, the King of the
holy government. (Galatians 3: 16-29) It is
God's "woman", symbolical of his organization, which is called 'Jerusalem above,
who is the mother of us all' who are in

Christ Jesus. (Galatians 4: 26-28) The seed according to the promise of Jehovah that shall destroy Satan is Christ our Lord. Jehovah announced at Eden that he would put enmity between the seed of the woman (that is, his beloved One, the seed of his organization) and the Devil. It has ever been so, as we well know from history and from experience, that there has been constant enmity between those who love the Lord and those who hate God: "And I will put enmity between thee and the woman, and between thy seed and her seed; it shall bruise thy head, and thou shalt bruise his heel." (Genesis 3: 15) That clearly shows why the Devil and his dupes always fight against Christ Jesus and his faithful followers. It is the Kingdom, the Holy City, The THEOCRATIC GOVERNMENT, that shall destroy Satan and all wickedness, and that government must be and shall be properly represented on the earth.

Abel, the second son of Adam and Eve, was the first man on the earth to show faith in the Almighty God. God never forgets a faithful creature. It was Abel's faith and obedience that pleased God. (Genesis 4: 4) "By faith Abel offered unto God a more excellent sacrifice than Cain, by which he obtained witness that he was righteous, God testifying of his gifts: and by it he, being dead, yet speaketh."—Hebrews 11: 4.

God counted Abel a righteous man because of his faith. Abel was murdered at the instance of the Devil, and every murder that has been committed on earth has been done at the instance of the Devil. Concerning Abel's righteousness and God's purpose to punish those who have practiced religion and used it to bring about the murder of many others, Jesus Christ said to the religionists on earth at his time: "Wherefore, behold, I send unto you prophets, and wise men, and scribes: and some of them ye shall kill and crucify; and some of them shall ye scourge in your synagogues, and persecute them from city to city: that upon you may come all the righteous blood shed upon the earth, from the blood of righteous Abel unto the blood of Zacharias son of Barachias, whom ye slew between the temple and the altar." (Matthew 23:34, 35) Abel was a good and faithful man, and it is written that "they that have done good" shall be resurrected. (John 5:29) God has a place for Abel.

The next man who had faith in God was Enoch. When it is said that a man walks with God, that means that his course of action is in harmony with God's appointed way or rules. Long ago, as it is written of Enoch, "Enoch walked with God; and he was not, for God took him." (Genesis 5:24) God did not permit the Devil to kill Enoch, and because of Enoch's faith God took him away: "By faith Enoch was translated that he should not see death; and was not found, because God had translated him: for before his translation he had this testimony, that he pleased God." (Hebrews 11: 5) Enoch prophesied that the Lord Jesus Christ, at his coming and his kingdom, will punish those who have fought against God. (Jude 14, 15) It was Enoch's faith that pleased God; and therefore it is written in connection with him and other faithful creatures: "But without faith it is impossible to please him: for he that cometh to God must believe that he is, and that he is a rewarder of them that diligently seek him."—Hebrews 11: 6.

Because of faith God counted Noah a righteous man, and "Noah walked with God". (Genesis 6: 9) In Noah's day the human race had become exceedingly wicked and filled the earth with violence. God informed Noah of His purpose to destroy that wicked generation, and Noah obeyed the Lord God and was saved from that destruction and brought over to the world beginning thereafter: "By faith Noah, being warned of God of things not seen as yet, moved with fear, prepared an ark to the saving of his house; by the which he condemned the world, and became heir of the righteousness which is by faith." (Hebrews 11: 7) That blessing of Noah and his family was because of his faith. God has a further blessing for Noah yet to be received.

Abraham resided in the land of Ur when God directed him to move into a land about which Abraham knew nothing. Having faith in God, Abraham obeyed and went into the strange land. Concerning him and his faith it is written: "By faith Abraham, when he was called to go out into a place which he should after receive for an inheritance, obeyed; and he went out, not knowing whither he went."—Hebrews 11: 8.

In that strange land of Canaan God made a covenant with Abraham and caused Abraham to perform his part in a great prophetic drama, wherein Abraham pictured God himself, and in which Abraham's son Isaac played a part picturing the coming of Christ Jesus and his great sacrifice: "For what saith the scripture? Abraham believed God, and it was counted unto him for righteousness."—Romans 4: 3.

Thereafter Abraham was called "the Friend of God". (James 2: 23) Abraham saw by faith the day coming when God would have his kingdom in operation under Christ Jesus the Messiah, and that filled his heart with joy. Jesus referred to this when he said: "Abraham rejoiced to see my day, and he saw it and was glad." (John 8: 56) The Bible magnifies the importance of faith and obedience unto God by frequent reference to the faith of Abraham, who is called the father of the faithful. "Even as Abraham believed God, and it was accounted to him for righteousness. Know ye therefore, that they which are of faith, the same are the children of Abraham."—Galatians 3:6, 7.

Abraham was swift to obey God, and that meant he was ready and willing, upon short notice, to move, and also shows that he had no fixed abiding place on the earth, but was looking for a better place. He dwelt in tents with his sons and grandsons; concerning which it is written: "By faith he sojourned in the land of promise, as in a strange country, dwelling in tabernacles with Isaac and Jacob, the heirs with him of the same promise: for he looked for a city which hath foundations, whose builder and maker is God." —Hebrews 11:9, 10.

Abraham had faith in God's government of righteousness, THE THEOCRACY, which is symbolized by a city, and God has fixed a place for Abraham. Sarah his wife was old and past the age of childbearing. She had no children; but when God sent his angel and informed Sarah that she would give birth to a son, Sarah had faith in God's promise and God blessed her: "Through faith also Sara herself received strength to conceive seed, and was delivered of a child when she was past age, because she judged him faithful who had promised. Therefore sprang there even of one, and him as good as dead, so many as the stars of the sky in multitude, and as the sand which is by the sea shore innumerable."—Hebrews 11: 11, 12.

Abraham and Sarah's only son, Isaac, grew to manhood's estate, and then God put a great test upon Abraham. God commanded Abraham to offer his son upon a fiery altar of sacrifice. Under that great test Abraham exhibited strong faith in God. "By faith Abraham, when he was tried, offered up Isaac; and he that had received the promises offered up his only begotten son, of whom it was said, That in Isaac shall thy seed be called: accounting that God was able to raise him up, even from the dead; from whence also he received him in a figure." (Hebrews 11: 17-19; Genesis 22: 9-18) It was on that occasion that Abraham and Isaac performed their parts in the great prophetic drama foretelling the sacrificial death and resurrection of the beloved Son of Jehovah God.

Faithful Isaac was also used of God to foreshadow the seed of promise, that is to say, those who would be made partakers of the great THEOCRACY. (Galatians 4: 28) The Scriptures tell of the faith of Isaac and of Jacob, who, because of their faith and obedience unto God, became heirs to the promise of God made first to Abraham; and concerning this it is written: "By faith Isaac blessed Jacob and Esau concerning things to come.

By faith Jacob, when he was a dying, blessed both the sons of Joseph; and worshipped, leaning upon the top of his staff."—Hebrews 11: 20, 21.

Moving on in the development of the typical theocracy, and looking further to the great and real THEOCRATIC GOVERNMENT, the Holy City that shall rule the world in righteousness, God makes note of the faith and faithfulness of Joseph, the beloved son of Jacob. Then he makes mention of Moses, who also was there used as a type of Christ Jesus. Moses was reared by the royal family of Egypt; but, upon receiving instruction from God and having faith in God's promise, he refused to be called the son of Pharaoh's daughter, and devoted himself to the service of Jehovah. "Choosing rather to suffer affliction with the people of God, than to enjoy the pleasures of sin for a season; esteeming the reproach of Christ greater riches than the treasures in Egypt: for he had respect unto the recompence of the reward. By faith he forsook Egypt, not fearing the wrath of the king: for he endured, as seeing him who is invisible."—Hebrews 11: 25-27.

By faith he saw the coming THEOCRACY and devoted his life to the service of God. He was chosen of God to lead the Israelites out of Egypt, and in this he played the part in one of Jehovah's great prophetic dramas foretelling the deliverance of God's faithful people from the power and oppression of Satan's organization. "Through faith he kept the passover, and the sprinkling of blood, lest he that destroyed the first-born should touch them. By faith they passed through the Red sea as by dry land: which the Egyptians assaying to do were drowned."—Hebrews 11: 28, 29.

Joshua succeeded to the place once occupied by Moses. He received command from Almighty God to lead the Israelites into Canaan, and in doing so God worked a great miracle, causing the raging waters of the Jordan river to stand still while Joshua led the host of Israel and they marched over dryshod into safety. (See Joshua chapter 3.) At God's command Joshua led the Israelites around the walled city of Jericho, behind which walls the enemies of God's people hid for safety, and it was God who threw down those walls; and concerning the faith of Joshua and those who were with him it is written: "By faith the walls of Jericho fell down, after they were compassed about seven days."–Hebrews 11: 30.

God would have it known that even harlots can turn away from a wrongful course and find the way of life, whereas those who practice religion and refuse to obey God fail to find life. (Matthew 21: 31) In Jericho resided a woman named Rahab, who was engaged in keeping a bawdyhouse. She learned of Jehovah's power and his blessing upon those who have faith in him and who serve Jehovah God. Upon learning these truths she readily made a covenant with God's servants to shield and protect them, and she exhibited her faith in God by agreeing to do what they requested her to do to protect them. Thereby she played a part in a prophetic drama foretelling that in the present time of wickedness on the earth those who show favor to God's servants shall be blessed by the Lord. Rahab's faith in God was rewarded, and she was saved from the fate that befell those of Jericho who had no faith in God; and concerning her it is written: "By faith the harlot Rahab perished not with them that believed not, when she had received the spies with peace." (Hebrews 11:31; Joshua 6:23) God has given his Word that he will not forget the faith of Rahab but in his own due time she is certain to receive his everlasting blessing because of her faith.

Although Israel as a nation turned to demonism or religion and for that reason God cast away the nation, there were amongst the Israelites some faithful men who exercised faith in God, and who looked forward to THE THEOCRACY, and who because of their faith rendered service unto God and received his promised blessing. Those men are mentioned in the Scriptures as receiving the approval of Almighty God because of refusing to yield to the influence of Satan and his agents, and because of their devotion to God it is written concerning them: "And what shall I more say? for the time would fail me to tell of Gedeon, and of Barak, and of Samson, and of Jephthae; of David also, and Samuel, and of the prophets."—Hebrews 11:32.

There was Gideon, a farmer, who was threshing his wheat when the angel of Jehovah appeared and told Gideon that God had selected him to be a deliverer of the Israelites from the Devil religionists, the Midianites, who were oppressing the Israelites. (See Judges sixth chapter.) With his little band reduced to only 300 men Gideon put to flight and destroyed the enemy host of the Midianites. Thus God rewarded him with service because of his faith and made a prophetic picture of greater blessings to come in future days.

Barak is another specifically named because of his faith. With him was Deborah, the prophetess of God, who worked with Barak. Deborah played a part in the prophetic drama, picturing the organization of God, while Barak, the commander of the loyal forces of Israel, played the part in that drama picturing Christ Jesus the Lord. With a small army of 10,000 men, poorly equipped, Barak joined battle with an overwhelming enemy host, which host was equipped with iron chariots under the leadership of Sisera. In that battle the angels of heaven fought with Barak and Almighty God sent a great storm and flood, which swept away the disorganized and disrupted army of Sisera, and then Barak destroyed the entire lot as they fled. (See Judges chapters four and five.) Barak is mentioned for his faithfulness, and God has a place for him.

Samson received favorable report from the Lord because of his faithful devotion to Almighty God. He was used by the Lord to deliver the Israelites from the bondage in which they were held by the demonized religionists, the Philistines. (See Judges chapters 13 to 16.) After faithful service to God Samson was taken prisoner and brought before the Philistines, who put out his eyes and brought him into a public place to exhibit him and taunt him and reproach his God. Samson there played a part in the prophetic drama picturing the faithful servants of the great THEOCRACY, who are blind to everything except Jehovah God and his kingdom. Blind Samson, held a prisoner, was given great strength by Jehovah to pull down the two pillars supporting the temple of the demons, where there were assembled thousands of religionists who reproached and defamed God's holy name. Samson was faithful even to the last and in his death slew a host of God's enemies. His faith secured for him God's approval.

Jephthah was another faithful servant of God, who led the loyal Israelites in battle against their enemy, the Ammonites, who were demon-worshipers. Jephthah gained by the Lord's grace a great victory in vindication of Jehovah's name. (See Judges 11: 1-33.) That which appears to have been pleasing to God, and which gained for Jephthah God's approval, was the keeping of his vow, which Jephthah made, the keeping of which put Jephthah to a great and crucial test.—Psalm 50: 14.

David when a lad, because of his faith and devotion to Almighty God, was permitted to slay the monster Goliath, foreshadowing Christ Jesus slaying the monster, the oppressor of humankind. David fought many battles, and, in every instance, those battles were for the vindication of Jehovah's name. Of David God said: 'He is a man after my own heart.' (1 Samuel 13: 14; Psalm 89: 20; Acts 13: 22) David's name means *beloved*. He was a type of Christ Jesus. It was David's faithfulness to God that gained for him His approval.

Samuel was a child of parents who were devoted to and served God. His mother consecrated Samuel to Jehovah before Samuel's birth, and when the babe was weaned she handed him over to the service of God. That was a specific instance in which the child was taught from his youth up to have faith in and to serve God, and from that

he never departed. He was yet a child when
God called Samuel to be a prophet and used
him thereafter as a prophet. Samuel was
faithful unto the end and repeatedly warned
the Israelites against demonism or religion.
He judged Israel with a righteous judgment, always showing his devotion to Almighty God. (See 1 Samuel chapters 1 to 7.)
Samuel prophesied the coming of The THEO-
CRATIC GOVERNMENT and the King thereof
and the setting up of that kingdom in power
and glory.—Acts 3:20-24.

Then favorable mention is made of the
prophets by and through whom God has
spoken, which prophets had faith in God
and in his coming government, THE THEOC-
RACY, and prophesied of its coming. Because
of their faithfulness they received God's
approval. A list of these names of faithful
prophets appears in the Bible. Their prophetic utterances were not their own con-
clusions, such as "wise men" of today utter,
but those faithful men wrote as they were
moved of the spirit of God to write.—2 Peter 1:21.

Valiant Fighters

Every one of those faithful men endured
great affliction, which was heaped upon them
by religionists and other dupes of the Devil,
and all these faithful men are mentioned as
valiant fighters. The Devil, in his effort to
make effective his wicked challenge to Al-

PRESENTATION OF SAMUEL FOR TEMPLE SERVICE

mighty God, fought against these faithful
men, endeavoring to turn them away from
God. In that fight the Devil employed religion or demonism as his chief instrument,
and applied physical force where he could
not succeed by fraud and deception. That
those men remained true and steadfast under the test and showed their faith and devotion to God, the Almighty caused to be
written in his Word concerning them the
following, to wit: "Who through faith sub-

dued kingdoms, wrought righteousness, obtained promises, stopped the mouths of lions, quenched the violence of fire, escaped the edge of the sword, out of weakness were made strong, waxed valiant in fight, turned to flight the armies of the aliens. Women received their dead raised to life again: and others were tortured, not accepting deliverance; that they might obtain a better resurrection: and others had trial of cruel mockings and scourgings, yea, moreover, of bonds and imprisonment: they were stoned, they were sawn asunder, were tempted, were slain with the sword: they wandered about in sheepskins and goatskins; being destitute, afflicted, tormented; (of whom the world was not worthy:) they wandered in deserts, and in mountains, and in dens and caves of the earth."—Hebrews 11: 33-38.

The Promise

Almighty God had given his word that he would raise up a seed and set up his government, by which the world shall be ruled in righteousness and by which obedient men shall be forever blessed. Later he renewed this word of promise to Abraham and bound his word with his oath. (Genesis 12: 3; 22: 16-18; Hebrews 6: 17-20) The faithful men described in the foregoing chapter who died before the coming of Christ Jesus trusted God implicitly. They believed his promises and relied upon them. They willingly bore

testimony to their faith in God's Word of
promise, and they sealed their testimony
with their own lifeblood. They did not expect the promised government in their day,
but they were firmly convinced that in his
due time God would carry out fully his word
of promise, and therefore they went into
death full of faith. Their faith is certain
to be rewarded by the Most High. Mark
here the Scriptural proof: "These all died
in faith, not having received the promises,
but having seen them afar off, and were per-
suaded of them, and embraced them, and
confessed that they were strangers and pil-
grims on the earth."—Hebrews 11:13.

They knew that the promise would not be
fulfilled completely while Satan continued
to be the invisible overlord or god of this
wicked world: "For they that say such
things declare plainly that they seek a country." (Hebrews 11:14) They were seeking a
country; which manifestly meant that they
were not devoted to the country wherein
they resided. They were seeking what country? The Scriptures answer: "The kingdom of heaven," "the Holy City," which
Jesus bought with his own lifeblood. They
willingly took that course, and they could
have turned back had they so desired. "And
truly, if they had been mindful of that country from whence they came out, they might
have had opportunity to have returned: but
now they desire a better country, that is, an

heavenly: wherefore God is not ashamed to be called their God; for he hath prepared for them a city."—Hebrews 11: 15, 16.

God has prepared a place for them in connection with the Holy City, his THEOCRATIC GOVERNMENT. A "city", or ruling organization, is specifically prepared for them. This "city" is not a part of the Holy City, but God's organization just the same, and which operates under the supervision of the Holy City.

When will those faithful men come into possession of what is prepared for them? The Scriptures answer that they received the approval of God as faithful men but, while they sojourned on earth, they did not come into possession of or bear away that which was promised. And why did they not receive it before their death? That question is specifically answered as follows: "And these all, having obtained a good report through faith, received not the promise: God having provided some better thing for us, that they without us should not be made perfect."— Hebrews 11: 39, 40.

Clearly the meaning of this scripture, last quoted, is that some "better thing" must first be provided for others, of whom Paul was one part, and before those faithful men of old could come into their reward or that which was prepared for them. That "better thing" here mentioned is the Holy City, the kingdom of God, The THEOCRATIC GOVERN-

MENT, and it is prepared for those who compose the capital organization, to wit, Christ Jesus and the members of his body, all of whom must prove faithful unto death. That would mean that all of the Holy City must be selected and the Kingdom must come before those holy men of old could receive what is prepared for them.

This is the order, as shown by the Scriptures: Jehovah God first revealed to his beloved Son the hidden treasure, which is The THEOCRATIC GOVERNMENT. The beloved Son gave up everything that he had that he might buy that treasure, and he bought it, including all obedient creatures. The purchase price was presented in heaven, and the first ones to receive the benefit thereof are those who are called and elected to be members of the Holy City or "holy nation", the kingdom of heaven. The Kingdom must be completed and set up, with Christ Jesus in full authority and glory as King, before these faithful men could be granted everlasting life on earth. The ransom sacrifice, by which the purchase price was provided for mankind, must first be paid over before any man could be released from the bondage of death, which had been inherited through Adam.

When Jesus became a man and when he was crucified as a man, at that time all the faithful men preceding him and herein mentioned had passed away. Where were they since they had been counted righteous and had received a good report from Jehovah? Had they gone to heaven? The Scripture answers that all were dead. No one could go to heaven before the purchase price was paid over in heaven and the heavenly way was open. Concerning David, 'the man after God's own heart,' it is specifically written: "For David is not ascended into the heavens: but he saith himself, The Lord said unto my Lord, Sit thou on my right hand, until I make thy foes thy footstool."—Acts 2:34, 35.

John the Baptist was one of the great prophets, and he can never be in heaven, because he had died before the crucifixion of the Lord: "Verily I say unto you, Among them that are born of women there hath not risen a greater than John the Baptist: notwithstanding, he that is least in the kingdom of heaven is greater than he."—Matthew 11:11.

All those men died and went out of existence into the grave, or "hell", but all are held in the memory of Almighty God, and whom he will resurrect from the dead in his own due time and according to his promise. Those men had faith in the resurrection, and therefore they endured the great fight of affliction even unto death in order "that they might obtain [the] better resurrection".— Hebrews 11:35.

Resurrection

Those who compose the royal house, the holy nation of which Christ Jesus is the Head, participate in the "first resurrection", that is to say, first in importance and first in time. (Revelation 20:4, 6) The apostle Paul wrote that he gladly suffered the loss of everything that he might share in that resurrection with Christ Jesus. (Philippians 3:7-14) Those who have a part in the resurrection of Christ are raised up out of death and made spirit creatures and are given like immortality, and their everlasting existence is in the spirit in heaven.

Faithful men of old, from Abel to the last one of the prophets, cannot have a part in the "first resurrection", for the reason that they died before the heavenly way was opened and before anyone was called to the heavenly kingdom. The life of those faithful men shall be forever human on the earth. They have a "better resurrection", however, than those of the human race in general have who are favored in the general resurrection. Those faithful men of old had their trial of faith before the purchase price or ransom was made available, but they had full faith in God's promise and they shall receive the benefit of the ransom sacrifice because of their faith and faithfulness. Other human creatures, that have lived on the earth for a season and died, are held in the memory of God and shall be resurrected, but not on equal terms with those faithful men of old who received God's approval before they died.

Invisible

Jehovah God is the great eternal Spirit. No human eye can ever see God: "And he said, Thou canst not see my face: for there shall no man see me, and live." (Exodus 33:17-23) Jehovah is the almighty Potentate, the King of eternity. (Jeremiah 10:10, *margin*) "[God] only hath immortality, dwelling in the light which no man can approach unto; whom no man hath seen, nor can see: to whom be honour and power everlasting. Amen."—1 Timothy 6:16.

The Lord Jesus Christ is "the express image" of his Father, Jehovah God. (Hebrews 1:3) He is that great Spirit, and, like Jehovah, no human eye can ever behold him. The members of the body of Christ in the resurrection are made in the likeness of Christ Jesus (1 John 3:2), made spirits and with Christ Jesus in the Holy City, and can never be seen by human eyes, because human eyes cannot see a spirit. Therefore The THEOCRATIC GOVERNMENT, the Holy City, will always be invisible to human eyes, but will exercise absolute control over all things in the earth.

Visible

When God set up his typical theocracy with Israel and ruled over Israel as his chos-

en people, none of the Israelites saw him;
yet they observed his power. When God
spoke to his faithful men he sent an angel
as his messenger, who appeared in human
form and delivered the message from the
Most High. (Genesis 22:11; Joshua 5:13-
15; Judges 6:11) God made the earth for
man and He made man for the earth, and
in due time righteous men shall live for ever
on the earth. They shall have an organization that shall govern in righteousness. That
organization will be, not a democracy, but
a government representative of the great
THEOCRACY, acting under the direct supervision of the King of the great THEOCRATIC
GOVERNMENT. Necessarily that representative government will be visible to human
eyes, and the people will receive the laws
and instructions through those visible representatives.

Princes

A "prince" is a sovereign ruler appointed by and acting under the direct command
of the supreme or higher powers. Jehovah
God and Christ Jesus his King are "the
Higher Powers". (Romans 13:1) Jehovah
is the King of eternity over all, and Christ
Jesus is the King of the Holy City and, as
the Chief Executive appointed by Jehovah,
has and exercises all power in heaven and
in earth. (Matthew 28:18; John 5:22, 26)
The Lord Jesus Christ is "the Prince of

Peace", and upon his shoulder the government of THE THEOCRACY shall rest. (Isaiah 9:6, 7) The chief ruler amongst men appointed by the Lord is a prince. — Genesis 32:28; 1 Kings 14:7.

"In All the Earth"

The faithful men of the nation of Israel were called 'fathers in Israel' and were so recognized by the Israelites, and are thus spoken of in the Word of God. (Acts 3:22) Those faithful men of old who had faith in the coming THEOCRATIC GOVERNMENT and were under the great test proved their faith and integrity toward God; and while a long time ago they died and went into the tomb or grave, yet in the memory and purpose of Almighty God they have lived, because it is his express purpose by and through Christ Jesus to resurrect them from the dead. (Exodus 3:6; Matthew 22:31, 32) Since those faithful men and servants of Jehovah God have opportunity of a "better resurrection", and since God gave his word of promise that he had "prepared for them a city", that is, an organization, where will their eternal existence be? and what position or place in God's great arrangement shall they have? This question is answered in the following scripture, to wit: "INSTEAD OF THY FATHERS SHALL BE THY CHILDREN, WHOM THOU MAYEST MAKE PRINCES IN ALL THE EARTH."— Psalm 45:16.

Christ Jesus bought those faithful men, and bought their rights to life with his own lifeblood. They must therefore receive life from God by and through Christ Jesus. It is the will of God that Christ Jesus shall raise them out of death and give them life. (Romans 6: 23; 5: 18, 19) Their resurrection shall take place, according to the Scriptures, when the Kingdom comes and begins to function. When raised from the dead and given life they will be the "children" of Christ Jesus because receiving life by and through him. Therefore it is certain that those faithful men will be raised from the dead as perfect human creatures, and be appointed to and occupy the high position of "princes [or visible overlords or sovereign rulers] in all the earth". They will not be a part of the Holy City, or THEOCRATIC GOVERNMENT, because that is spiritual; but they will occupy the high position of visible representatives of the Holy City, or THEOCRACY, and will govern or rule the peoples of the earth, and all the people will look to them to receive instruction from them.

In full corroboration of this note the words, to wit, "Behold, a king shall reign in righteousness, and princes shall rule in judgment." (Isaiah 32: 1) The King James or Authorized Version uses the word *judgment* as to the manner of the rule of these princes, whereas another translation renders the word *justice*. Both are correct. The

judgments or judicial determinations are
made by the Lord, and those faithful princes
will carry out or execute those judgments
previously written and made by the Lord,
and they will carry out these judgments or
orders with exact justice to all. All the peoples that live on earth shall come under their
visible rule or command. That will be a rule
that will be a joy to the whole earth and all
the people in it. "When the righteous are
in authority, the people rejoice."—Proverbs 29: 2.

_____

"That is certainly thrilling," said John.
"Eunice, by the grace of the Lord we may
see those faithful princes soon. We shall be
anxious to see them and follow their lead.
As Jesus said, 'Abraham by faith saw the
day of His kingdom, which shall rule in
righteousness, and he rejoiced.' Abraham
saw it by faith. Now by faith we see the
righteous government or rule of the world,
and we do now rejoice. Let us continue our
studies and learn from the Scriptures what
may be our position or place in the Lord's
gracious arrangement."

CHAPTER 6

OTHER SHEEP

> "After this I beheld, and, lo, a great multitude, which no man could number, of all nations, and kindreds, and people, and tongues, stood before the throne, and before the Lamb, clothed with white robes, and palms in their hands."
> – Revelation 7:9.

JEHOVAH builds up Zion, his capital organization, and then makes provision for faithful and obedient men to acquire that which Adam forfeited by reason of his disobedience. Man is the highest element of animal life, but God employs the names of lower animals to illustrate both disobedient and obedient men. Goats are used to symbolize disobedient human creatures; sheep used to symbolize obedient men. It is those obedient men that are called by the Lord "other sheep".

THE THEOCRACY is the government created and built up by the Almighty God as his capital organization and which shall rule the world. Those who are made members of that government are selected and elected by Jehovah. Their number is definitely fixed before the selection begins, and this is emphasized at Revelation 7:1-8. It is mainfestly certain that when THE THEOCRACY is completed there is no further opportunity for creatures to be installed into that government. Jesus uttered a parable concerning the Kingdom and concluded it with the statement: 'When the Bridegroom [which is Christ Jesus] came, they that were ready went in with him, and the door was shut.' (Matthew 25:1-10; Luke 13:24, 25) Those received by the Lord and made members of the Kingdom he calls the "little flock" of his sheep, because the number is comparatively small and is definitely fixed. (Luke 12:32) Such are the ones that are associated with Christ Jesus in heaven.

Aside from those who compose the "little flock" there are human creatures that get life everlasting and must live on the earth. God did not make the earth in vain, but he made it to be inhabited by perfect men. (Isaiah 45:12, 18) For centuries the Devil has attempted to prevent there being a perfect man on earth, and this effort on the Devil's part has been put forth by him to carry out his wicked challenge to Jehovah that God could not put men on earth that would remain faithful to him. The Devil's challenge shall fall flat.

God's purpose cannot fail, because he is all-powerful. Jehovah says, "I have spoken it, I will also bring it to pass; I have purposed it, I will also do it." (Isaiah 46:11) "So shall my word be that goeth forth out of my mouth: it shall not return unto me void; but it shall accomplish that which I please, and it shall prosper in the thing whereto I sent it."—Isaiah 55:11.

His announced purpose is to make the earth a fit place for righteous human creatures to live. "The earth abideth for ever." (Ecclesiastes 1:4) That means that the earth shall be the everlasting home of righteous, perfect men. Righteous men shall rule the earth under the direction and supervision of the Lord Jesus Christ. What place has the Lord provided for his "other sheep"?

Identification

It appears to be the rule that Jehovah brings about conditions in fulfillment of his prophecy and, after that, permits his faithful servants to see the fulfillment of the prophecy and sometimes to have a part in the fulfillment. Jesus uttered a great prophecy concerning his coming in glory and in power to begin his reign, and this prophecy began to have fulfillment in 1914, and his coming to the temple of God took place in 1918. Before that time no human creature could understand whom the Lord meant by his statement 'the sheep on my right hand'. Note the prophecy, which reads: "When the Son of man shall come in his glory, and all the holy angels with him, then shall he sit upon the throne of his glory."— Matthew 25:31.

That fixes the time for the Lord's appearing at the temple for judgment, and which came to pass in A.D. 1918. Thereafter he conducts his judgment, separating those persons of good-will toward his kingdom from those who are against his kingdom. Those of good-will he calls 'the sheep on my right hand', which manifestly are the "other sheep" mentioned at John 10: 16. Such human creatures, pictured by his "other sheep", cannot go to heaven, and therefore must find life on the earth. God's purpose from the beginning was that righteous men under his kingdom should receive the benefit of the Kingdom, which Jesus purchased with his own lifeblood: "And he shall set the sheep on his right hand, but the goats on the left. Then shall the King say unto them on his right hand, Come, ye blessed of my Father, inherit the kingdom prepared for you from the foundation of the world; for I was an hungred, and ye gave me meat; I was thirsty, and ye gave me drink: I was a stranger, and ye took me in."—Matthew 25: 33-35.

The apostle John, who wrote down The Revelation at the dictation of the Lord, specifically represented or pictured the faithful servants of the Lord who are on the earth at the time of the coming of Christ

Jesus to the temple. When he wrote, John
was in banishment on the isle of Patmos.
God's faithful people now on the earth are
in banishment so far as other peoples of
the earth are concerned. They are hated by
all the nations because they are faithful to
the Lord, even as Jesus foretold. (Matthew
24: 9) John had made inquiry as to the identity of the "great multitude" which he first
beheld, as described at Revelation 7: 9 and
Revelation 7: 13, 14. Likewise at the time
of his coming to the temple the faithful followers of Christ Jesus did not know the
identity of the "great multitude", and so
they had to inquire, and in due time the
Lord revealed the identity of that multitude. It appears clearly from the Scriptures
that no one on the earth could identify the
"great multitude" until after the coming
of the Lord to the temple. Thereafter it is
the will of God that his faithful people
on the earth shall understand. (Revelation
1: 11; Daniel 12: 10) Now they see that the
"great multitude" are the same as the
Lord's "other sheep".

Prior to the coming of the Lord to his
temple sincere students of the Bible had
understood that the "great multitude" mentioned at Revelation seven is a spiritual company of secondary importance, possessing a
less degree of faith than that of those who
shall reign with Christ. That view could not
be correct, for the following reasons: No

one can please God unless he has and exercises faith and is faithful. "God is no respecter of persons," and he changes not. (Acts 10:34; Malachi 3:6) All of mankind who get life must maintain their integrity toward God, and hence must have and exercise faith and must prove faithful. It is only such that have part in the vindication of Jehovah's name. 'A secondary class of less faith,' therefore, is wholly inconsistent with God's purpose.

John records the fact that 144,000 members are of "the body of Christ", which reign with him. Before he had a vision of such he had no vision of the "great multitude". Then he says: "After this I beheld, and, lo, a great multitude, which no man could number, of all nations, and kindreds, and people, and tongues, stood before the throne, and before the Lamb, clothed with white robes, and palms in their hands." (Revelation 7:9) It therefore clearly appears that the spirit class are a fixed number, because these are a part of the Kingdom. Those of the "great multitude" are not a limited number, but rather the Lord opens the way for as many to come as may desire to serve him. He puts no limitation on the number. These come from all nations. They stand "before the throne", which shows that they are not in the throne and not a part of the Kingdom. They do not have to be in heaven in order to be be-

190 CHILDREN

fore the throne of judgment, but, on the contrary, their judgment takes place on earth; and this is shown by the words of Jesus at Matthew 25: 31, 32. They stand before the Lamb, that is, before Christ Jesus, the great Judge and King. They have a standing and are thus received by the Lord. They are, as symbolically stated, "clothed with white robes." Each one has a robe, showing that the robe is a means of identification of the individual members. Their being white robes symbolizes that they are clean and pure.

How do they get clean and have pure robes? The Scriptures answer that they "have washed their robes . . . in the blood of the Lamb" (Revelation 7: 14); that is to say, they have exercised faith in the Lord Jesus Christ, the Lamb of God, who takes away the sin of the world. (John 1: 29) They have exercised faith by coming to the Lord and obeying his commandments. They also appear with "palms in their hands". "Palms" symbolize that they are recognizing Christ Jesus as the King, and they welcome him with shouts of joy. This was foreshadowed at the time Jesus rode into Jerusalem and offered himself as King, and at that time "a great multitude . . . took the branches of the palm trees, and went forth to meet him" and hailed him as King. (John 12: 12, 13, *Am. Rev. Ver.;* Matthew 21: 8, 9) In symbolic phrase of Revelation 7: 9, that "great multitude" stood before the Lord's throne of judgment and there received the Lord's approval, and they recognized and accepted Christ Jesus as their Lord, Redeemer and King. Those pictured there as the "great multitude" gave expression to their joy, as is stated: "[They] cried with a loud voice, saying, Salvation to our God which sitteth upon the throne, and unto the Lamb." (Revelation 7:10) Thus they show that they have learned and believed that to Almighty God belongs salvation, which he is giving to man by and through Christ Jesus, the purchaser and Redeemer. — Psalm 3:8; Acts 4:12; Romans 6:23.

Revelation 7:11, 12 describes the heavenly creatures joining in the praise of Jehovah because the time has come for the gathering of the Lord's "other sheep". Then it was that the question was propounded concerning the multitude: "What are these which are arrayed in white robes? and whence came they?" (Vs. 13) The answer is given: "These are they which came out of great tribulation, and have washed their robes ... in the blood of the Lamb." (Vs. 14) That means that they have been gathered unto the Lord in troublesome times.

Physical Facts

When the physical facts that have come to pass fit the prophecy, then we may be sure that we have a proper understanding of the prophecy. The seventh chapter of Revelation is prophecy. Note the facts that have been brought to pass and made clear in recent times. In the religious denominations, called "churches", there have been and still are many persons who are made sad by reason of the practices that are carried on in those organizations in the name of the Lord. These sad persons have a desire to know about God and Christ that their hearts may be filled with joy. These are the ones that hunger and thirst for righteousness. Jehovah's faithful witnesses, acting under the command of Christ Jesus, give to such sincere persons information of and concerning God's kingdom, and this they do by taking to them the knowledge of the truth and thus "set a mark upon the foreheads [seat of intelligence] of the men that sigh, and that cry, for all the abominations that be done in the midst thereof [that is, in the midst of the religious congregations]". (Ezekiel 9:4) For several years Jehovah's witnesses have been carrying the Kingdom message to those other persons who have hungered and thirsted for righteousness, and in recent months many have fled from the religious institutions and have taken their stand firmly on the side of Jehovah and his THEOCRATIC GOVERNMENT under Christ Jesus. Such are the ones to whom Jesus referred when he said: "Blessed are they which do hunger and thirst after righteousness: for they shall be filled."— Matthew 5 : 6.

Jehovah's witnesses have been going from house to house with the message of the Kingdom, and multitudes of people have come and are coming to the Lord, and are learning of his purpose and taking their stand firmly on the side of God and his kingdom. By exercising faith in the shed blood of Christ Jesus and his kingdom they have identified themselves as being blessed of God and his King, and they are receiving his blessing. They have every reason to rejoice, and do rejoice and attribute salvation and all blessings to the Almighty God and to his King.

How do they serve the Lord and his kingdom? They "serve him day and night", meaning, all the time, continuously. (Rev. 7:15) They have received the truth of and concerning God's kingdom and have learned that Jesus has bought all the Kingdom interests and all the rights of obedient men, and with joy they go about telling others who have a hearing ear, and thus sing the praises of Jehovah God, his Kingdom, and his King. These facts, now well known and understood, exactly fit the prophecy and thus are proving that the present is the time when the Lord is gathering unto himself his "other sheep", that shall compose the "great multitude".

Tribulation

"These are they that come out of the great tribulation." (Vs. 14, *Am. Rev. Ver.*) Christ Jesus was enthroned as King in 1914 and came to his temple in 1918, and from that time onward tribulation upon the earth has continuously increased, and in that time the Devil has done all within his power to turn the people away from God and his kingdom. (Revelation 12:12) During this time of tribulation upon the earth the Lord gathers to himself those of good-will, and these, taking their stand on the side of God and his kingdom, find peace of mind and joy of heart, and these go to make up the "great multitude". No more do they need to hunger for the truth, because the Lord feeds them from his own storehouse of truth. (Revelation 7:16, 17) Multitudes of people in the earth have hungered and others do hunger for the truth. They want something different from the husks which they have been receiving from religious institutions. Learning the truth, therefore, from God's Word, they flee to the Lord. It has been the privilege and it is the privilege of Jehovah's witnesses to carry this spiritual food to the hungry ones, and when such hungry ones are fed upon the truth concerning the Kingdom their joy is great and they quickly join themselves with "the remnant" to carry that message of good news to others, and thus the number of the Lord's "other sheep" continuously increases.

Peace

Woe, sorrow, distress and great suffering now afflict the peoples of all nations of the earth. The Devil and his host of demons have taken all peace from the earth, but there is a company of persons who amidst all the strife and turmoil have peace and contentment. And who are they? These are the ones who are of good-will toward God and who exercise faith in him and his King. When the man-child Jesus was born, the angels of God, at his command, sung this anthem: "Glory in the highest unto God! and on earth peace, among men of good-will."—Luke 2:14, *Rotherham.*

Only those who are now of good-will toward God and his King can have and enjoy peace of mind that passes understanding of all others. (Philippians 4:7) Those who put their trust in God and his kingdom well know that God is their salvation and that he will make things work together for the good of those who love and serve him. They clearly see from the Scriptures that Satan the Devil has brought all the woe upon the nations and peoples of the earth and that this he is doing in his effort to carry out his challenge to turn all men away from God. The faithful servants of Jehovah hear the message, and believe and rely upon it, to

wit, "The God of peace shall bruise Satan
under your feet shortly." (Romans 16:20)
The "great multitude" share in this knowledge and rejoice.

Refuge

Any ceremony or practice indulged in,
and which is contrary to the will of Almighty God, is religion, because such is always prompted by the chief of demons,
Satan. Nazism, Communism, Fascism, and
suchlike, are against God, and their practices are religious. The religious institutions called "church denominations" teach
doctrines that defame God's name and oppose his kingdom; for instance, such doctrines as the immortality of all souls; conscious suffering of the dead in "purgatory"
or "hell torment"; the doctrine concerning
Peter as the foundation of the church, and
that he has successors on earth; the doctrine of worshiping images, and suchlike.
These doctrines have been a means to en-
snare many good, honest and sincere people. God has repeatedly warned against such
snares. (Deuteronomy 7:16) The Scriptures
clearly point out that every people on earth
that has followed religion has sooner or
later met disaster.

Foreknowing the many pitfalls and difficulties in the way of men which are provided by the Devil to deceive men, God has
made provision to relieve men from these

difficulties when they sincerely seek to know the right way. When the chosen people of God, the Israelites, were on their way to the Promised Land God commanded Moses to provide certain cities known as "cities of refuge". (Deuteronomy 4:41-44; Joshua 20:1-7; Numbers 35) The cities of refuge were provided for the benefit of the children of Israel and 'for the strangers or sojourners amongst them'. (Numbers 35:15) God's "everlasting covenant" concerning the sanctity of human life forbids the taking of human life except it be done officially by one authorized by the Lord to do so. (Genesis 9:6) The law concerning the cities of refuge, briefly, was this: If a man killed another willfully, intentionally and with malice, he must be put to death as a murderer, and the one executing him is called the "avenger of blood", that is, the official executioner. If one killed a man accidentally or unawares and without malice, his means of protection was to flee to the city of refuge and remain within the bounds of that city, obedient to the laws thereof, until the death of the high priest; and while he remained within the bounds of the city and obeyed the laws thereof he was safe from being punished. (For a detailed discussion see *Salvation,* page 211, and *Riches,* page 106.)

The entire matter relating to cities of refuge was typical, and foreshadowed greater things to come to pass at the end of the world, where we now are. (Hebrews 10:1; 12:12-29; 1 Corinthians 10:11; Romans 15:4) The cities of refuge represented the Lord's organization, to which persons of good-will may now flee. All nations have some kind of religion, which is a reproach upon the name of God. The controlling or ruling elements of the nations are, to wit, religious, political, and commercial. Such ruling powers have willfully violated or broken God's "everlasting covenant" concerning the sanctity of life, and God declares his purpose to punish them for the same. (Isaiah 24:5) But in all those nations there are many persons of good-will who have been induced by the ruling powers to participate in breaking the everlasting covenant, and which persons of good-will have thus done ignorantly or unawares. All nations hate and persecute the servants of God, and do so willfully; but in those nations there are many persons who are kind to the servants of God and show kindness to them because they are serving God, and there are others who indulge in the persecution of God's people ignorantly but learn later of their wrongdoing and repent. The one who continues in willful wrongdoing receives due punishment at the hands of the Lord, whereas those who have committed a wrong unwittingly, that is, ignorantly, and afterwards repent and seek to rectify their

wrongdoing, may find refuge if they flee to
the Lord Jesus Christ. The "avenger of
blood" is the Lord, Christ Jesus, the official Executioner of Jehovah, who at Armageddon will execute all willful wrongdoers.

The antitypical city of refuge, therefore,
is God's organization under Christ the King.
After the coming of Christ Jesus to the temple, the antitypical city of refuge is open to
receive for protection those who flee from
Satan's organization to the organization of
the Lord. They flee by having and exercising faith in the shed blood of Christ Jesus
as their Redeemer and by consecrating themselves to God and his King, agreeing to do
and then doing the will of the Lord. Those
who thus flee to the antitypical city of refuge must remain there until the battle of
the great day of God Almighty, that is to
say, until the antitypical high-priestly class
is fully completed. It is at the battle of
Armageddon that the official execution by
Christ Jesus takes place upon the wicked,
but those who have found refuge under the
Lord's organization are promised protection. All such are included in those called
the Lord's "other sheep", which he is now
gathering. The fact that the provision of
the cities of refuge in the type would receive strangers and sojourners shows that
in the antitype the protection is for those
who are not of the elect Kingdom class, but
those who are the "other sheep" of the Lord

and who shall constitute the "great multitude".

Other Prophetic Pictures

There are many prophetic pictures set forth in the Bible foretelling the "great multitude". Jehu was anointed by the command of God to be king over Israel. He was commissioned by the Lord to destroy demonism or religion amongst the Israelites. (1 Kings 19:16; 2 Kings 9:2-8) Jehu, whose name means "Jehovah is He", was a type of Christ Jesus, God's official Executioner. Jehu proceeded to destroy the Baal-worshipers, or demon-religionists, amongst the Israelites. While in performance of that duty Jehu came upon a man named Jehonadab, or Jonadab. Those in the antitype who form the "great multitude" were pictured by Jonadab. The antitypical Jonadabs are people of good-will toward God. In the type the Jonadabs were not Israelites, but they shunned religion and refused to have anything to do with it. They were particularly known for their faithfulness in the performance of their word and obedience to that which was right.—Jeremiah 35:18, 19.

When Jonadab heard that Jehu was engaged in destroying demonism or religion, he went out to meet Jehu; and seeing him coming, Jehu stopped his chariot and spoke to Jonadab. (2 Kings 10:15, 16) In reply to a question propounded to him Jonadab there declared that he was on the side of Jehu, hence of good-will toward Jehu and God, whom Jehu served. Jehu immediately invited Jonadab to join him in his chariot (which he did) and to accompany Jehu when he went to slaughter the Baal-worshipers. In this prophetic drama Jonadab pictured those persons of good-will toward the Lord who put themselves under the organization pictured by the chariot of God, and who continue on the Lord's side, become companions of the faithful remnant, and thus work with the remnant until Armageddon. They join with the remnant in testifying to the Kingdom message. (For a detailed discussion see book *Riches,* chapters two and three; also *Salvation,* chapter three.)

**KING JEHU AND JONADAB
SEE DEMONISM DESTROYED**

Live on Earth

Those who will compose the "great multitude" are gathered to the Lord Jesus Christ before the day of God's wrath is expressed at Armageddon. Their selection takes place while Christ Jesus, the great Judge, has before him all nations of the earth for judgment, and that judgment day is the present time. Selection of the "great multitude" differs in some things from the selection of the "little flock" of sheep, in this, that those who compose the "little flock" are called, begotten and proved, and their number is fixed at 144,000. Those who compose the "great multitude" are not limited in number; they flee to the Lord and find refuge under his organization, and, abiding there faithfully until after Armageddon, receive the full benefit of the ransom sacrifice.

As the little flock must first exercise faith in God and in Christ Jesus before being called, even so the "great multitude" must have faith in God and in Christ Jesus before they can take their stand on the side of The THEOCRATIC GOVERNMENT. Men having the desire to be on the side of God and his kingdom begin to seek the way of righteousness, which is God's appointed way for all those who shall ever receive life everlasting. Learning that Jehovah is the Almighty God and Christ Jesus is the Redeemer of all who obey him, such persons of good-will begin to exercise faith by trusting in Christ Jesus as the Redeemer, and by agreeing to do the will of God and of Christ. The ransom sacrifice is now available for all such, who believe on the Lord Jesus Christ, that his precious blood is the purchase price of mankind who obey him. Note that the Scriptures say that Christ Jesus is the "author of eternal salvation unto all them that obey him". (Hebrews 5:9) All who obey the Lord must first take their stand firmly on the side of Christ Jesus the King and then continue to be obedient to God's law as announced by the King.

How can one take his stand on the side of Jehovah and his kingdom under Christ Jesus and make this fact known? By consecrating himself to God and Christ, that is, by solemnly agreeing to do the will of God; then by performing water immersion, which is symbolic and constitutes an outward testimony that one is of good-will toward the Lord and has taken his stand on the side of God and his kingdom. Then he must faithfully carry out his agreement to do God's will by learning from the Scriptures the will of God and faithfully obeying what he there learns. The faithful men of old manifestly consecrated themselves unto God by agreeing to do his will and then faithfully carried out that agreement by obeying his will. Those of the "little flock" who become members of the Kingdom must

first exercise faith, fully consecrate themselves to God and Christ, and then be diligent to carry out their agreement. Those of
the "great multitude" must do likewise, because there is no such thing as "degrees of
faith". The ransom sacrifice is for those who
believe and who publicly show their faith in
God and in Christ. Faith and obedience are
absolutely essential to all who find life everlasting, whether in the spirit or on the earth.

Christ Jesus being now at the temple of
God conducting judgment of the nations,
the way is now open for the people of good-
will to take the necessary steps to be of the
"great multitude". For some time the faithful servants of the Lord have carried the
message of the Kingdom to the people, and
those of good-will toward God and his King
have heard and now give heed to that message, and many others are still doing so.
Now is the time when the following scripture applies, to wit: "For whosoever shall
call upon the name of the Lord shall be
saved." (Romans 10: 13) This clearly proves
that those who fail or refuse to call upon
the name of the Lord cannot have the benefit of the ransom sacrifice. And how do they
call upon the name of the Lord? The Scripture answer is: "That if thou shalt confess
with thy mouth the Lord Jesus, and shalt
believe in thine heart that God hath raised
him from the dead, thou shalt be saved.
For with the heart man believeth unto right-

eousness; and with the mouth confession is made unto salvation. For the scripture saith, Whosoever believeth on him shall not be ashamed."—Romans 10: 9-11.

When one duly takes his stand on the side of The THEOCRATIC GOVERNMENT he is not ashamed, but desires it to be known that he is for God and his kingdom, and he desires to carry that message to others. What hope is set before those who do now fully consecrate themselves unto God and Christ his King? Life everlasting on the earth, which God has provided for obedient men under the reign of Christ. The Lord Jesus Christ is clothed with full power to resurrect and to give life to the obedient ones. As he stated: "I am the resurrection, and the life, . . . and whosoever liveth and believeth in me shall never die." (John 11: 25, 26) Such are the ones who shall receive life at the hand of Christ Jesus the King. It is to such of the Lord's "other sheep" that these words are addressed: "Then shall the King say unto them on his right hand, Come, ye blessed of my Father, inherit the kingdom prepared for you from the foundation of the world." (Matthew 25: 34) These go away into everlasting life (Matthew 25: 46): "And these [the wicked] shall go away into everlasting punishment; but the righteous into life eternal."

"Flee to the Mountains"

Jehovah God is symbolized by a mighty
Rock or Mountain. Christ Jesus is also
known under the symbol of Rock or Mountain. The kingdom of God, of which Christ
Jesus is the great King, is in symbolic language described as "a stone . . . cut out without hands", hence by Jehovah, and which
Stone "became a great mountain, and filled
the whole earth", and which "mountain"
destroys Satan's organization.—Daniel 2:
34-45.

The kingdom of God is called "Mount
Zion", that great mountain that God pre-
pares for his own habitation and as his capital organization. "Jerusalem" is a symbol
of Jehovah God's universal organization.
Now is the day when all persons of good-
will who desire salvation must flee from
Satan's organization that controls the present wicked world and flee to God's organization under Christ and which is called "the
mountain".

In his great prophecy recorded at Matthew 24 Jesus tells of the conditions that
shall exist at the end of the world, when
he comes in power and glory to judge the
nations, which he is doing at the present
time. At the same time he commands that
this good news of the Kingdom shall be
publicly declared throughout the nations as
a witness and that this must be done before

the final end at Armageddon. In this connection he addresses all persons of goodwill toward God in these words: "When ye, therefore, shall see the abomination of desolation, spoken of by Daniel the prophet, stand in the holy place, (whoso readeth, let him understand:) then let them which be in Judæa flee into the mountains."—Matthew 24: 15, 16.

The "abomination of desolation" is that religious, political organization which claims the right to rule the world in the place of and instead of the Lord; and from this the people of good-will must flee, and flee to the Lord's organization, pictured by the mountains.

Safety can be found only under Jehovah's THEOCRATIC ORGANIZATION. Religious organizations furnish no protection whatsoever to the people. Religion is entirely contrary to the will of God and is a snare, as he has declared. Today religion is fully united with dictators or arbitrary rulers of the earth, and these jointly claim their right to rule the earth. They therefore stand where they "ought not" to stand. Instead of supporting THE THEOCRACY, they defy it. The facts, therefore, show that this is the time that all persons of good-will must flee to the organization of Jehovah under Christ Jesus, that is, "to the mountains." All opposers to THE THEOCRACY the Lord will destroy at Armageddon, because such constitute an abomination in his sight. (Mark 13: 14-20) Safety is to be found and deliverance had only in the organization of Jehovah under Christ Jesus.

"Permit me, Eunice, at this time, to read from *The Watchtower* of September 1, 1939, beginning at paragraph 36, on page 265:

" 'Since 1925 particularly Jehovah's witnesses have carried the kingdom message and placed it within the hearing of the people, which message tells of the day of vengeance of our God, and that it is very near. Such is their part in God's "strange work", and such work appears to the religionists as a very strange thing. This witness work must be done before Jehovah shows to the enemy his great power, which he will do at Armageddon. Causing his name and his kingdom to be proclaimed throughout the earth, Jehovah thus gives warning to the enemy and at the same time extends his mercy toward those practitioners of religion who have been and are deceived and held as prisoners in the religious organizations, and who unwittingly have walked with religionists. Now in this day Jehovah makes it clearly to appear that religion is doomed, and the sounding of such warning of doom provides the opportunity to all persons of good-will to flee to the kingdom for protection before the wrath of God is expressed against Satan's organization.

" 'WHO MAY ESCAPE

" 'To now be permitted to declare the name and kingdom of Jehovah and the approaching hour of his wrath upon all wickedness, is an unspeakable privilege granted to those upon whom he has put his spirit. The message boldly announces the supremacy of Jehovah, and this done in the midst of religious opposition makes it possible for those who hear and who obey to find protection and salvation; and this God foretold through the prophecy of Joel 2:32: "And it shall come to pass, that whosoever shall call on the name of the Lord shall be delivered: for in mount Zion and in Jerusalem shall be deliverance, as the Lord hath said, and in the remnant whom the Lord shall call."

" 'Necessarily it follows that whosoever shall not call upon the name of the Lord shall not be delivered. That makes it imperative for Jehovah's witnesses to carry out their commission to proclaim [to the people] his name, his kingdom and his vengeance at the present time.

" 'When must one call upon the name of Jehovah, THAT DELIVERANCE MAY BE HAD? NOT AFTER THE BATTLE OF ARMAGEDDON BEGINS, at which time all may discern by the natural sight of the eyes the expression of God's vengeance against wickedness. Faith must be exercised by those who find protection. One must first believe that the Almighty God is Jehovah and that protection and salvation belong to him. (Hebrews 11:6; Psalm 3:8) He must believe that Jesus Christ is the Redeemer and Deliverer, and then take action in harmony with that belief. Otherwise the inherited condemnation abides on such one to destruction. (John 3:36) He must call upon the name of Jehovah before the battle of Armageddon begins; and this he must do by hearing, believing and acting upon the information of truth brought to him by those who are witnesses for Jehovah, and particularly upon whom God has placed his spirit. For this reason Jehovah sends forth his anointed witnesses to declare his name and his purposes: "How then shall they call on him in whom they have not believed? and how shall they believe in him of whom they have not heard? and how shall they hear without a preacher [one who bears testimony to the truth or proclaims the truth]? And how shall they preach, except they be sent [who are sent by receiving the anointing of the spirit and commission from Jehovah to go and preach this gospel of the kingdom]? as it is written, How beautiful are the feet of them that preach the gospel of peace, and bring glad tidings of good things!" (Romans 10:14,15) It is concerning these faithful witnesses that the prophecy is written: "How beautiful upon the mountains are the feet of him [Christ]

that bringeth good tidings, that publisheth
peace; that bringeth good tidings of good,
that publisheth salvation; that saith unto
Zion, Thy God reigneth!''—Isaiah 52: 7. . . .

" 'Organized religion began with Babylon,
and ever since then the religionists and their
organizations have been designated in the
Scriptures under and by the name of ''Babylon''. As God sent Jeremiah to warn those
of Israel who were of good-will that they
might flee out of the Devil's organization,
so now he sends his anointed ones, accompa-
nied by their companions, the Jonadabs, to
give warning to all others who desire protection and salvation, and to those [who *desire* protection and salvation, and to those]
warned Jehovah now says: ''Flee out of the
midst of Babylon, and deliver every man
his soul; be not cut off in her iniquity; for
this is the time of the Lord's vengeance;
he will render unto her a recompence.''
''My people, go ye out of the midst of her,
and deliver ye every man his soul from
the fierce anger of the Lord.''—Jeremiah
51: 6, 45.

" 'This message must be carried to the
people now, and upon every one who has
received the anointing of the holy spirit
God has placed the responsibility to participate in delivering that message. A fail-
ure or refusal to perform the commission
thus given is certain to be disastrous to the
ones thus failing or refusing.

" 'In the typical days Jerusalem and Zion were located on adjoining mountains, and pictured the universal and the capital organization of Jehovah. Zion was a type of Jehovah's capital organization, made up of Jesus Christ and the 144,000 members of his body, anointed by the holy spirit, and upon which mountain, antitypically, now Jesus Christ and his body members stand, and there they are strongly fortified against the enemy. (Revelation 14: 1, 3) Those who will compose the "great multitude" are not pictured as standing upon Mount Zion. All persons of good-will who flee to the mountains as commanded, and faithfully abide there under the protection of Christ until the end of Armageddon, will be delivered and will form the "great multitude". "For in mount Zion and in Jerusalem shall be deliverance," says the prophecy. Here the word "deliverance" means "an escaping", and may be properly applied to the act of escaping and to those who do escape. (Isaiah 4: 2, 3) Jehovah's provision for those of good-will is by and through Christ Jesus, the Head of his organization Zion. "But upon mount Zion shall be deliverance, and there shall be holiness; and the house of Jacob shall possess their possessions." (Obadiah 17) Mount Zion is THE THEOCRACY, or Kingdom, and deliverance shall be there because Jehovah God will fight for his organization, as it is written: "For thus hath

the Lord spoken unto me, Like as the lion
and the young lion roaring on his prey,
when a multitude of shepherds is called
forth against him, he will not be afraid of
their voice, nor abase himself for the noise
of them: so shall the Lord of hosts come
down to fight for mount Zion, and for the
hill thereof. As birds flying, so will the Lord
of hosts defend Jerusalem; defending also
he will deliver it; and passing over [cover-
ing it with complete protection] he will preserve it." (Isaiah 31:4,5) Thus the Lord
shows that protection and salvation come
only from him by and through his royal
organization. This he makes known for the
benefit of the Jonadabs, or persons of good-
will.

" 'Escape and deliverance shall be found
in no other place than in the Lord God's
organization, "as the Lord hath said." Repeatedly God has thus said by his prophets, the "holy men of old". He has said it
through Christ Jesus and his apostles, and
now he uses the remnant, or the anointed
ones, to bring this message to the attention
of the people of good-will. All of these, from
the faithful men of old, and including the
remnant, have been and are witnesses to the
name of Jehovah and his purpose. The remnant now bear this message which the Lord
has said, and they must continue to carry
that message to the people, because that is
the purpose of their anointing.' "

"John, dear, don't you think we should have *The Watchtower* and study it regularly, that we might be informed of the unfolding of Jehovah's prophecies?"

"It is published twice each month. We shall have it, Eunice."

Multitude Gathering

Tribulation came upon the nations of the earth in 1914 and has continued to increase each year since that day. Now all the nations of earth are in distress. It is during this time of tribulation that the people of good-will hearing the message of the Kingdom are seeking refuge under the Lord's organization. Both the "little flock" and the Lord's "other sheep" are the ones that the world has no use for. Hence they do not desire them. To these obedient ones the Lord addresses these words: "Gather yourselves together, yea, gather together, O nation [God's 'holy nation' and companions] not desired; before the decree bring forth, before the day pass as the chaff, before the fierce anger of the Lord come upon you, before the day of the Lord's anger come upon you. Seek ye the Lord, all ye meek of the earth, which have wrought his judgment; seek righteousness, seek meekness; it may be ye shall be hid in the day of the Lord's anger."—Zephaniah 2:1-3.

The way of the Lord is the way of righteousness. To "seek meekness" means to be

diligent to learn what is God's will. God
has promised to lead those who are thus
meek and endeavor to learn. "The meek
will he guide in judgment, and the meek
will he teach his way. All the paths of the
Lord are mercy and truth unto such as keep
his covenant and his testimonies."—Psalm
25:9, 10.

———

The brief silence was broken by Eunice
speaking. "John, the Lord has been very
gracious to us. Each one of these studies becomes more profitable and the truth learned
more precious to us. From our childhood
we have desired to serve God. Would it not
be well for us to now make a consecration
unto God and unto Christ Jesus and then
to seek the first opportunity to emphasize
that consecration in baptism, publicly declaring our covenant with God?"

"To that I fully agree, Eunice. We don't
need to make such consecration to any man.
Our agreement is with the Lord, to whom
we can go directly. Note this text addressed
to those who seek him and who agree to do
his will: 'And Jesus said unto them, I am
the bread of life; he that cometh to me shall
never hunger; and he that believeth on me
shall never thirst. All that the Father giveth me shall come to me; and him that cometh to me I will in no wise cast out.'—John
6:35, 37.

"Faith and obedience are the necessary things. We have faith and now we are striving to obey, and we should obey by symbolizing our consecration in water baptism. There must be much work for those to do who are faithful to the Lord, and we must do our part. You remember that water hole in the creek near the big sycamore tree, where we used to go swimming as children? It will be a delight for us to go there and symbolize our consecration by water immersion. We have learned from the Scriptures that we don't have to be immersed by some religious person, but anyone who loves God can immerse us. Both your father and my father love the Lord, and let us invite one of them to do the immersing, and all the family to go with us to that water hole, and then we will be immersed next Sunday."

It is agreed.

"John, the Lord will surely reveal to us what we must do after we have taken this step of obedience, and then we must do it."

CHAPTER 7
HIS WITNESSES

"Ye are my witnesses, saith Jehovah, that I am God." —Isaiah 43:12.

OVER a period of many centuries Jehovah God has been developing his capital organization, which shall rule the world in righteousness, and against which THEOCRATIC GOVERNMENT no power shall ever prevail. That organization will be a complete vindication of Jehovah's name and to his everlasting glory. All power resides in Jehovah. He is the Almighty God, besides whom there is no other. For him to will that a thing be done means that it is certain to be accomplished. He could have built up the capital organization instantly had that been his will and purpose. That was not his purpose. As the Scriptures disclose, the development of God's capital organization, or kingdom, was for ages a mystery. That mystery he first revealed to his beloved Son, and then, after Jesus had been crucified, raised from the dead, and exalted to heaven, Jehovah made known to men for the first time the meaning of that mystery. Does God's Word now revealed to man make clear the reason for the long period of time he was developing his kingdom? Yes; and the Scriptural answer to that question magnifies the name and power of the Most High.

The garden of Eden was a perfect place and one of beauty and glory. Therein God had placed the perfect human pair and issued to them his mandate to "multiply and fill the earth". Before doing anything to carry out that divine mandate Satan came upon the scene. Concerning that wicked one, Satan, the record reads: "In [the garden of] Eden the garden of God didst thou abide; . . . thou wast a cherub with outspread covering (wings); and I had set thee upon the holy mountain of God (as) thou wast; in the midst of the stones of fire [that is, covered with a blaze of glory] didst thou wander. Perfect wast thou in thy ways from the day that thou wast created, till wickedness was found in thee." (Ezekiel 28: 13-15, *Leeser*) Almighty God then declared his judgment of complete destruction of Satan. God made known that he would bring forth a seed that would destroy Satan, and which seed the Scriptures identify as Christ.—Genesis 3: 15; Galatians 3: 16, 29.

Satan defiantly challenged the supremacy and power of Jehovah God. He declared that God could not put on earth a man that would remain faithful and true when put to the most severe test. (Job 2: 4, 5) Almighty God could have immediately brought into existence his capital organization and immediately have destroyed Satan. But that was not his purpose. Being all-wise, God purposed and arranged that all creatures should have a free choice as to whom they would serve, and that there must be demonstrated before creatures who is supreme and who is righteous. Those choosing to serve the Devil should suffer destruction; those choosing to obey and serve Jehovah God should live; and to carry into completion his purpose God committed the work into the hand of his beloved Son, the Logos, that is, Jesus. That means that every man and every angel is free to choose whom he will serve, and hence he fixes his own destiny by his choice: "Know ye not, that to whom ye yield yourselves servants to obey, his servants ye are to whom ye obey; whether of sin unto death, or of obedience unto righteousness?"—Romans 6: 16.

It now clearly appears from the Scriptures that one means of keeping his purpose a mystery until due time to reveal it was to employ cryptic language and use symbols to represent realities. An instance is found in connection with the declaration of God's answer to the wicked challenge of Satan. Pharaoh of Egypt was an arbitrary ruler of the first world power, which world power particularly stood for avarice, conquest and commerce. Pharaoh was the earthly representative of the Devil, or god of this wicked world, and Jehovah's answer to Satan's challenge was recorded at the time as though it were addressed to Pharaoh, but in fact is addressed to Satan. In answer to that wicked challenge Jehovah said: "Even now I might have stretched out my hand, and I might have smitten thee . . . but for this cause have I allowed thee to remain, in order to show thee my power; and in order that they may proclaim my name throughout all the earth."—Exodus 9: 15, 16, *Leeser*.

Mark here the two things which God declared as his reason and purpose in deferring the execution of Satan until a time later: (1) to show God's supreme power; and (2) the making known of His name.

Said the Lord: "In order to show thee my power; and in order that THEY MAY PROCLAIM MY NAME THROUGHOUT ALL THE EARTH." The word THEY here used manifestly means all men on earth who would choose to faithfully serve Almighty God and obey his commandments. Therefore it follows that every person that receives the approval of Almighty God, and that receives from him life everlasting, *must be a witness for Jehovah God.* There could be no exception to this rule, because God's rules do not change, and he is no respecter of persons.—Malachi 3: 6; Acts 10: 34.

"Jehovah's witnesses"

The name "Jehovah's witnesses" means but one thing, to wit, that each one is to bear witness for Jehovah, the Almighty God, and for none other. They are Jehovah's witnesses, and not members of some sect or cult as the Devil would have others believe. They are selected by the Lord God. They are not subject to the control of human organizations or human power. Their allegiance is to Almighty God. They must obey his commandments and are responsible to God for their action.—Romans 14: 4.

This wicked world is now in the "last days" thereof. These are "perilous times", and the day for the execution of the wicked is just at hand and the Devil knows that his time is short. (2 Timothy 3: 1; Revelation 12: 12) "The battle of that great day of God Almighty," which shall destroy Satan's organization and all wickedness, is about to be fought. (Revelation 16: 13-16) In these last days God has on the earth a comparatively small number of persons who are really devoted to him and his THEOCRATIC GOVERNMENT, and who now bear testimony to the name of God and his kingdom. The Devil would have all believe that this small company of faithful servants of Almighty God constitute a religious sect or cult following the lead of some man. No human power or organization could lead or control the witnesses of the Most High God. Even some countries, which are under the power and control of demonism, now declare by law that Jehovah's witnesses are illegal. Such worldly organizations show complete ignorance of the purpose and power of Almighty God. No earthly government or power has any authority to declare Jehovah's witnesses illegal; and in doing so such nation commits the rankest blasphemy and in due time shall receive a just recompense from the Lord's Executioner.

Jesus

One of the titles which God gave his beloved Son Jesus is "The Faithful and True Witness, the beginning of the creation of God". (Revelation 3:14) He is the Head and the first of all witnesses of Jehovah. All true and faithful followers of Christ Jesus are witnesses of Jehovah God. Almighty God appointed his beloved Son his Witness and sent him to the earth to bear witness before the people of the name and kingdom of the Most High. (John 8:14-18) Says Jehovah God of his beloved Son, Christ Jesus: "Behold, I have given him for a witness to the people, a leader and commander to the people."—Isaiah 55:4.

Before the ruling power of Jerusalem Jesus said: "To this end was I born, and for this cause came I into the world, that I should bear witness unto the truth. Every one that is of the truth heareth my voice." (John 18: 37) From these scriptures it necessarily follows that every person who becomes a follower of Christ Jesus and performs his covenant must be a witness to the truth and to the name and majesty and kingdom of Jehovah God, and is therefore one of Jehovah's witnesses. (1 Peter 2: 21) To his faithful followers Jesus says: "And ye also shall bear witness, because ye have been with me from the beginning."—John 15: 27.

A witness is one who testifies before others to that which is the truth. Every one, therefore, who proclaims to others the name, majesty and kingdom of Jehovah God is a witness for Jehovah.

Human Witnesses

Abel was the first righteous man on the earth after the tragedy in Eden. He was a witness to the name of Almighty God: "By faith Abel offered unto God a more excellent sacrifice than Cain, by which he obtained witness that he was righteous, God testifying of his gifts; and by it he, being dead, yet speaketh."—Hebrews 11: 4.

All faithful men specifically named at the eleventh chapter of Hebrews were witnesses to the name of Jehovah God, both by word of mouth and by their course of life. By faith they saw THE THEOCRACY and declared themselves for that government of Almighty God, and thus they were witnesses to the name and majesty of Jehovah. All the faithful prophets of God were Jehovah's witnesses. Concerning that great prophet John the Baptist, it is written: "There was a man sent from God, whose name was John. The same came for a witness, to bear witness of the Light, that all men through him might believe. He was not that Light, but was sent to bear witness of that Light."—John 1: 6-8.

The faithful men of old above mentioned, and who included all the holy prophets, were witnesses of Jehovah. The word translated "witnesses" is the same word from which is translated "martyrs". Those faithful men of old were martyrs, sealing their testimony with their lifeblood. They were faithful witnesses of Jehovah. The Scriptures hold them forth as shining examples to be followed by those who should become members of the "holy nation" of God and also those who shall be their "companions"; as it is written: "Wherefore seeing we also are compassed about with so great a cloud of witnesses, let us lay aside every weight, and the sin which doth so easily beset us, and let us run with patience the race that is set before us, looking unto Jesus the author and finisher of our faith; who, for the joy that was set before him, endured the cross, despising the shame, and is set down at the right hand of the throne of God."—Hebrews 12:1, 2.

So necessary and important is it to be a witness for Jehovah that each one who agrees to follow in the footsteps of Jesus is admonished to lay aside every weight, that is, everything that hinders the full performance of his duty to serve God; also that he must put aside the sin that "doth so easily beset" every creature, which sin is religion, because it is so very easy to fall under the influence of religion. This great sin, the Scriptures declare, must be laid aside and the Christian must become a faithful and true follower of Christ Jesus and, as such, be a faithful and true witness of Jehovah God.

Ordained

The word *ordained,* as defined by the best authority (Doctor Strong), means "to make; to appoint; to anoint; to constitute; to commission". Only the Lord, therefore, could truly and properly ordain one to become a witness for Him. Jesus applied the following prophecy to himself, and to all who are his true footstep followers: "The spirit of the Lord God is upon me; because the Lord hath anointed me to preach good tidings unto the meek; he hath sent me to bind up the brokenhearted, to proclaim liberty to the captives, and the opening of the prison to them that are bound; to proclaim the acceptable year of the Lord, and the day of vengeance of our God; to comfort all that mourn."—Isaiah 61: 1, 2.

One who becomes a true and faithful servant of God and Christ, and who has received the spirit of the Lord, is ordained or commissioned to preach the good news of the Kingdom and to magnify Jehovah's name, and hence is an "ordained minister" of the gospel.

Not only are such persons appointed and commissioned by the Lord to preach the gospel of the Kingdom, but such are emphatically commanded that they must preach the gospel of this kingdom. (Matthew 24: 14) When Christ Jesus appeared at the temple and put his consecrated followers to the test, he sent forth the approved ones to "offer unto the Lord an offering in righteousness". (Malachi 3: 3) Such means that they must employ their lips and every other faculty possessed to bear witness to the truth of Jehovah's name and his kingdom. (Hebrews 13: 15) Each one of such is appointed and commissioned to preach the good news by telling the people of the Kingdom, or THEO-CRATIC GOVERNMENT. This positive command the Lord Jesus gives, to wit: "And this gospel of the kingdom shall be preached in all the world for a witness unto all nations; and then shall the end come."—Matthew 24: 14.

All such sincere followers of Christ Jesus who obey this commandment are Jehovah's witnesses, bearing testimony to his name and to his kingdom. No earthly power has any authority to interfere with their preaching "this gospel", because they are the witnesses of the Most High, or Almighty God, acting under his commandment.

In modern times the colleges and universities, and particularly so-called "theological schools", teach anything and everything but the gospel of God's kingdom. There are numerous religious denominations, which preach their own doctrines based upon the traditions or teachings of men. Prior to the coming of the Lord Jesus to the temple for judgment in 1918 many consecrated persons who were preaching to the people of and concerning his second coming were known as Millennial Dawnites, or Russellites, or International Bible Students, and other like sectarian names. But when the Lord Jesus cleansed the temple and the approved ones were sent forth to "offer unto the Lord an offering in righteousness", God separated his faithful servants from all others. The approved ones, brought into the temple, were made a part of Zion, the elect organization of Jehovah; and to such the Lord says: "For Zion's sake will I not hold my peace, and for Jerusalem's sake I will not rest, until the righteousness thereof go forth as brightness, and the salvation thereof as

"YE ARE MY WITNESSES"

a lamp that burneth. And the Gentiles shall see thy righteousness, and all kings thy glory: and thou shalt be called by a new name, which the mouth of the Lord shall name."—Isaiah 62: 1, 2.

What Name?

All who now truly offer unto the Lord an offering in righteousness must be witnesses to the name of Jehovah. They must go amongst the people and declare his name and his kingdom, and the message which such servants bear is contrary to that which religionists teach. Therefore the Almighty God separates his faithful witnesses from religious organizations, and this takes place at the time Christ Jesus, the great Judge, is dividing his "sheep" from the "goats".

(Matthew 25:32) In this division the Lord God calls upon the tradition teachers to make their proof or else admit they are wrong; and thus it is recorded: "Let all the nations be gathered together, and let the people be assembled: who among them can declare this, and shew us former things? let them bring forth their witnesses, that they may be justified: or let them hear, and say, It is truth."—Isaiah 43:9.

Then the Lord addresses his faithful servants, who are wholly devoted to him, and says: "Ye are my witnesses, saith the Lord, and my servant whom I have chosen; that ye may know and believe me, and understand that I am he: before me there was no God formed, neither shall there be after me. I have declared, and have saved, and I have shewed, when there was no strange god among you: therefore ye are my witnesses, saith the Lord, that I am God." (Isaiah 43:10, 12) Here is the clear distinction between religionists and Christians. Jehovah's witnesses are his servants, and not the servants of any earthly organization.

It is these faithful servants of Almighty God and Christ who must fulfill the command and purpose of Jehovah God to 'declare his name in all the earth' just preceding the battle of Armageddon, at which time and place God will exhibit his supreme power against the Devil and all wickedness. —Exodus 9:16.

Companions

The "other sheep" of the Lord, the Jonadabs, who shall form the "great multitude",
now flee to God's organization and find refuge under Christ the King. Hearing the message of the Kingdom, they choose to serve
God and Christ. They become the companions of "the remnant", that is, the spirit
company yet on the earth. As the companions of the remnant they too must be witnesses to the name and kingdom of Almighty
God. The following prophecy now applies,
because the remnant are taken into the house
of the Lord and their companions are serving before the throne; hence it is written:
"I was glad when they said unto me, Let
us go into the house of the Lord. Our feet
shall stand within thy gates, O Jerusalem.
Jerusalem is builded as a city that is com-
pact together; whither the tribes go up, the
tribes of the Lord, unto the testimony of
Israel, to give thanks unto the name of the
Lord. For there are set thrones of judgment,
the thrones of the house of David. Pray for
the peace of Jerusalem; they shall prosper
that love thee. Peace be within thy walls,
and prosperity within thy palaces. For my
brethren and companions' sakes, I will now
say, Peace be within thee. Because of the
house of the Lord our God I will seek thy
good." (Psalm 122:1-9) Therefore the Jonadabs join with the remnant in taking part

in the testimony to the name of Jehovah and to the great THEOCRACY, which is the only hope of mankind.

Invitation

Christ Jesus is that great Spirit, who is Head and King of Zion, the capital organization of Jehovah. The members of the church, that is, of "the body of Christ", of which Christ Jesus is the Head, are designated in the Scriptures as "the bride" of Christ. (Ephesians 1: 22, 23; John 3: 29; Revelation 21: 9) The Lord Jesus at the temple takes the lead in declaring the name and kingdom of Jehovah, and such witness work is done within the hearing of those persons of good-will that they may choose to serve God and live. Therefore the divine command is given: "And the Spirit and the bride say, Come. And let him that heareth say, Come. And let him that is athirst come: and whosoever will, let him take the water of life freely."—Revelation 22: 17.

That means that Christ Jesus and all those of "the remnant" on the earth will proclaim the name of Jehovah and his kingdom and thereby invite all who are of good-will toward him to come and find the way to life. The "companions" of those witnesses, that is, those who will form the "great multitude", hearing the Kingdom message, give heed and come to the Lord, and they too join in the invitation to all who hunger and thirst for righteousness to come, that whosoever will may come and take of the water of life freely. Thus the general invitation is now open to all of good-will, without limitation of number, to come to the Lord. The present is the time, therefore, when the way is open to those who seek the Lord, and this is the time mentioned in the Scriptures, to wit: "And it shall come to pass, that whosoever shall call on the name of the Lord shall be delivered: for in mount Zion and in Jerusalem shall be deliverance, as the Lord hath said, and in the remnant whom the Lord shall call." (Joel 2:32; Romans 10:13) Since the coming of the Lord to the temple this message of the Kingdom is the general invitation to all of good-will to come and take of the water of life freely, that is, to find the way to life and then to join in declaring that message throughout the earth.

"Strange Work"

Jehovah's witnesses and companions go from house to house calling the attention of the people to the Scriptures concerning Jehovah and his kingdom. That message of God's Word necessarily exposes religion as the instrument of Satan, used to deceive the people, and against which Almighty God has repeatedly given warning to those who will hear. While the apostles were on the earth they shunned religion, warned the people against it, and preached this gospel of the kingdom of God. The apostle Paul, particularly, pointed out that religion is demonism. (Acts 17:22, *Moffat, Rotherham;* Galatians 1:6-16) Within a few years after the apostles had passed away professed Christian men, taking the lead in Christian organizations, fell victims to religion and religious practices and taught traditions of men rather than God's Word. They mixed God's Word with their traditions, and thus the people were easily deceived. That practice continued for centuries and is carried on to this day. Then in due time God sent his Messenger, Christ Jesus, to prepare the way before Him (Malachi 3:1); and doing such work, the Lord called out from religious systems those sincere persons who desired to see and looked for the coming of the Lord and his kingdom in glory. It was those faithful ones who, being tested at the temple, became Jehovah's witnesses of modern days, and such the Lord sends forth to preach "this gospel of the kingdom" as a witness to the nations of the earth before the final end of Satan's organization. The message of the Lord, therefore, discloses that religion, which is practiced by the denominations, is demonism and the religionists are blinded by the influence of the enemy and cannot see the truth. The Lord warns all sincere Christians to flee from religion and to serve God and Christ the King. He warns them that the day of his wrath against all ungodliness is near, and therefore the people must abandon religion or demonism and serve God and his kingdom if they would be saved.

As Jehovah's witnesses go from place to place giving the warning from the Lord and proclaiming Jehovah's name and his purpose the religious leaders observing their work think Jehovah's witnesses are strange people and engage in a strange work, and they often say words to this effect: "It is strange that these people, who claim to be Christians, have to go about finding fault with our religion." It is the message of truth that exposes religion as a wrong thing. This "strange work" is God's work: "For the word of God is quick and powerful, and sharper than any two-edged sword, piercing even to the dividing asunder of soul and spirit, and of the joints and marrow, and is a discerner of the thoughts and intents of the heart."—Hebrews 4: 12.

This work of preaching "this gospel of the kingdom", giving warning to the people, is not the work of any man or men. It is God's work, and his servants engage in it because commanded by the Lord to do so. (Matthew 24: 14) It is not done for the benefit of the wicked who oppose God, but is done for the benefit of sincere persons who are of good-will and who, because of wrongful influence, are held in restraint by religious organizations. The message of

truth is sounded and the warning is given
that those who have faith in God and in his
kingdom may flee to the place of safety and
find the way to life when the wrath of God
is expressed against the world. It is inform-
ative work, that those who desire righteousness may know how to choose the way that
leads to safety and life. This work is not
done for the purpose of holding up persons
or groups of persons to ridicule or hatred;
it is done in honor of the name of the Lord.
The witness work points to Jehovah God
and his kingdom as the only hope for human creatures who desire to live, and the
doing of this work necessarily exposes ungodliness and all who are going in the wrong
way.

God used Noah to give warning of His
purpose to destroy all flesh because of the
wickedness and violence which the demons
had brought upon the people in that day.
(2 Peter 2:5; Genesis 6:11-17) The Israelites fell away to idolatry or demonism, called
"religion", and God sent his prophets, Jeremiah, Ezekiel and others, to warn them of
his purpose to destroy that nation because
they had violated their covenant, turned
away from him and turned to demonism.
The Lord Jesus specifically warned the Israelites against religion and religious leaders in order that those of good-will who desired to choose righteousness might do so.
(Matthew 23:1-36) He emphatically told

the religious leaders that they had made the Word of God of none effect amongst the people because of teaching their traditions and that therefore they were the servants of Satan the Devil.—Matthew 15:1-9; John 8:40-44; Matthew 3:7.

There are many religious organizations in the earth today, not one of which advocates and supports THE THEOCRACY. All of them teach and follow the traditions of men, which is against the Lord, and all are an abomination in God's sight. There is a great and old religious institution that during the past 1500 years has spread all over the earth and has drawn into its clutches millions of persons, many of whom are very sincere, yet blind to the truth, and these are held in restraint by reason of the influence exercised over them by religious leaders. Such persons of good-will, God will see to it, shall have an opportunity of hearing the truth, that they may escape. That great religious institution is closely allied with commerce and politics and is a part of Satan's world. That great religious institution uses constantly as its slogan these words: "The gates of hell shall not prevail against us." Furthermore they say: "When God's wrath comes, it will not touch us, because we have made a covenant with death, and an agreement with hell." The leaders of that great religious institution are proud, austere and scornful men that rule within their institutions and exercise a powerful influence outside there-of. God, through his prophet and for the benefit of those who are held in restraint by such great religious institution, answers the boastful words of those scornful men in this manner: "So shall be wiped out your covenant with death, and your vision with hades [shall] not stand; when the overflowing scourge sweepeth past, then shall ye be thereby beaten down: as often as it sweepeth past, it shall take you away, for morning by morning shall it pass along, by day and by night; and it shall be nothing less than a terror to make out the message."— Isaiah 28: 18, 19, *Rotherham*.

That work of giving witness and warning is the work which Almighty God has arranged and commanded must be done just preceding the great battle of Armageddon. Note the prophecy in this connection: "For the Lord shall rise up as in mount Perazim, he shall be wroth as in the valley of Gibeon, that he may do his work, his strange work; and bring to pass his act, his strange act." —Isaiah 28: 21.

And when is that "strange work" to be done? and when completed? The foregoing texts show that it immediately precedes God's "strange act", which "strange act" is the expression of his wrath at the battle of Armageddon, which is "the battle of that great day of God Almighty" and which shall completely wreck Satan's organization. This is exactly in harmony with the declaration of Jehovah to Satan, to wit: 'For this cause have I permitted thee to remain, that I might show thee my power, and that they [my witnesses] may proclaim my name throughout all the earth.'—Exodus 9: 16.

Just before God exercises his supreme power in the destruction of Satan's organization he does his "strange work" on earth, and this is done by sending his servants amongst the people to give warning to the honest and sincere ones who desire righteousness and to make known his own great name. This he does "for his name's sake". It therefore clearly appears that when God's "strange work" is done, which work is now in progress and which shall be done by the proclamation of his name and kingdom, that work will immediately be followed by the greatest tribulation that the world will ever have known, about which Jesus said: "And this gospel of the kingdom shall be preached in all the world for a witness unto all nations; and then shall the end come. For then shall be great tribulation, such as was not since the beginning of the world to this time, no, nor ever shall be."—Matthew 24: 14, 21.

Everyone who loves righteousness must take his stand now on the side of THE THEOCRACY and must participate in the "strange work" of proclaiming the name and kingdom of the great THEOCRAT, Jehovah God, and his King, Christ Jesus. It is those people who now hear his warning and give heed to it, and who turn to the Lord and find refuge in Christ, and who immediately become his servants, that will be saved and receive his blessings. None other shall escape: "Blessed is the people that know the joyful sound; they shall walk, O Lord, in the light of thy countenance. In thy name shall they rejoice all the day: and in thy righteousness shall they be exalted."–Psalm 89: 15, 16.

"Oh, John, we must immediately become witnesses to the name and kingdom of Jehovah, and we must do our part in telling others about Him and his kingdom."

"To that I fully agree, Eunice. In this hour of world distress it is our privilege to be on the Lord's side and proclaim his name. Our eternal salvation depends upon our faithful service to God and his King from henceforth. What may we expect from others if we engage in this witness work?"

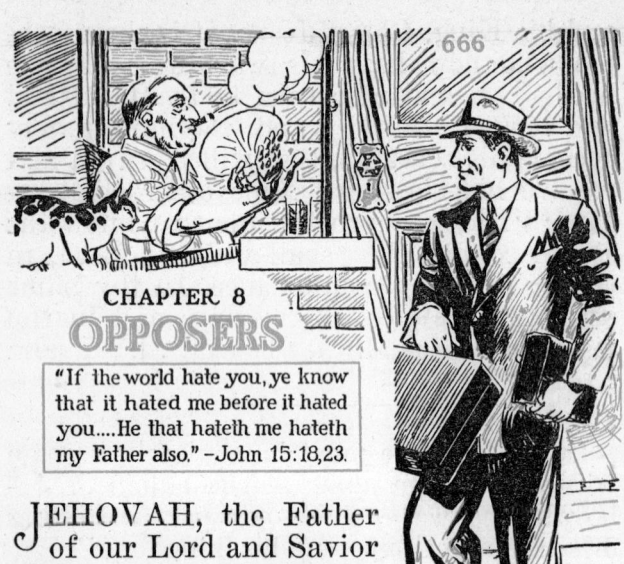

CHAPTER 8
OPPOSERS

"If the world hate you, ye know that it hated me before it hated you....He that hateth me hateth my Father also." –John 15:18,23.

JEHOVAH, the Father of our Lord and Savior Jesus Christ, is righteous and all things with him are righteous. "The LORD is righteous in all his ways, and holy in all his works." (Psalm 145:17) "For the righteous LORD loveth righteousness; his countenance doth behold the upright." (Psalm 11:7) Likewise Jehovah's beloved Son is righteous, holy and pure; and because he loves righteousness at all times Jehovah has exalted him to the highest place next to the Almighty himself. "Thou lovest righteousness, and hatest wickedness: therefore God, thy God, hath anointed thee with the oil of gladness above thy fellows."—Psalm 45:7.

Who could hate Jehovah God, and who could plant hatred in the mind of another against the Almighty God, who is love? Only the wicked one, Satan the Devil. His name Satan means adversary or opposer of God. Satan is the prince of the world, from the time of Eden onward to Armageddon, and the entire world is under the power and influence of Satan, that wicked one. (John 12:31; 1 John 5:19) Therefore all creatures that hate Jehovah, the Almighty God, are the servants of the Devil. All who hate the Lord Jesus Christ are likewise servants of the Devil. All who hate the faithful servants of God and Christ are also of the Devil. These scriptures should convince all sincere persons who desire righteousness that those who hate Jehovah's witnesses and persecute them are instruments of "that wicked one", who hates God and Christ, and that all such opposers of Jehovah and his kingdom are doomed for destruction. But why does the world hate the Lord Jesus Christ, as stated in the text? His answer is: 'The world hateth me because I testify of it, that the works thereof are evil.' (John 7:7) The world hates all who faithfully follow in the footsteps of Jesus by giving testimony to Jehovah's name.

What is meant in these texts just cited by the term "the world"? The people and nations of earth that are under the influence of demons, of which Satan the Devil is the prince or chief of demons, constitute the world that lies in the wicked one. (1 John 5:19, *Diaglott*) The world is made up chiefly of three ruling elements, to wit: religion, politics, and commerce; and all persons who thus rule practice some kind of religion, which is demonism, because their practice is contrary to God's Word. The world, therefore, consists of the organization of the peoples of earth into forms of government which are dominated by the power and influence of the invisible overlord, Satan. The new world will consist of all people who survive Armageddon, and who love righteousness and hate wickedness, and such will live on the earth under the supervision and control of the invisible, righteous overlord, Christ the King. Thus it is seen that all people and all nations must now be separated or divided into two classes, that those who love righteousness and who serve righteousness shall live, and that those who choose wickedness shall be destroyed. "The Lord preserveth all them that love him; but all the wicked will he destroy."–Psalm 145:20.

The name Devil means traducer or slanderer. The name Jehovah God means the Almighty's purpose toward his creatures. The Devil began to defame the name of Almighty God when he told the first lie to Eve. From that time till now the Devil has constantly slandered the name of Jehovah, and the Devil has caused multitudes of creatures to become slanderers and haters of the name of Almighty Jehovah God. For this purpose the Devil put Nimrod forward as one equal to or above God, and hence Nimrod was honored as "a mighty one" "before the Lord". (Genesis 10: 8-10) Nimrod was the leader of the first organization of religion following the flood. The Devil and his servants have continuously reproached the name of Jehovah God; and His beloved Son, Christ Jesus, has always magnified the name of Jehovah. For that reason the Devil has continuously reproached the name of Jesus Christ. For this reason it is written of Christ Jesus: "The reproaches of them that reproached thee are fallen upon me." —Psalm 69: 7, 9.

Every creature who has been faithful to Almighty God has suffered reproach, slander, opposition, persecution and cruelty. The faithful men of old, from Abel onward, suffered all manner of reproach and cruel punishment for the reason that they were for and declared the name of Almighty God and his coming kingdom. No one who loved God could be guilty of inflicting punishment upon those faithful men who proclaimed the name of Almighty God. The Devil was the one who brought reproach upon them and caused their suffering, and this the Devil did because those faithful men proclaimed the name of the Most High.

From the very day that Jesus began to proclaim the name and kingdom of Jehovah the Devil opposed him and sought to bring about his destruction. (Matthew 4: 1-11) The Devil and his associate demons continued to reproach, slander and persecute Jesus, and to falsely charge him with crime, and finally brought about his crucifixion. The faithful servants of Jesus Christ spend their days declaring the name of Jehovah and Christ Jesus the King, and the Devil and his agents constantly reproach them and persecute them. And why? Because they uphold the name of the Lord and joyfully proclaim his name and his kingdom.

Devil's Servants

A Christian is one who is a follower of Christ Jesus and who therefore proclaims the name of Jehovah and his kingdom. No true Christian ever persecuted another Christian. A person may claim to be a Christian and indulge in reproaching God and Christ and in persecuting true Christians, but that claim of being a Christian is false. No one who loves God and his kingdom could hate, reproach or persecute a true follower of Christ Jesus. Any person who reproaches the name of God and Christ thereby shows himself to be an enemy of God and Christ, and a servant of the Devil: "Know ye not, that to whom ye yield yourselves servants to obey, his servants ye are to whom ye obey; whether of sin unto death, or of obedience unto righteousness?"—Romans 6:16.

If a person claims to love the Lord and at the same time indulges in slander, reproach and persecution of others who are serving God and Christ, that slanderer shows that he is the servant of Satan. Says Jesus: 'He that is not for me is against me.' (Matthew 12:30) It follows, therefore, that every one who is not for the Lord and his Kingdom is a servant of Satan, and that of necessity is true, whether such person realizes it or not.

Religionists

The unbroken line of Bible testimony shows that at all times those who have indulged in reproaching the name of Almighty God and Christ and in the persecution of God's servants have been and are those persons who indulge in and practice religion. This is further proof that religion is demonism and religion is brought into action by the chief of demons, Satan, for the very purpose of bringing reproach upon the name of God and Christ and all those who serve him. For this reason Jehovah warned his chosen people that they must shun religion or demonism because the same is a snare unto all who attempt to serve righteousness. (Deuteronomy 7:1,16) The nation of Israel yielded to religion, disobeying God's commandment, and that nation suffered destruction. It was the scribes, priests and Pharisees, the religious leaders of Israel, that persecuted the prophets of God, and this Jesus plainly told them, as set forth at Matthew 23: 33-36.

It was the same class of religious leaders that reproached the name of Jesus and sought to kill him because Jesus preached the truth of and concerning Jehovah and his kingdom. Jesus told them that they were servants of the Devil. (John 8: 40-44) It was that same class of religionists who made the Word of God of none effect by their teaching the traditions of men, and at the same time those religionists claimed to be servants of God. Their claim was false, and in fact they served the Devil.—Matthew 15: 1-9.

The men who falsely charged Jesus with treason and caused him to be put to death were religious men and leaders in religious practices. Not willing to have Jesus tried upon truthful testimony, those same religious leaders sought false witnesses in order to convict Jesus and bring about his death. (Matthew 26: 57-62) It was those same religious leaders that raised up a mob of ignorant persons to reproach the name of Jesus and to howl for his lifeblood. (Matthew 27: 25) It was that same class of religious leaders that bribed witnesses to deny the resurrection of Jesus, whom God had raised up out of death. (Matthew 28: 11-15)

Without a doubt the Devil used those religious leaders to reproach the name of God and his beloved Son.

Will God forgive those religious leaders and permit them to have the benefit of the ransom sacrifice and a resurrection from death? The Scriptures answer that question, No! because those men were willful wrongdoers and never repented of their wrongdoing. In this connection it appears that many have improperly applied the words accredited to Jesus, which appear to have been spoken by him, to wit: "Father, forgive them; for they know not what they do." (Luke 23:34, *Am. Rev. Ver.*, margin) Those words had no application to the religious leaders who brought about Jesus' death. The context plainly shows that those words were spoken by the Lord Jesus on behalf of the two thieves that were crucified at the same time with Jesus. One of them railed on Jesus, repeating the words that had been used by the Pharisees to reproach the name of God and Christ, and the malefactor no doubt repeated those words, without knowing the force and meaning thereof. Those thieves were ignorant men. But the religionists, who brought about the crucifixion of the Lord, were willful and deliberate murderers. Upon such the wrath of God abides forever.—John 3:36.

The ransom sacrifice results beneficially to those only who repent of their wrong,

JESUS FALSELY ACCUSED BEFORE CAIAPHAS

and who believe on the Lord God and on
Christ Jesus as the Savior, and who then
render themselves in full obedience to the
Lord. Instead of repenting, those religious
leaders, who brought about Jesus' death,
continued to reproach his name and to persecute those who proclaimed the name of
Jehovah and Christ. It was that same class
of religious leaders who caused the faithful witness Stephen to be stoned to death.
(Acts 6: 8-15; 7: 1-59) One religious prac-
titioner, who stood by and witnessed the
death of Stephen, did afterwards repent
and turn fully to the Lord, and the Lord
forgave him. But those wrongdoers who did

not repent died in their sins. — Galatians 1:13-17; Acts 9:1-20.

For his name's sake the faithful disciples inquired of Jesus as to what would be the conditions existing on earth at the time of the end of the world and the coming of his kingdom. To their question Jesus uttered the great prophecy recorded at Matthew 24. All the physical facts that have come to pass show that the end of the world of Satan's rule without interruption began in 1914, when Jehovah God sent forth Christ Jesus to begin his reign. (Psalms 2:6; 110:2) From 1918 onward the persecution of the Lord's servants on earth increased. In answer to the above question as to conditions Jesus spoke the prophecy which must apply to and be fulfilled upon his faithful servants on earth from and after 1918 until Armageddon. To them Jesus says: "Then shall they deliver you up to be afflicted, and shall kill you: and ye shall be hated of all nations for my name's sake." — Matthew 24:9.

The World War was on at the time this prophecy began to apply, and every nation involved in that war hated the faithful servants of Christ Jesus and persecuted them, and from then till this day that hatred and persecution has increased. Why have the nations thus hated the Lord's servants? For the sake of the name of God and of Christ. The faithful servants have continued to proclaim Jehovah's name and kingdom, and the Devil has seen to it that those faithful servants of God have suffered all manner of persecution and continue thus to suffer.

In Germany during the reign of the dictator thousands of Jehovah's witnesses have been imprisoned and cruelly beaten and many of them killed, all because those witnesses proclaimed the name and kingdom of Jehovah God and Christ. In all the nations of Continental Europe the servants of God's kingdom are cruelly persecuted today. The same is true of the countries of Asia and Africa. In Canada, now ruled by a religious dictator, Jehovah's witnesses are declared an "illegal" organization and are imprisoned because they dare speak the name of Jehovah God and Christ Jesus or have in their possession anything that makes known the name of God and his kingdom. Puny, insignificant man declares illegal the witness work of the Almighty Jehovah God!! Let the honest people judge as to whose servants such dictators are.

In the United States, which from its foundation has stood for freedom of worship, thousands of Jehovah's witnesses are arrested, imprisoned, and cruelly abused, their property destroyed, and their names cast out. For what reason? Because those faithful witnesses proclaim the name of Jehovah and his King. At whose demand are such cruelties and persecutions carried on? In every instance it is done at the demand of powerful religious organizations, and particularly that old and great religious organization which boasts that the gates of hell shall not prevail against it. That great religious organization, in particular, demands that the political and judicial officers shall punish Jehovah's servants, and hence they have harassed and persecuted Jehovah's witnesses even as the religionists did Jesus and his apostles. Such religious leaders see to it that mischief is framed by law against those who faithfully serve Jehovah and his King, even as the Lord foretold. (Psalm 94:20, 21) At the present time thousands of Jehovah's witnesses are subjected to trial and punishment by the courts. Mark how the words of Jesus apply to the present day, to wit: "If ye were of the world, the world would love his own: but because ye are not of the world, but I have chosen you out of the world, therefore the world hateth you. Remember the word that I said unto you, The servant is not greater than his lord. If they have persecuted me, they will also persecute you; if they have kept my saying, they will keep yours also. But all these things will they do unto you for my name's sake, because they know not him that sent me."–John 15:19-21.

"Oh, John, I can now understand why mobs in Texas, Alabama, Louisiana, Maine, Illinois, and in many other places have cruelly assaulted and ill-used Jehovah's witnesses. Many of the newspapers have made many false reports about them, and also they encourage the mobs. It is now clear to me that the Devil, the chief of demons, has used and is using blinded religionists to incite ignorant persons to form mobs and to ill-treat faithful servants of the Lord. These facts exactly fit the prophetic words of Jesus."

"Yes, Eunice, it is even so. You recall that in his great prophecy concerning the present day Jesus also said: 'As it was in the days of No'e, so shall it be also in the days of the Son of man.' (Luke 17:26) The demons had debauched all the people except Noah and his family. They dared tell the truth, and hence the demons and their dupes reproached Noah and his family. Likewise in the days of Lot the demons overreached the people, and caused Lot to be persecuted.

"Today the entire world is gone mad because of the influence and power of the Devil and his host of demons exercised over the people. Amidst all the turmoil that is upon the nations and the fanatical hysteria that is sweeping over the earth, the testimony concerning God and his kingdom must be given and God is seeing to it that it is given. Now it is the great privilege of the people who love God and righteousness to go about telling others who are of good-will concerning Jehovah's name and his kingdom in order that such persons may flee to the place of safety. Eunice, we must do our part and go and tell those people who will hear that God's kingdom is their only hope. We must be witnesses to his name, regardless of the persecution that may come upon us. Here I am reminded of the words of the apostle Paul, that he rejoiced in tribulation because of the opportunity of serving God and Christ the King.

Dividing the People

"The people are rapidly being separated into two companies: the 'goats' and the 'sheep'. The great Judge, Christ Jesus, is placing the 'goats' on his unfavorable side. All such are marking themselves by opposing the King and his servants. The people of good-will are fleeing to Christ because they are his 'other sheep', and he is putting 'his sheep' on his favorable side. Armageddon, the battle of that great day of God Almighty, is drawing near.

"There is another class designated the 'evil servant'. Such company is made up of persons who had the advantage of the ransom sacrifice, agreed to do the will of God, and then proved unfaithful, and now they reproach the name of Jehovah and his King, and persecute the faithful servants of God. They have become offended at the Lord and his way of carrying on his work and have become lawless, and these are gathered out and their lot is fixed. (Matthew 25: 41; 2 Thessalonians 2: 1-12) The fate of the 'evil servant' is the same as that of the hypocrites and other defamers of Jehovah's name.—Matthew 24: 51.

Armageddon

"What is Armageddon? The word means the place of the gathering of troops under Christ Jesus. These servants of the Lord are opposed by Satan and his servants, and in God's due time He will command the Lord Jesus Christ to lead the host of heaven against all the wicked ones in the great battle of that day of God Almighty and destroy the wicked. That is called 'the battle of Armageddon'. In that battle all the opposers of THE THEOCRACY shall be destroyed. Only persons of good-will, who flee to the Lord before Armageddon is fought and who remain faithful and obedient under Christ, shall survive, and these shall be the ones that will form the 'great multitude'. In that great conflict the wicked, and particularly the religious leaders, will find no way of escape. (Jeremiah 25: 33-35) Armageddon will be the worst tribulation the world will ever have known. (Matthew 24: 21) Jehovah's kingdom is the only refuge."

CHAPTER 9

ADMONITION TO CHILDREN

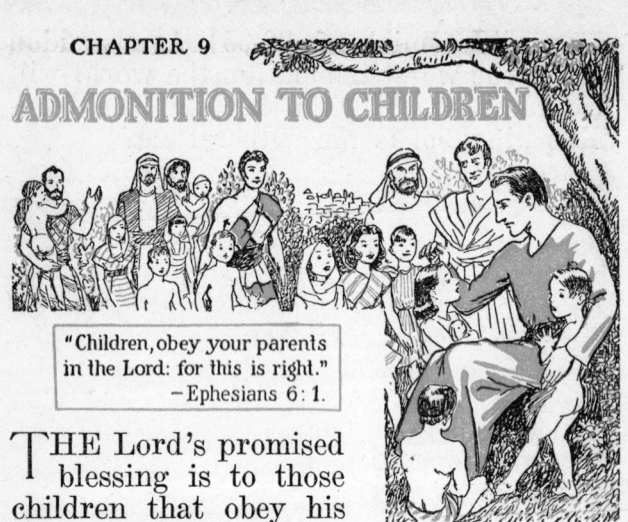

"Children, obey your parents in the Lord: for this is right."
—Ephesians 6:1.

THE Lord's promised blessing is to those children that obey his laws. Almighty God is the Father, or Life-giver, to all and he has delegated to Christ Jesus the authority and power to administer life to all obedient ones. Hence Christ Jesus the King is called in the Scriptures "The Everlasting Father", meaning the One who administers life everlasting. (Isaiah 9:6) The 'first command with promise' given to children is this: "Honour thy father and thy mother; that thy days may be long upon the land which the Lord thy God giveth thee." — Exodus 20:12.

The words "father" and "mother", in this text, are used symbolically as well as literally. Symbolically this command means

256

that the Almighty God, the Life-giver, is the Father, and his organization is the "mother", of all who receive life everlasting. Hence every one who receives life must honor God the Father and his organization, the mother, through which life is administered. For this reason it is written in the Scriptures: "Children, obey your parents in the Lord: for this is right." The emphasis here is on the words "in the Lord", that is to say, parents who are devoted to Jehovah and his kingdom.

Marriage and childbearing is God's arrangement for humankind that shall live on the earth. Parents who have made a covenant to do the will of God and who have children are properly said to be "in the Lord", within the meaning of the foregoing text. Their children, therefore, must be taught by the parents in the Lord to be obedient to the Lord and to their human parents as they follow the Lord. Such parents, who are in the Lord, must be "taught of God" and obey him. (Isaiah 54: 13) It follows that they should require their children to be obedient to His commandment or rules, which the Lord has put in his Word. Upon all parents who are in a covenant to do God's will there is laid a duty and specific obligation to teach their children the Word of God, and it is the duty of the children to obey their parents who give such instruction. There can be no question about the responsibility that rests upon the parents as well as the children. To the parents this admonition is given: "And, ye fathers, provoke not your children to wrath: but bring them up in the nurture and admonition of the Lord."—Ephesians 6: 4.

Let the words of the text be emphasized, to wit: "Children, obey your parents in the Lord: for this is right." The only inference to be drawn therefrom is that parents in the Lord must teach their children that which is right, therefore that which is righteous. The words "right" and "righteous" are from the same root and mean the same thing. This is shown by the following proof texts: "For the righteous Lord loveth righteousness; his countenance doth behold the upright." (Psalm 11: 7) "For the eyes of the Lord are over the righteous, and his ears are open unto their prayers: but the face of the Lord is against them that do evil." (1 Peter 3: 12) "The Lord knoweth the days of the upright; and their inheritance shall be for ever. They shall not be ashamed in the evil time; and in the days of famine they shall be satisfied. The righteous shall inherit the land, and dwell therein for ever." (Psalm 37: 18, 19, 29) "Light is sown for the righteous, and gladness for the upright in heart." (Psalm 97: 11) These and many like promises of God are given to those who love and obey righteousness. Parents in the Lord will be glad to instruct their children in righteousness, and the children should be obedient with real joy. They should have in mind the words of the beloved Son of God: "I delight to do thy will, O my God." —Psalm 40: 8.

How may parents and children learn of and know the way of righteousness? Only by receiving and obeying instructions given by Jehovah and recorded in his Word: "Thy word is a lamp unto my feet, and a light unto my path. Thy righteousness is an everlasting righteousness, and thy law is the truth. The righteousness of thy testimonies is everlasting: give me understanding, and I shall live. My tongue shall speak of thy word; for all thy commandments are righteousness."— Psalm 119: 105, 142, 144, 172.

Religious ceremonies produce no good results and are in vain and injurious, because contrary to the Word of God. Note the clear distinction made between such religious ceremonies and the truth. "Study to shew thyself approved unto God, a workman that needeth not to be ashamed, rightly dividing the word of truth. But shun profane and vain babblings; for they will increase unto more ungodliness."—2 Timothy 2: 15, 16.

The word here rendered "profane" means heathenish. Religion is heathenish and is a reproach to the name of Almighty God. The words "vain" and "babblings" translate the same root word, and both mean empty, fruitless, and therefore detrimental. The theory of "human evolution" could not possibly lead to righteousness, but rather to increase selfishness, arrogance, and disobedience to God. Evolution denies the creation of man as stated in the Bible, and the theory is equivalent to saying, "There is no Almighty God." Religious ceremonies that pay tribute, honor or praise to any creature are likewise contrary to God's will and are degrading and reproach Jehovah's name. Many persons sincerely indulge in fixed religious ceremonies and think that by so doing the same will bring to them good results. But such persons are woefully deceived. To lean to the information or instruction of men, to the effect that any kind of religion is good just so the person sincerely believes it, not only is harmful but leads to destruction.

If one desires to be taught in the right way he must not follow the teachings of men, which teachings are contrary to God's Word, nor even lean to his own theories. To prate about, talk about or participate in such things as religion and evolution, is vain babbling. God's instruction to those who would find the right way is this: "Trust in the Lord with all thine heart; and lean not unto thine own understanding. In all thy ways acknowledge him, and he shall direct thy paths. Be not wise in thine own eyes; fear the Lord, and depart from evil."— Proverbs 3: 5-7.

Sane persons desire to live, because without life nothing else could be enjoyed. How may one get life? Jesus answers: "This is life eternal, that they might know thee, the only true God, and Jesus Christ, whom thou hast sent." (John 17:3) To know means to receive and perceive the truth. Where is the truth concerning life to be found? Jesus answers: "Thy word is truth" (John 17:17); which means that the truth concerning life is found only in the Word of God the Creator. To receive and perceive the truth one begins to gain knowledge. God's visible creation imparts information or knowledge that a mighty power, far above man, exists. (Psalm 19:2) The sincere person would fear to offend that great power: "The fear of the Lord is the beginning of knowledge: but fools despise wisdom and instruction." —Proverbs 1:7.

The fear of God, therefore, is the beginning of knowledge. How does such a person become wise? One becomes truly wise by receiving and perceiving the truth of God as set forth in his Word, and then by pursuing a course of action in harmony with that knowledge. Fear of God, therefore, is the beginning of true knowledge, and also the beginning of wisdom. The "fear of God" means to believe that Jehovah is the Almighty Creator, from whom all good proceeds, and therefore one fears or dreads to pursue any course that is contrary to God's

will. The wise person is he who is diligent
to do that which is pleasing to God, perceiving that God grants his favor of life everlasting only to those who joyfully do his
will: "The fear of the Lord is the beginning
of wisdom; and the knowledge of the holy is
understanding. For by me thy days shall be
multiplied, and the years of thy life shall be
increased." (Proverbs 9: 10, 11) "The fear
of the Lord is the beginning of wisdom: a
good understanding have all they that do
his commandments: his praise endureth for
ever."—Psalm 111: 10.

Mark that the fear of God is the beginning of knowledge and wisdom; and that
fear of God must continue in the heart and
mind of the person who would please him.
Such person must first have some knowledge of God and his purpose, and then,
by taking the course pointed out by God's
Word, that person begins to grow wise.
When he appreciates God's instruction as
set forth in the Bible, and then shows that
appreciation by his obedience, he begins
to have understanding. Knowledge, wisdom
and understanding, therefore, are progres-
sive and advance in this order: First knowledge, then wisdom, then understanding. By
"understanding" is meant the creature's
proper appreciation of the relationship he
bears to the great Creator, Almighty God.

To further illustrate the point: The child
beholds the stars and planets at night, and

his reasoning faculties conclude the star did
not make itself, it is not the result of evolution, but the great and mighty One made
all stars and planets. To himself he says:
'I would like to know more about the Creator and his purpose, and I would fear to
do anything that displeases him.' That is
the beginning of knowledge. The child then
learns that the Bible contains the Word of
God. He seeks and studies the Bible and
gains more information and knowledge and
begins to follow the course pointed out by
the Scriptures as to what he shall do, fearing lest he should go wrong, fearing to displease God; and that is the beginning of
wisdom. Then he begins to see and appreciate that God is the Almighty One, and that
he, the child, is but a small creature, and
that God's goodness and mercy are extended to all creatures who know and obey him;
and then he tries to obey, and thus he gains
understanding. He is appreciating his relationship to the almighty Creator, Jehovah.

To the child or person who has faith in
God and who desires to learn of him, the
Almighty says: "My son, if thou wilt receive my words, and hide my commandments with thee; so that thou incline thine
ear unto wisdom, and apply thine heart
to understanding; yea, if thou criest after
knowledge, and liftest up thy voice for understanding; if thou seekest her as silver,
and searchest for her as for hid treasures;

then shalt thou understand the fear of the Lord, and find the knowledge of God. For the Lord giveth wisdom: out of his mouth cometh knowledge and understanding. He layeth up sound wisdom for the righteous: he is a buckler to them that walk uprightly. He keepeth the paths of judgment, and preserveth the way of his saints. Then shalt thou understand righteousness, and judgment, and equity; yea, every good path. When wisdom entereth into thine heart, and knowledge is pleasant unto thy soul, discretion shall preserve thee, understanding shall keep thee."—Proverbs 2:1-11.

Discretion would require such a person to follow the way God has pointed out; and understanding, which is a proper appreciation of the relationship between the creature and the Creator, will keep one in the right way.

Parents who have covenanted to do the will of God have a special responsibility resting upon them concerning their children. That responsibility cannot be side-stepped or avoided by placing their children under another to be instructed, and particularly when that other person, the teacher, is not "in the Lord". Parents are the ones who brought their children into the world, and it is their duty and responsibility to teach their children. There is but one right way to teach them, and that is in harmony with God's Word and what is contained in the

Word of God. They should avoid teaching
them anything that is contrary to God's
Word. Hence they must avoid and shun evolution concerning men, and shun religion,
because it is false.

When?

When shall the parents begin to teach
their children? Preparation should be made
before the child is born, by properly inform-
ing themselves. From the time the child is
born it should be taught obedience, because
to obey that which is right is essential to
life. Obedience in small things, as well as
in the more weighty matters, should be required of the child. As the child increases
in years and in ability to receive and perceive the truth, the parents should enlarge
upon the teaching of that child, particularly
concerning the Word of God.

The foundation of the child's education
must be laid in the Word of God, because
that is the one way that leads to life everlasting. In order to be equipped to teach
their children, the parents must first learn.
For their own good, and for the good of
their children, the parents must faithfully
keep their covenant with God, and that covenant includes learning for themselves and
teaching the child God's commandments. In
this connection note the following instruction: "But the mercy of the Lord is from
everlasting to everlasting upon them that

fear him, and his righteousness unto children's children; to such as keep his covenant, and to those that remember his commandments to do them. The Lord hath prepared his throne in the heavens; and his kingdom ruleth over all."–Psalm 103: 17-19.

Teaching of children by the parents that which is contained in the Word of God will result to them in the greatest of all blessings; and hence such is the greatest blessing the parent can bestow upon the children. Generally those of the world who are parents desire to provide their children with a college education and a training in religion, commerce, and politics, with the ability to make money and shine in the world. Good that is enduring does not result from such worldly teaching. It is of far greater importance to the child to teach it God's Word, that it may gain knowledge, wisdom and understanding, which lead to endless blessings: "How much better is it to get wisdom than gold! and to get understanding rather to be chosen than silver!" (Proverbs 16: 16) "Receive my instruction, and not silver; and knowledge rather than choice gold. For wisdom is better than rubies; and all the things that may be desired are not to be compared to it."—Proverbs 8: 10, 11.

He who follows the course of religion, politics and commerce usually ends his career in sorrow. He who pursues the course of wisdom, which is pointed out by God's

Word, receives the blessings of the Lord
and enters into everlasting joy: "The blessing of the Lord, it maketh rich; and he add-
eth no, sorrow with it." (Proverbs 10:22)
"Happy is the man that findeth wisdom,
and the man that getteth understanding:
for the merchandise of it is better than the
merchandise of silver, and the gain thereof
than fine gold. She is more precious than
rubies; and all the things thou canst desire
are not to be compared unto her. Length of
days is in her right hand; and in her left
hand riches and honour. Her ways are ways
of pleasantness, and all her paths are peace.
She is a tree of life to them that lay hold
upon her; and happy is every one that re-
taineth her."—Proverbs 3:13-18.

Where?

Shall the child be sent to the Sunday
school of some religious organization to
there receive instruction? No; for the reason that religious organizations do not teach
the Bible, which is the way of righteousness. If the parents love their children they
must and will instruct them at home in the
Word of God and will take their children
with them to the class or company where
the Bible is carefully and systematically
studied, and there require the children to
sit quietly and learn; and when they have
advanced sufficiently they will let the children participate in the study. Such is the

rule which God has made known, and that is the only proper rule to follow. The rule or rules which God made known to the Israelites, his typical chosen people, apply to all persons who enter into a covenant with God to do his will. These rules, applying to the typical people, with stronger reasoning apply to the antitypical. When a person believes that God is the Almighty and that Christ Jesus, the beloved Son of God, is the Redeemer of men, and when that person relies upon these truths and willingly agrees to do the will of God, that person then and there covenants to do what God's Word commands him to do. God's rules do not change, even as he does not change. (Malachi 3:6) Therefore the rules announced in his Word from Genesis to Revelation apply to those who have agreed to do God's will. God is the great Teacher or Instructor, by and through Christ Jesus, of all His people; and the rules relative to such instruction apply to all persons who have *agreed to do God's will,* even as it is written: "For this cause I bow my knees unto the Father of our Lord Jesus Christ, of whom the whole family in heaven and earth is named."—Ephesians 3:14, 15.

What, then, are the rules which God has announced concerning the parents and their responsibility to teach their children? Let the Word of God answer: "Only take heed to thyself, and keep thy soul diligently, lest thou forget the things which thine eyes have seen, and lest they depart from thy heart all the days of thy life; but teach them thy sons, and thy sons' sons; specially the day that thou stoodest before the Lord thy God in Horeb, when the Lord said unto me, Gather me the people together, and I will make them hear my words, that they may learn to fear me all the days that they shall live upon the earth, and that they may teach their children."—Deuteronomy 4: 9, 10.

After announcing to his covenant people the rules which they must obey God says to them: "Therefore shall ye lay up these my words in your heart and in your soul, and bind them for a sign upon your hand, that they may be as frontlets between your eyes. And ye shall teach them your children, speaking of them when thou sittest in thine house, and when thou walkest by the way, when thou liest down, and when thou risest up. And thou shalt write them upon the door posts of thine house, and upon thy gates; that your days may be multiplied, and the days of your children, in the land which the Lord sware unto your fathers to give them, as the days of heaven upon the earth."— Deuteronomy 11: 18-21.

Note these specific commandments concerning the teaching of the children: "Observe and hear all these words which I command thee, that it may go well with thee, and with thy children after thee for ever,

when thou doest that which is good and
right in the sight of the Lord thy God.''
(Deuteronomy 12: 28) ''And he said unto
them, Set your hearts unto all the words
which I testify among you this day, which
ye shall command your children to observe
to do, all the words of this law.''—Deuteronomy 32: 46.

The parents who have agreed to do the
will of God must teach their children to
love God: ''And thou shalt love the Lord
thy God with all thine heart, and with all
thy soul, and with all thy might. And these
words, which I command thee this day,
shall be in thine heart: and thou shalt
teach them diligently unto thy children,
and shalt talk of them when thou sittest
in thine house, and when thou walkest by
the way, and when thou liest down, and
when thou risest up. And thou shalt bind
them for a sign upon thine hand, and they
shall be as frontlets between thine eyes.''
—Deuteronomy 6: 5-8.

To 'love God', as commanded in verse five
above, means to be unselfishly devoted to
doing the will of God, and doing so with
a genuine delight. ''If ye love me, keep my
commandments.'' ''If ye keep my commandments, ye shall abide in my love; even as I
have kept my Father's commandments, and
abide in his love.'' (John 14: 15; 15: 10)
Jesus emphasized the necessity of obeying
God's commandments. (Matthew 22: 37-40)

Parents who love God will keep always in mind concerning their children that the life of the child is involved and that it is of the greatest importance that the child should be instructed from its youth onward as to what God requires of those who shall find life everlasting.

Human Laws

Nations enact laws, and it is the duty of parents and children to obey all such laws as are in harmony with God's law, because such is right. Laws are made for transgressors, but if one always does that which is right, according to God's law, he will not be a transgressor of either the law of man or the law of God. Suppose the state enacts a law, and the keeping of that law by a child who is in covenant with God would make the child an idolater and hence a violator of God's law, what shall the child do? God's law provides that all who practice idolatry shall be everlastingly destroyed. Human laws, that is, laws of nations, punish those who disobey their laws, and sometimes the punishment is death. As to what a person in a covenant with God shall do under such circumstances Jesus gave the correct answer, a similar question being propounded to him: "Render to Cæsar the things that are Cæsar's, and to God the things that are God's." (Mark 12: 17) "Cæsar" here stands for the state, nation, or human laws. The law of God is supreme. All human laws that are valid derive their authority from God's law. One must choose to obey either the law of man or the law of God, and those in a covenant with God and having agreed to do his will must obey the law of God, if they would live. Such is the Scriptural authority, and that authority is controlling so far as persons who have made a covenant to do God's will are concerned. (Acts 3: 22, 23; 4: 19, 20; 5: 29; Daniel 3: 15-28) The person who is always diligent to obey God's law, and who does obey God's law, will never infract any law of any state that is just, proper and right.

Parents are often required to suffer punishment because they teach their children the Word of God, but such suffering does not deter them from teaching the child what God has commanded. If the parents or children are punished by the state for rendering obedience unto God's law, then that suffering is suffering for righteousness' sake: "And who is he that will harm you, if ye be followers of that which is good? But and if ye suffer for righteousness' sake, happy are ye: and be not afraid of their terror, neither be troubled. For it is better, if the will of God be so, that ye suffer for well doing than for evil doing."—1 Peter 3: 13, 14, 17.

Punishment being inflicted upon the children of God because they obey his command-

ments will receive due attention from the
Lord himself, and in his own due time he
will recompense those who punish the children for obeying God's law. He will avenge
his faithful servants, and his due time for
doing so is just at hand.—Luke 18: 7, 8.

It has ever been the practice of Satan to
put the fear of man into the heart and mind
of Christians, and this he has done in his
endeavor to turn them away from God. The
true child of God has no fear of what man
or Devil may do to him, because he knows
that the fear of man leads into the snare of
the Devil. (Proverbs 29: 25) The greatest
punishment human laws can inflict upon one
is death. The greatest punishment God in-
flicts upon the violators of his law and covenant is complete destruction. Christians who
suffer death at the hands of the state because they obey God, such persons are guar-
anteed a resurrection out of death by the
power of the Lord. Therefore Jesus admon-
ishes the Christian in these words: "And
fear not them which kill the body, but are
not able to kill the soul: but rather fear him
which is able to destroy both soul and body
in hell."—Matthew 10: 28.

If the child of God is put to death because he obeys the law of God, which is supreme, God will not forget that faithful soul
but will raise him up out of death and grant
to that faithful one life everlasting. Fear
God, and live.

Obey

All parents who are consecrated to God, and hence in a covenant to do God's will, must obey his commandments; and one command concerning their children is this: "And, ye fathers, provoke not your children to wrath: but bring them up in the nurture and admonition of the Lord."—Ephesians 6: 4.

"Nurture" means to discipline and train the child in the way of righteousness; and such way of righteousness God has marked out in his Word. 'Admonish' means to teach and instruct, to counsel and advise, the children of and in accord with the will of God as set forth in the Scriptures. The parents who love their children will not neglect to obey this injunction of the Scriptures. They will see to it that their children receive instruction as God has commanded. If the parents claim to love and serve God, and at the same time fail or refuse to teach their children the Word of God, such course of the parents is certain to cause the children to lose respect for the parents, and thus the parents will be provoking their children to do wrong or to wrath. For this reason the admonition is given to the parents to bring up their children in the nurture and admonition of the Lord.

Gathering His Own

The present is the time when the Lord is gathering his "other sheep", which shall form the "great multitude". Both parents and children are of the "other sheep". Both should walk together with the Lord, seeking always to know and to do the will of God. The hope of the parents and of the children who are Jonadabs or persons of good-will is that they may live forever on the earth, serving and praising God and his King. Rendering themselves now in obedience to the Lord's law their hope is to be forever together, that is to say, real partners or companions in doing righteous deeds to the glory of God and his King. That companionship should begin now, and both parents and children should together study the Word of God and be diligent to obey his commandments and to inform others who will hear, of the blessings that await all who obey God and his King. God has laid this great obligation upon the parents, even as he laid a similar obligation upon his typical people.

First take note of what the Lord says to all those who would find the way of life: "Give ear, O my people, to my law: incline your ears to the words of my mouth. . . . which we have heard and known, and our fathers have told us. We will not hide them from their children, shewing to the generation to come the praises of the Lord, and his strength, and his wonderful works that he hath done. For he established a testimony in Jacob, and appointed a law in Israel, which he commanded our fathers, that they should make them known to their children: that the generation to come might know them, even the children which should be born, who should arise and declare them to their children: that they might set their hope in God, and not forget the works of God, but keep his commandments."—Psalm 78: 1-7.

The consecrated parents who make confidants of their children will take their children to the company studies where the Bible is studied, and both will have a part in the study. Also they will pursue their studies of the Scriptures together in the home, and will talk about the Lord and his kingdom as they go about their work. Also they will go together in the witness work from house to house, telling the people of God's gracious provision for those who love and obey him. Parents who pursue this course win the highest respect of their children and set them an example and lead them in the way to the fountain of life. Both have in mind the same great objective, that is, looking forward to the day of their deliverance from unrighteousness and when righteousness shall fill the earth, to the glory of God

and to the good of all who obey THE THE-
OCRACY.

Children Witnesses

A child of tender years often shows itself
as a good and effective witness for Jehovah
and his King. The child mind is free from
errors of religion, if it is receiving proper
training at home from consecrated parents.
Naturally that child speaks to others of the
most important thing in its mind, and the
most important thing is the Kingdom and
the vindication of Jehovah's name. In simple phrase the child tells of the blessings
that are soon to come to mankind through
THE THEOCRACY, and that testimony given
by a child is frequently received by elder
persons, as well as others, and by them given
deep consideration. On many occasions children have brought the Kingdom message to
grownups in such a simple and forceful manner that grownups could not fail to consider
it. The consecrated parents will teach their
children to be witnesses to the name and
kingdom of God.

The Lord made a marvelous picture foretelling exactly what is today observed by
those who love God and his kingdom. Jesus
rode into the city of Jerusalem in the manner that ancient kings presented themselves
to the people. (Matthew 21: 2-16) Men, wom-
en and children hailed Jesus as King, thus
publicly giving testimony that they recog-

nized and accepted Christ Jesus as man's King and Deliverer. That was a prophetic picture, the fulfillment of which is now in progress, when Christ the King has come and sits in judgment and is separating his "other sheep" from those who are against him. As the great King he is now enthroned, and his reign has begun. That prophetic picture points to the present when men, women and children now recognize and hail Christ Jesus as the great King of The THEOCRATIC GOVERNMENT which shall rule the world in righteousness and bless all obedient ones. As it was in the picture, so it is now in reality. Christ the King has come, and his "other sheep" are proclaiming his name and praises: "And a very great multitude spread their garments in the way; others cut down branches from the trees, and strawed them in the way. And the multitudes that went before, and that followed, cried, saying, Hosanna to the son of David! Blessed is he that cometh in the name of the Lord; Hosanna in the highest!"—Matthew 21: 8, 9.

After riding into the city, as shown in the prophetic picture, Jesus went into the temple and there the multitude, including the children, followed him. Their presence there offended the religious leaders, even as today the testimony of the multitude, including minor children, offends the religious leaders. Now Jesus is in the temple and the children cry out, hailing him as King and Deliverer. Mark the words of Jesus speaking then, and which words apply now with greater force and effect: "And when the chief priests and scribes saw the wonderful things that he did, and the children crying in the temple, and saying, Hosanna to the son of David! they were sore displeased, and said unto him, Hearest thou what these say? And Jesus saith unto them, Yea: have ye never read, Out of the mouth of babes and sucklings thou hast perfected praise?" (Matthew 21: 15, 16) Encourage your children now to be witnesses and their testimony will be effective.

The hour has now come when children who are taught and who love God and his King will give the greatest witness to the name of Jehovah and his King that has yet been given. These little ones who now fearlessly and faithfully proclaim the name of the great THEOCRACY and continue faithfully to do so are certain to receive the approval of the Lord and be granted an everlasting inheritance in this earth, here to enjoy endless life, peace and joy beyond anything man has ever known. This is the most favorable time children have ever had on earth, because it is the time when they may serve God in sincerity and in truth and bear testimony to his name and his kingdom.

CHILDREN HAILING JESUS – RELIGIONISTS OPPOSE

Requirements

To receive God's approval his covenant people must meet his requirements. "Behold, to obey is better than sacrifice." (1 Samuel 15:22) Faith, faithfulness and obedience are required of all who shall receive life. The servant of God inquires: "Wherewith shall I come before the Lord, and bow myself before the high God? . . . He hath shewed thee, O man, what is good; and what doth the Lord require of thee, but to do justly, and to love mercy, and to walk humbly with thy God?"–Micah 6:6, 8.

"Parents in the Lord" will be diligent to obey God by 'bringing up their children in the nurture and admonition of the Lord', as commanded. They will teach their chil-

dren to be obedient, and particularly to love
and obey the commandments of God and
Christ. Together they will study God's commandments in the home, that they may understand them and that they may obey the
Lord. This done, parents and children will
walk together in righteousness with God,
that is, in the way he has commanded. Being diligent to seek righteousness and to be
guided by God's Word, they will be guided
in the right way: "The meek will he guide
in judgment, and the meek will he teach his
way. All the paths of the Lord are mercy
and truth unto such as keep his covenant
and his testimonies." (Psalm 25: 9, 10) To
his "other sheep", who in this day walk
according to the commandment of the Lord,
he will give protection until his wrath be
overpast.

The children of tender years, as well as
the older ones, who have given their sincere, heart devotion to God and his King,
and who in obedience to the Lord's commandment continue faithfully and joyfully
to bear testimony to his name and to the
kingdom of the great THEOCRAT, will soon
see the earth cleansed of all wickedness,
which will come in the expression of God's
wrath leveled against Satan's entire organization. During that time of greatest crisis
God will keep in the hollow of his hand and
under his complete protection all those that

love and serve him faithfully. For centuries a great divine mandate has waited God's due time to be carried into full effect. After Armageddon the faithful "other sheep", who will form the "great multitude", will come forth from their place where God has hidden and protected them, and they shall be advanced to a place under the capital organization and given a service of great importance in the favor of the Lord. The Lord will assign them to a place prepared for the "great multitude" from the time of Eden, and, performing their assigned duty, they will participate in the vindication of the name of the Most High. Today the greatest favor to children is to know God and Christ Jesus and to be witnesses to the name of Jehovah and to his glorious government, THE THEOCRACY.

"Permit me to make this observation, Eunice, concerning the capital organization of Jehovah: The Scriptures, as we have learned, show that the marriage of man and woman pictures the relationship of Christ and his church. Christ Jesus is the Bridegroom, and the body members collectively constitute his bride. It is written to the faithful followers of Christ Jesus by the Lord's true servant: 'I have espoused you to one husband, that I may

present you as a chaste virgin to Christ.'
(2 Corinthians 11:2) Now, Eunice, I re-
mind you that you have agreed to be my
wife, and since seeing the relationship of
Christ and his bride we appreciate more
than ever the beauty and sacredness of such
relationship. I am grateful to the Lord that
I am to have the companion of my youth,
who has always been so faithful, soon to be
my wife and companion, that together we
may forever serve the Lord. By His grace
we will bring up our children in the nurture and admonition of the Lord. It now
seems to be the appropriate time to name
the day when we shall consummate our marriage contract. Shall we do so?''

"You are very kind and considerate, dear
John. Our hope is that we shall be of the
'great multitude' that shall forever serve
the King of Eternity. Before consummat-
ing our marriage and beginning to bring
children into the world, would it not be well
for us to learn more from the Scriptures
about what position or place the 'great
multitude' will have in God's gracious and
blessed arrangement, and whether that multitude shall rear children?''

"Yes, Eunice dear, that is a timely suggestion. In our next study let us ascertain
from the Scriptures, if we can, what the
Lord will have the 'great multitude' to do,
both now and in the future. We must thus

be instructed, that we may properly teach our children, if the good Lord permits us to have children.''

CHAPTER 10

THE MANDATE

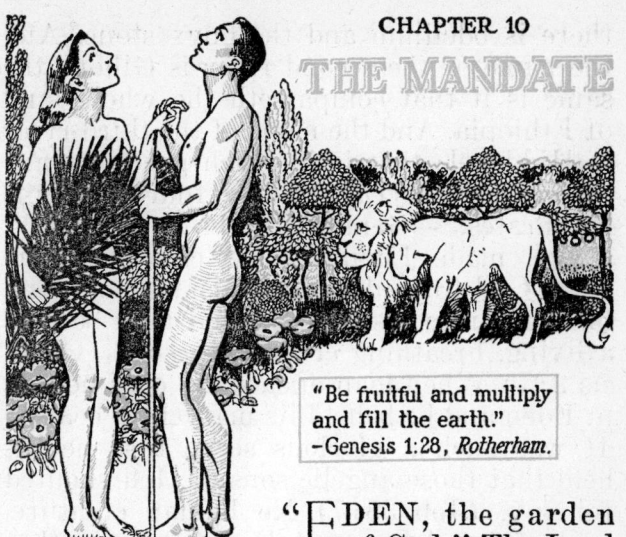

"Be fruitful and multiply
and fill the earth."
—Genesis 1:28, *Rotherham.*

"EDEN, the garden of God." The Lord God planted that garden, and it was perfect. The name "Eden" means a paradise or place of beauty and pleasantness. In it grew everything perfect man could desire. "And out of the ground made the Lord God to grow every tree that is pleasant to the sight, and good for food; the tree of life also in the midst of the garden, and the tree of knowledge of good and evil. And a river went out of Eden to water the garden; and from thence it was parted, and became into four heads. The name of the first is Pison: that is it which compasseth the whole land of Havilah, where there is gold; and the gold of that land is good:

there is bdellium and the onyx stone. And the name of the second river is Gihon: the same is it that compasseth the whole land of Ethiopia. And the name of the third river is Hiddekel: that is it which goeth toward the east of Assyria. And the fourth river is Euphrates."—Genesis 2: 9-14.

God made Eden for his creature man. Then God formed the organism of man and breathed into his nostrils, and man became a living, breathing creature, a soul. (Genesis 2: 7) When man opened his eyes he was in Eden and he beheld its marvelous beauty. It was such a glorious scene that he beheld that those angelic sons of God shouted for joy. (Job 38: 7) No human creature, aside from Adam and Eve, ever saw that garden of perfection and glory. When man violated God's law he was expelled from Eden and the gates thereof were closed, and never again can Adam see it. None of Adam's offspring have ever seen Eden.

In the brief time Adam and Eve were in Eden they would revel in its grandeur. They would walk amidst the trees by the rivers, inhale the fragrance of the sweet-scented flowers, eat the perfect fruit, and join with the birds in song to the praise of the great Creator. It was at that time and in that place that the Almighty God issued to the perfect pair his mandate, to wit:

"BE FRUITFUL AND MULTIPLY AND FILL THE EARTH."

Only Eden was made a paradise. Other parts of the earth God cursed with thorns and thistles and weeds that sinful man might be required to labor for his food. (Genesis 3: 17) That it is Jehovah's purpose to some day have the entire earth a paradise there is not the slightest doubt. That being Jehovah's purpose in the beginning, it must be carried out in his due time.—Ezekiel 36: 35.

The Almighty God created the earth to be inhabited forever by righteous men. He created man a righteous creature for the earth. All of God's creation is perfect and done in righteousness. These statements are fully supported by the infallible Word of God and cannot be successfully called in question. (Isaiah 45: 12, 18) "His work is perfect." (Deuteronomy 32: 4) "For the word of the Lord is right; and all his works are done in truth." (Psalm 33: 4) "His work is honourable and glorious: and his righteousness endureth for ever. He hath made his wonderful works to be remembered: the Lord is gracious, and full of compassion. The works of his hands are verity and judgment; all his commandments are sure." (Psalm 111: 3, 4, 7) "All thy works shall praise thee, O Lord; and thy saints shall bless thee."—Psalm 145: 10.

Adam, the man whom God created, was perfect and righteous when created, and therefore had the right to life, conditioned upon obedience. Likewise Eve was perfect and righteous when created. To that perfect and righteous pair God gave the commandment: "Be fruitful and multiply and fill the earth." The Authorized Version of the Bible uses the word "replenish" (the earth), but the many other translations render that same word "fill". (See *Leeser, Douay, Margolis, Rotherham, Strong,* and others) Necessarily the mandate could be carried out only by righteous men and righteous women. By reason of disobedience of God's law Adam and Eve became unrighteous before an effort was made to perform the divine mandate. For that reason the mandate failed as to them, but it could not fail as to God. It shall be performed.—Isaiah 46: 11.

At the time when the mandate was given to Adam and Eve by Jehovah that perfect pair was under the supervision of an invisible overlord, to wit, Lucifer, who also was then perfect. Lucifer led that human pair into sin and death. Lucifer became Satan, that wicked one who at all times since opposes the Almighty God. It would follow that at the time when the divine mandate is carried out, human creatures who carry it out, even though perfect and righteous, must be under the supervision of a righteous overlord. Almighty God does not deviate one jot or tittle from his purpose, and nothing that is done by wicked men and wicked spirit creatures can prevent the carrying out of his purpose, which

BIBLICAL LIBRARY

POINTED DISCOURSES

he will do in his own time and good way. With God there is nothing impossible. All persons who have faith in God may with full and complete confidence expect to find that the Scriptures clearly point out how and when Jehovah God's great mandate to fill the earth shall be carried out.

A "mandate" is an authoritative statement, and the divine mandate, above mentioned, is stated with absolute authority from Jehovah, the Almighty God, and must stand.

Adam Disqualified

The divine mandate, so far as it related to Adam and Eve, was canceled because they became unrighteous. Not so, however, with Almighty God. That mandate had been issued and must stand. God had given his word, and that must stand for ever: "For as the rain cometh down, and the snow, from heaven, and returneth not thither, but watereth the earth, and maketh it bring forth and bud, that it may give seed to the sower, and bread to the eater; so shall my word be that goeth forth out of my mouth: it shall not return unto me void; but it shall accomplish that which I please, and it shall prosper in the thing whereto I sent it."— Isaiah 55: 10, 11.

After being expelled from Eden Adam and Eve began to multiply, but not in righteousness, and therefore it was impossible for them to carry out the divine mandate. They were sentenced to death by the judgment of Jehovah; hence they were deprived of any right to life and of the power to transmit that right to their offspring. (Genesis 3: 15-19) That judgment and the effect thereof still stand as to all human creatures who have not taken their stand entirely on the side of Jehovah: "Man that is born of a woman is of few days, and full of trouble. He cometh forth like a flower, and is cut down: he fleeth also as a shadow, and continueth not."—Job 14: 1, 2.

All the offspring of Adam were born under condemnation by reason of inherent imperfection. (Romans 5: 12) "Behold, I was shapen in iniquity, and in sin did my mother conceive me." (Psalm 51: 5) In order for the divine mandate to be carried out God must make some human creatures righteous and therefore qualified to carry out the mandate.

The Flood Prophetic

Approximately 1600 years after Eden's tragedy the offspring of Adam had grown to a large number, all of which were exceedingly wicked, with but a few exceptions. Only three men within that time God counted righteous because of their faith and obedience. Within that period of time the Devil had put forth his strongest endeavors to debauch and completely degrade humankind. Even a host of angels, that is, spirit creatures, the Devil had led into wickedness. Some of the spirit creatures materialized in human form and cohabited with women and produced a crop of rebels against God. After Noah had lived 500 years he had a family. (Genesis 5: 32) Aside from Noah and his family all human creatures turned to wickedness: "The earth also was corrupt before God, and the earth was filled with violence. And God looked upon the earth, and, behold, it was corrupt; for all flesh had corrupted his way upon the earth. And God said unto Noah, The end of all flesh is come before me; for the earth is filled with violence through them; and, behold, I will destroy them with the earth." —Genesis 6: 11-13.

Then God brought the great flood of waters, or deluge: "And every living substance was destroyed which was upon the face of the ground, both man, and cattle, and the creeping things, and the fowl of the heaven; and they were destroyed from the earth: and Noah only remained alive, and they that were with him in the ark."—Genesis 7: 23.

Only eight souls were saved from that deluge: "And spared not the old world, but saved Noah, the eighth person, a preacher of righteousness, bringing in the flood upon the world of the ungodly." (2 Peter 2: 5) These scriptures fully prove the cancellation of the divine mandate so far as Adam and Eve and their offspring were concerned.

The flood, which destroyed all flesh as stated in the foregoing text, prevented Satan's scheme to corrupt all creatures on the earth. Therefore the saving of Noah and his family from the flood is proof of the supremacy of Jehovah: "And, behold, I, even I, do bring a flood of waters upon the earth, to destroy all flesh, wherein is the breath of life, from under heaven; and every thing that is in the earth shall die. But with thee will I establish my covenant; and thou shalt come into the ark; thou, and thy sons, and thy wife, and thy sons' wives with thee."—Genesis 6: 17, 18.

The result of the flood was the cleansing off the earth everything of humankind that willfully defiled it. God used the flood, the ark, Noah and the members of Noah's family, to make a great prophetic picture, the fulfillment of which takes place in God's due time and is performed chiefly by Christ Jesus.

Learning the meaning of the prophetic picture made by the flood enables one to see the means by which God will carry out his purpose to cleanse the earth of all wickedness and then to fill the earth with a righteous race of human creatures. That the flood was typical and foreshadows what shall come to pass at the end of Satan's uninterrupted rule and with the coming of

Christ Jesus in power and glory, is made certain by the words of Jesus: "And as it was in the days of No'e, so shall it be also in the days of the Son of man." "Even thus shall it be in the day when the Son of man is revealed."—Luke 17: 26, 30.

Before the flood of waters fell upon the earth God caused Noah to build an ark, and he commanded Noah to take into that ark all the members of his family, to there be hidden in safety until the flood was passed: "But Noah found grace in the eyes of the Lord." (Genesis 6: 8) "And the Lord said unto Noah, Come thou and all thy house into the ark; for thee have I seen righteous before me in this generation."—Genesis 7: 1.

In the last quoted text note that Jehovah said to Noah: "For thee have I seen righteous before me in this generation." Because of Noah's faith and obedience God counted him as a righteous man. Noah, therefore, pictured the One who was to come and who is righteous, and also those associated with him in righteousness, they too being made righteous by reason of their faith and obedience unto God. Noah, therefore, pictured Christ Jesus, the righteous One, and also all the members of "the body of Christ", which together compose the royal house or kingdom of God. It is the Kingdom, of which Christ Jesus is the Head, that Jehovah uses to carry out his purpose. That great prophetic drama in which Noah and his family played a part was made and recorded long ago, and is now made understandable by those who love God and is for their comfort and hope, and enables them to see and to understand what the things that are now coming to pass on the earth really mean. (Romans 15:4) God permits his faithful servants now to be in his light and to see and appreciate his works.

God commanded Noah to take with him into the ark the members of his family, and these, together with Noah, constituted eight persons only who were carried over and were saved from the destructive deluge of waters. Noah builded the ark at the command of Almighty God, and which was a picture of God's organization. The Greater-than-Noah, Christ Jesus, builds the capital organization of Jehovah, and therefore the ark pictured Jehovah's capital organization. Noah and his family remained in the ark during the deluge, and there they were completely hidden in safety and carried over the flood.

Likewise all in Christ Jesus are granted safety during the antitypical deluge, that is, Armageddon. Those who were hidden with Noah in the ark pictured those who shall find refuge and safety under the capital organization of Jehovah. The members of Noah's family, therefore, foreshadowed or pictured the "other sheep" of the Lord, who are gathered unto him and who find protection from the devastation of "the bat-

tle of that great day of God Almighty",
called "Armageddon". The great deluge of
waters that fell upon the earth as soon as
the eight persons were safely in the ark
pictured the battle of Armageddon, which
shall begin its destructive work when all
the "other sheep" of the Lord are gathered
under the protection of the Lord's organization. This is strong proof that only those
who are in Christ and those who are of the
"other sheep" of the Lord, together with
the "princes", shall survive Armageddon.
All others now on the earth will die at Armageddon. It is the "sheep", that is to say,
the obedient ones, that are saved; and it is
the "goats", or disobedient ones, that shall
suffer destruction. (Matthew 25:31-46) It
follows, therefore, that all those who survive Armageddon must be counted righteous in the sight of God. That righteousness comes only from God through Christ
Jesus, and comes to those who by reason of
their faith and obedience unto God and
Christ are made righteous.

The flood having ended, Noah and his
family went forth out of the ark at the command of God: "Go forth of the ark, thou,
and thy wife, and thy sons, and thy sons'
wives with thee. Bring forth with thee
every living thing that is with thee, of all
flesh, both of fowl, and of cattle, and of
every creeping thing that creepeth upon
the earth; that they may breed abundant-

ly in the earth, and be fruitful, and multiply upon the earth." "And Noah went forth, and his sons, and his wife, and his sons' wives with him." (Genesis 8: 16-18) All the animals in the ark went forth with Noah. "And Noah builded an altar unto the Lord; and took of every clean beast, and of every clean fowl, and offered burnt offerings on the altar." (Genesis 8: 20) Noah then offered animals in sacrifice before the Lord, and that sacrificial offering was pleasing to God. "And the Lord smelled a savour of rest." (Genesis 8: 21, *margin*) That appears clearly to refer to the rest and comfort that will come to the survivors at the end of the battle of Armageddon; and this shows that the sacrifice offered by Noah was a part of the prophetic picture.

Noah and his family were the only human creatures then on the earth, and, all of them having found favor in the sight of God, all were counted righteous by reason of their faithfulness and obedience. This also was a part of the prophetic picture foretelling that immediately following the battle of Armageddon all the survivors will be righteous in the sight of God.

Mandate Restated

After Noah had offered the sacrifice before the Lord, God restated the mandate originally given to Adam and which Adam had failed to perform: "So God blessed

TYPICAL FULFILLMENT OF MANDATE AFTER THE FLOOD

Noah and his sons, and said to them, Be fruitful and multiply and fill the earth.'' (Genesis 9: 1, *Rotherham*) Since Noah and his family in connection with the ark and the flood were making a prophetic picture, of necessity also the restatement of the mandate to Noah and his sons was a part of that prophetic picture, foretelling God's purpose to carry out his mandate and foretelling the righteous ones that he would use to carry it into operation.

The mandate was first stated to Adam when he was a righteous man. It was restated to Noah and his sons when they were counted righteous and when making the prophetic drama, as above mentioned. That necessarily means that the mandate must be and will be carried out by the ones whom Noah's sons represented and who must be righteous. Noah pictured Christ Jesus and the members of "his body", who are righteous. The divine mandate must be carried out by those men and women who are under the direction and command of the Greater-than-Noah, namely, Christ the King, and the human creatures who must carry out that mandate must be righteous in God's sight when they do carry it out.

It must be kept in mind that Noah was typical. Noah did not carry out the divine mandate, although he lived on the earth 349 years after he came out of the ark. The Divine Record does not show that Noah brought into the world any children after the flood. His three sons, Shem, Japheth and Ham, were born before the flood, and those three, according to the Scriptures, are the three primary branches of the human race. If Noah had more than these three sons, there would have been more than three primary branches of the human race. Since the Divine Record does not show that he had any other than these three sons, this must mean that they are the only sons he had.

Since Noah in the picture represented the spiritual or heavenly company, or royal house of which Christ Jesus is the Head, and since Noah had no sons after the flood, this shows that the divine mandate to multiply and fill the earth does not apply to the spiritual class as to performance, but that the mandate must be carried out by human creatures acting under direct supervision of Christ Jesus, the antitypical Noah, and who is "the Everlasting Father" who administers life everlasting to all who live.—Isaiah 9: 6; Romans 6: 23.

The Bible record of the three sons of Noah, to wit, Shem, Japheth and Ham, sets forth the names of their children and grandchildren, all of which were born after the flood and after the restating of the divine mandate, and this record discloses seventy names or generations from the divine viewpoint. (Genesis 10: 1-32) From the record it appears that Nimrod had no children and died childless and in wickedness, and for that reason his name is not included in the seventy. Memory of Nimrod shall cease for ever. "The memory of the just is blessed: but the name of the wicked shall rot."— Proverbs 10: 7.

Neither Noah nor his three sons could actually carry out the divine mandate; and this also clearly shows that each one of them played his part in the prophetic drama foretelling the carrying out of the mandate by those whom the picture foretold. Why could not Noah and his sons carry out the divine mandate? Because the ransom sacrifice had not then been paid and they did not have and possess the right to life everlasting. They could receive such only through Christ Jesus, after the paying of the ransom price, and they all died before that time. In the picture they were counted righteous and played the part picturing a class of persons that must be actually righteous before they can carry out the divine mandate to "fill the earth". Adam was a righteous one when the mandate was given, and only righteous men can carry out that mandate in fact. Before the mandate can be carried out according to the expressed will and purpose of Almighty God, the human race must be purchased by the lifeblood of Christ Jesus, God's beloved Son, and then life and the right thereto must be administered to men by Christ Jesus in order that they could be qualified to carry out the mandate. It is expressly stated, at Hebrews eleven, that Noah and the other faithful men there named were counted righteous by reason of their faith and obedience, and that all of those died without having received life and must await the completion of the Kingdom before they can come into possession of life and the right thereto. It follows, then, that Noah and his sons, being without the right to life, could not carry out the divine mandate to fill the earth, but that they each played their parts in the prophecy relative to the fulfilling of that divine mandate.

Prophecy Fulfilled

In due time Jehovah sent his beloved Son into the earth to carry out His purpose. Christ Jesus, by his own lifeblood, purchased the human race, and to him is given full power and authority to administer life to all men that believe God's Word, believe on Christ and choose to obey Christ, and that do faithfully obey God and Christ. (Matthew 28:18; John 5:22, 26; 17:3) Christ Jesus, being exalted to the highest place, proceeded to build up God's capital organization in harmony with his Father's will, and which organization is the Kingdom, or THEOCRATIC GOVERNMENT, of which Christ Jesus is the Head. That capital organization is spiritually made up of Christ and the 144,000 members of "his body" and designated in the Scriptures under the symbol of "little flock" of sheep, which "little flock" share the Kingdom with Christ Jesus, their Head. The faithful men of old who are to be princes in the earth must wait until that capital organization is completed, and then they shall be granted life everlasting. The "other sheep", called "Jonadabs", and which shall form the "great multitude", are gathered unto the Lord Jesus Christ, and ultimately all of these, together with all in God's organization, must be of one fold. "And other sheep I have, which are not of this fold: them also I must bring, and unto my voice will they hearken [*Rotherham*], and there shall be one fold, and one shepherd."—John 10:16.

All must be in full harmony, and therefore all must be right and entitled, as provided by Jehovah God, to receive life everlasting through Jesus Christ. These "other sheep", that will form the "great multitude", must be gathered unto the Lord and hidden in the antitypical ark, that is to say, under the protection of the Lord's organization, and must there abide in safety until the wrath of God be passed, which wrath is expressed at Armageddon. All the members of the "great multitude" must and do receive a test, and they must prove their integrity before they receive life and the right to life everlasting.

By faith God's servants now see that the antitypical ark, that is, the Lord's capital organization, has been builded up; that Christ Jesus, the Head thereof, is on his throne of authority and has gathered to himself his associates, the members of "his body"; that before him are now gathered all the nations of earth for judgment; and that the Lord is now separating the people by putting his opponents on one side and the obedient ones on the other side, the opponents being designated as "goats" and the obedient ones designated as his "sheep". This is the time of God's "strange work" being done in the earth, when his name and his kingdom are being declared by his witnesses in accordance with his expressed will. (Exodus 9: 16) That "strange work" is about completed, and when it is completed the "other sheep" will have been gathered. What next?

Antitypical Deluge of Fire

God promised that the earth should not again be destroyed by water. (Genesis 9: 15) He has plainly warned, however, that the world shall be destroyed by fire, the "fire of his jealousy" or anger. (Zephaniah 3: 8; 2 Peter 3: 7) Jesus says: "And as it was in the days of No'e, so shall it be also in the days of the Son of man." "Even thus shall it be in the day when the Son of man is revealed." (Luke 17: 26, 30) The demons, under the command of the chief of demons, Satan the Devil, had in Noah's day completely overrun and debauched all the human race aside from Noah and his family. Likewise today the demons, under the influence, power and control of the Devil, now influence and control all the nations of the earth aside from those who have taken their stand firmly on the side of THE THEOCRACY. The small number who have turned away from demonism, and who are turning away, and who have faith in God and his kingdom and take their stand on the side of THE THEOCRACY, have the promise to be hid in the place of safety. The nations of the earth, both the rulers and the people who fail or refuse to believe in God and Christ, are blind to the truth of God's purposes. They are in complete darkness and are oblivious to what is about to befall the world. (Isaiah 60: 2) A like condition existed in Noah's day, 'until the flood came and destroyed them all.' The nations of the earth today are gathered into the "valley of concision" (Joel 3: 14, *margin*), and shortly the battle of that great day of God Almighty will be fought, and in that battle Christ Jesus shall completely destroy all creatures and things that are opposed to The THEOCRATIC GOVERNMENT. As Jehovah God will then exhibit his supreme power, all creation shall know that he is the Almighty God, "whose name alone is Jehovah."—Psalm 83: 18.

Survivors

The survivors of Armageddon will be made righteous. The Lord's "other sheep", who have sought righteousness and meekness as God has commanded, and who are hidden under the Lord's organization, the antitypical ark, will be carried over from the old world that shall suffer destruction and shall find their place in the "new earth, wherein dwelleth righteousness". (2 Peter 3: 13) Jesus states that his "other sheep", who will form the "great multitude", shall be righteous and that these go into eternal life, having received from him, as God's Executive, the right to life. — Matthew 25:46.

The "great multitude", then made up of those who are brought over from the present wicked world and who find life in the new world of righteousness, will be righteous in the sight of God. Those who will compose the "great multitude" will constitute the first ones on earth since perfect Adam that will qualify to carry out the divine mandate to fill the earth. Only righteous men and women can carry out that mandate. It follows, therefore, that the Lord's "other sheep", who will, by His grace, form the "great multitude", are to be the ones to fulfill that marvelous mandate, and that they receive their commission of authority to do so from Christ Jesus, the King, the One who ministers life everlasting to human creatures. In the prophetic picture Noah represented Christ Jesus, and his sons pictured the "other sheep" of the Lord. Noah had no children after the flood. That was prophetic. Noah's sons began to bring forth children after the flood. They pictured the "great multitude", and hence that part of the prophecy must be fulfilled by the "great multitude" after Armageddon.

The "other sheep" of the Lord, which form the "great multitude", could not be gathered to the Lord until after Christ Jesus came to the temple in 1918. Nor could his "other sheep" qualify to carry out the divine mandate until after such have been put to the test and approved and made righteous, and receive the full benefit of the ransom sacrifice; and this could not be fully accomplished until after Armageddon. Therefore from the time of perfect Adam in Eden until the "great multitude" is completely formed, no human creatures have appeared on the earth that could meet the requirements to carry out the divine mandate.

As the earth was clean and entirely free from sin when Jehovah God first issued or stated the mandate to "multiply and fill the earth", even so the earth must be clean and free from wickedness and under the complete control and supervision of the righteous Overlord, Christ, before the divine mandate can be carried out. Under the control of the righteous Overlord the following prophecy must be fulfilled, because such is the purpose of Jehovah, to wit: "Drop down, ye heavens, from above, and let the skies pour down righteousness; let the earth open, and let them bring forth salvation, and let righteousness spring up together. I the Lord have created it." "For thus saith the Lord that created the heavens; God himself that formed the earth and made it; he hath established it, he created it not in vain, he formed it to be inhabited; I am the Lord, and there is none else."—Isaiah 45:8, 18.

Satan corrupted the earth. (Ezekiel 28: 16-18) Satan and his wicked organization must be removed before the earth can be filled with righteous men as the mandate directs. The supervision of the work of filling the earth God has not committed to angels, but he has committed the supervision and control thereof to the Lord Jesus Christ, who has purchased all those who will compose the "great multitude" and whom he gathers unto himself according to the will of Jehovah. (Hebrews 2: 5-9) "Light is sown for the righteous." (Psalm 97: 11) Christ Jesus, the Redeemer and King, is the One who bears that light to righteous men in the earth. He is the great Morning Star. "I Jesus have sent mine angel to testify unto you these things in the churches. I am the root and the offspring of David, and the bright and morning star." (Revelation 22: 16) The "other sheep" of the Lord, in obedience to God's commandment, now seek righteousness, and they flee to God's organization for protection; and they must flee and take their position on the side of the Lord before Armageddon, and there find refuge, and, doing so, they are now permitted to see and to enjoy the light of God's Word now revealed concerning them.

Time

The "other sheep" of the Lord must prove their faith by their works, and hence must stand a test of faithfulness and must maintain their integrity toward God, before they receive life and the right to life at the hands of Christ Jesus. In the prophetic picture concerning the cities of refuge, which pictured the Lord's capital organization, the wrongdoer was permitted to flee to and find refuge in that city (organization) and, being there, he must be fully obedient to the rules or regulations of that city or organization. He must remain within the bounds of the city; and if he was found outside of the bounds he was subject to immediate execution; as it is written: "He shall abide in it [the city of refuge] unto the death of the high priest, which was anointed with the holy oil. . . . But after the death of the high priest the slayer shall return into the land of his possession."—Numbers 35:25-28.

As to the fulfillment of that prophetic picture, the antitypical high priest is the Lord Jesus Christ, and all the members of his body are counted in as of the high priest. (Revelation 1:6; 20:6; 1 Peter 2:5-10) All such have been anointed with the holy oil, that is to say, the holy spirit of God, and which anointing of the last members of the priesthood takes place after the coming of Christ Jesus to the temple. "The death of the high priest" means the end of the high priesthood or priestly class on the earth, which takes place when the "strange work" of the Lord has been completed, that is, when the preaching of "this gospel of the kingdom" is done. The "death of the high priest" is the change of all who form the priestly or the spiritual class from human to spirit, as stated in 1 Corinthians 15:49-52. Until the members of the royal priesthood are complete the "other sheep" find refuge in the antitypical city of refuge, that is, under the organization of Christ Jesus, and *must there remain and work* in harmony with the Lord's organization. They must remain in that condition until Armageddon has ended. Those "other sheep" are not justified to life until the royal priesthood is fully completed. The "other sheep", having proved their faith and obedience and maintained their integrity toward God prior to and during Armageddon, thereafter receive the full benefit of the ransom sacrifice and are justified and are granted life everlasting with the right to life on earth forever thereafter. Then such are righteous, and they possess the qualifications to carry out the terms of the divine mandate to multiply and fill the earth.

One who has sought the Lord, who has exercised faith in God and in Christ Jesus and has fled to Christ and found refuge under his organization, and who then withdraws himself from that protection by forsaking the Lord, that person suffers everlasting death. Therefore it is after having fled to Christ for refuge that the "other sheep" are tested as to their faith and obedience; and meeting the terms of that test and maintaining their integrity towards the great THEOCRACY, all such receive life and the right to life. The great and crucial time comes at the battle of Armageddon, and if those "other sheep" have obeyed the Lord's commandment to seek righteousness and meekness they have the promise of being hidden and protected by the Lord through that flood of fire.—Zephaniah 2:2-4.

As the sons of Noah were carried through the flood in the ark, even so the "other sheep" of the Lord are carried through the fiery flood of Armageddon in the antitypical ark, that is, Christ's organization. They pass over from the world of wickedness to the new world, wherein dwells righteousness. (2 Peter 3:13) For a more detailed consideration see *Riches,* chapters two and three; and *Salvation,* chapter seven; also *The Watchtower* 1938, pages 307-314.

It therefore clearly appears from the Scriptures that the time when the divine mandate begins to be carried out is after Armageddon, when the earth has been cleansed of wickedness. 'As it was in the days of Noah, so shall it be in the days of the Son of man.' (Luke 17:26-30) All these things pertaining to Noah, his sons, and the flood were typical and were recorded for the admonition of those upon whom the end of the world has come.—1 Corinthians 10:11.

Childbearing

Marriage and childbearing are the means of carrying out the divine mandate to multiply and fill the earth. This mandate was given to righteous man and woman in Eden, and even so the mandate must be carried out by righteous men and women on the earth after Armageddon and who have received righteousness and the right to life from God, by Christ Jesus. (Romans 6:23; John 17:3) From Eden to Armageddon it was not possible for the divine mandate to be carried out, for the reason that no righteous human creatures appeared on the earth qualified to carry it out. The divine mandate is unto life everlasting to righteous human creatures on the earth. After Armageddon only righteous human creatures will be on the earth. The Devil and all his wicked agents will then be completely disposed of, so that no wicked influence can be exercised over those of the earth. Then the children that are conceived in righteousness and brought forth in righteousness, by righteous parents, will be righteous, and they, being righteous, in due time will be qualified to participate in carrying out the divine mandate. It was God's command that righteous Adam and Eve, without any hindrances or limitations such as set forth in the seventh chapter of First Corinthians and at First Timothy 5:11-14, should bring forth children. Clearly the men and women of the "great multitude", because of their being righteous and having the right to life, will marry and bring forth children without hindrance. They will occupy and fill the place that no human creature could fill from the time of Eden to the Kingdom.

Should men and women, both of whom are Jonadabs or "other sheep" of the Lord, now marry before Armageddon and bring forth children? They may choose to do so, but the admonition or advice of the Scriptures appears to be against it. Being married before Armageddon and both continuing faithful and surviving Armageddon, their marital relationship shall continue and persist after Armageddon. They receive their right to life everlasting after Armageddon, and after receiving that right to life their children then born would be born in righteousness. Children born before Armageddon of parents who had not received the right to life would not be born with the right to life, but would have the privilege of choosing to serve God and Christ and live if they prove their integrity. Otherwise stated, each one must individually choose and individually be tested.

The prophetic picture seems to set forth the correct rule, to wit: The three sons of Noah and their wives were in the ark and were saved from the flood. They did not have any children, however, until after the flood. They began to have children two years after the flood. (Genesis 11:10, 11) No children were taken into the ark and none were born in the ark, and hence none were brought out of the ark. Only eight persons went in and eight came out of the ark. (1 Peter 3:20; Genesis 8:18) That would appear to indicate it would be proper that those who will form the "great multitude" should wait until after Armageddon to bring children into the world.

It is only a few years from the time the "other sheep" are gathered to the Lord until Armageddon. That entire period is a time of much tribulation, concluding with the greatest tribulation the world will ever have known. Speaking of that very time, Jesus says: "Woe unto them that are with child, and to them that give suck in those days!"—Matthew 24:19, 21.

That would seem to mean that those who would have infants during Armageddon would suffer much greater woe because of their care of the same. It is a great responsibility to rear children and care for them now, and it would be far greater difficulty to care for them during the time of the great tribulation upon the earth.

Jonadabs, or "other sheep" of the Lord, who are now married and have children are blessed with the great opportunity and the obligation to teach their children the Word of God and to show them the necessity of choosing the Lord and taking their stand on the side of THE THEOCRACY and being fully obedient and loyal to the Kingdom. There is but one possible way their children can find protection and blessing, and that is by choosing the Lord and fleeing to the Lord and serving him. Each one must choose for himself.

Satan knows that his time is short, and therefore he is desperately trying to turn all persons, including the children, against God. (Revelation 12: 12, 17) Therefore Satan influences public officials and others to compel little children to indulge in idolatrous practices by bowing down to some image or thing, such as saluting flags and hailing men, and which is in direct violation of God's commandment. (Exodus 20: 1-5) That is why in the last few years rules are made and enforced in the public schools compelling children of the Jonadabs, who are in a covenant to do God's will, to indulge in the idolatrous practice of flag-saluting and hailing men. It is the influence of that subtle foe, the Devil, that has brought about this state of affairs, and now Satan's agents cause great persecution to be brought upon the parents and the children who insist on obeying the commandments of God. This makes the way of both parents and children more difficult, but at the same time it puts a test upon them and affords them the opportunity to prove their faith and obedience and to maintain their integrity toward God and his King. Both parents and children who are now consecrated to do the will of God should rejoice in their privilege of bearing the reproaches that fall upon them because of their faithfulness to THE THEOCRACY under Christ. If they remain true and faithful to the Lord amidst such great persecution and opposition they may be fully assured that the Lord will shield and protect them and give them his great blessing through Armageddon and take them over into the new world to serve with joy forever. The Lord never forgets or forsakes those who are faithful to him.

Unto Life

The divine mandate to multiply and fill the earth was to life of the creature. That mandate to the "great multitude" is to life of the children they shall bring forth. The parents, then being justified and having the right to life which Adam lost and which Jesus bought for obedient men, will, by the Lord's grace, transmit life and the right to life to their children. There is no Scriptural reason why such child should ever die as a child. If that child, upon coming to the point of knowing good and evil, and hence to the point of individual, personal responsibility, then continues to obey God, it will live. God's law never changes, and it is written: "The soul that sinneth, it shall die."

(Ezekiel 18:4) If a descendant of the "great multitude", after reaching personal responsibility, willfully sins, then he would suffer the penalty, not as a child, but as a grown-up. Righteous parents will bring up their infants in righteousness, and these will receive the blessings of the Lord. Such children will not inherit the result of Adam's sin. There would be no reason to conclude that the child would die as a child. But if as a grown-up person it becomes a willful lawbreaker of THE THEOCRACY it will suffer destruction, from which there is no resurrection. — Jeremiah 31:29, 30; Hebrews 6:4-6.

The promise to those of the "great multitude" is that they shall bring forth children, not for trouble and pain, but to have joy. "There shall be no more thence an infant of days, nor an old man that hath not filled his days: for the child shall die an hundred years old; but the sinner, being an hundred years old, shall be accursed. They shall not labour in vain, nor bring forth for trouble; for they are the seed of the blessed of the Lord, and their offspring with them." —Isaiah 65:20, 23. (This prophecy is considered at length in the book *Salvation,* chapter seven.)

His Organization

The "great multitude" will be of God's universal organization, which is designated under the symbol of "Jerusalem". "Zion" is the name of God's capital organization, which organization executes and carries out God's purposes. The Lord's "other sheep" do not become a part of the universal organization of the Lord until they receive life and the right thereto, and then they will constitute the "great multitude". Note that Jesus says to them: "And other sheep have I which are not of this fold: those also I must needs bring, and unto my voice will they hearken, and there shall come to be one flock, ONE SHEPHERD." — John 10:16, *Rotherham.*

Christ Jesus is the Shepherd, and all who receive life from Jehovah by and through Christ Jesus must of necessity come into his flock, that is, be one of his obedient, loyal and faithful servants. All of that flock must be and shall be righteous. No unrighteous creature will be permitted therein. Since God has committed to Christ Jesus all power in heaven and in earth and to bring all creation under Christ Jesus, he is the "one Shepherd", and all of that flock, being obedient to righteousness, as Jesus states, "shall hear my voice," which means all such will be subject to and be obedient to the Lord. Jehovah, the Almighty God, is the GREAT SHEPHERD thereof: "One God and Father of all, who is above all, and through all, and in you all."—Ephesians 4:6; Psalm 23:1, *Am. Rev. Ver.*

The "other sheep" of the Lord, which are now being gathered by the Lord and which shall after Armageddon form the "great multitude", shall be of the general flock of the Lord, therefore of the general organization of the Lord, and must be righteous and in full accord with the Lord. The "great multitude" will therefore constitute a part of Jehovah God's organization that shall participate in carrying out Jehovah's purpose, and they shall likewise be under the supervision of Christ Jesus, the King and Shepherd of the flock. Their children will be conceived in purity and brought forth in righteousness. Note the expression by the faithful apostle: "Nevertheless we, according to his promise, look for new heavens and a new earth, wherein dwelleth righteousness."—2 Peter 3: 13.

The "new heavens" is The Christ, invisible to human eyes, and which rules the world in righteousness. The "new earth" is the organization upon the earth which is representative of the new heavens, and which carries out the commandments given by the new heavens.—Isaiah 65: 17-23. (See *Salvation*, page 333, and *Riches*, chapter eight.)

"John, dear, permit me to say just here that my heart is filled with joy, and I repeat the words of Mary: 'My soul doth magnify the Lord.' Appropriate to us now are the words of the Psalm: 'My heart shall

rejoice in thy salvation. I will sing unto
the Lord, because he hath dealt bountifully
with me.' (Psalm 13:5,6) Now I can appreciate the vision had by the apostle of
Christ Jesus when he heard the joyful shout
of the 'great multitude': 'Salvation to our
God, which sitteth upon the throne, and
unto the Lamb.'"

"I join with you, Eunice dear, in that
song now. The purpose of Jehovah in building his marvelous organization continues to
clarify in our minds. But let us in our next
study ascertain, if possible, why the Lord
has shown us such great favor in revealing
to us these marvelous truths now."

CHAPTER 11

FOR HIS NAME'S SAKE

"He saved them for the sake of his name, to make known his mighty power."
— Psalm 106:8, *Rotherham*.

JEHOVAH'S name is above all things and of supreme importance. His name stands for everything that is good, pure, righteous and holy. His name stands for his purpose toward all creation. His name means that he is the Maker of heaven and earth and the Giver of life to all that shall ever have life. Centuries ago Satan challenged the name of the Most High, and from then till now Satan has brought great reproach upon the name of Almighty God. Under the influence of that wicked one the masses of human creation have defamed Jehovah's holy name. The Almighty God is long-suffering and permits the wicked to pursue their course of wickedness until his own due time to exalt and vindicate his name. The day of complete vindication of Jehovah's holy name is nigh. During the

long period of time from the rebellion to
the time of vindication Jehovah has shown
his favor to those who obey him, and this
he has done primarily for his own name's
sake.

Men of the world generally think more
highly of themselves than they ought to
think. Many Christians likewise fall into
the same error. Men usually take themselves too seriously and magnify their own
importance. Rulers and leaders amongst the
nations receive some power, authority and
honor from the people and for that reason
become highly exalted in their own mind.
The religious leaders, although claiming to
serve God, do not give the honor and glory
to God's name that is due him, but they
take the honor and praise to themselves.
They scorn the counsel of Jehovah's Word
and put forward the counsel and tradition
of men in the place and stead of the Word
of God. They rule the religious organizations according to their own worldly wisdom and thus turn the people to themselves
and away from Almighty God. Jehovah has
permitted them to go on in their own way
of selfishness and has not hindered them in
their work which has reproached his name,
but in his due time, as God announces, he
will take notice of those who reproach his
name and will duly recompense them. Because the name of Jehovah is of the highest importance the redemption and salva-

tion of men is of secondary and far less importance. Therefore human creatures should learn to think of themselves as dependents upon the Lord.

When Saul of Tarsus was a member of the Sanhedrin, and a teacher of "the Jews' religion", he reproached the name of Jehovah God and the Lord Jesus Christ. But when he saw his great error he straightway faced about and devoted himself wholly and unselfishly to the service of God and Christ. Then he admonished his fellow followers of Christ Jesus in these words: "For I say, through the grace given unto me, to every man that is among you, not to think of himself more highly than he ought to think; but to think soberly, according as God hath dealt to every man the measure of faith." —Romans 12: 3.

Manifestly a man who has no faith in God and his Word cannot think soberly of himself. The greater a man's faith, the more he appreciates his relationship to the Creator.

Many Christians who have leaned to their own selfish understanding have come to the conclusion that God has called them to the heavenly calling because he needs them to operate the universe. In this they are very wrong. They swell up and exhibit their importance, but they appear ridiculous in the sight of the Lord. God selected the Israelites as his typical people for himself, to the exclusion of all other nations. The Israelites then regarded themselves as of very great importance and indispensable to the Lord. For this reason they fell easy victims to religion or demonism. They committed sins and forgot God; but when they repented and cried unto the Lord he heard them and returned them to his favor. Did Jehovah forgive them and receive them again into his favor because he needed them or because they were worthy? No; but he did so for his own name's sake. Jehovah's name was at issue, and for his name's sake he continued to be long-suffering toward his typical people and continued to show his mercy toward them. God addressed these words to the Israelites, and they apply with stronger force to all who have since made a covenant to do his will, to wit: "Then said I unto them, Cast ye away every man the abominations of his eyes, and defile not yourselves with the idols of Egypt: I am the Lord your God. But they rebelled against me, and would not hearken unto me: . . . But I wrought for my name's sake, that it should not be polluted before the heathen, among whom they were, in whose sight I made myself known unto them, in bringing them forth out of the land of Egypt."— Ezekiel 20: 7-9.

The Israelites time and again turned to religion, or demonism, amongst the heathen or non-Israelite nations whither they went: "But I had pity for mine holy name, which

the house of Israel had profaned among the
heathen, whither they went. Therefore say
unto the house of Israel, Thus saith the Lord
God, I do not this for your sakes, O house
of Israel, but for mine holy name's sake,
which ye have profaned among the heathen,
whither ye went. And I will sanctify my
great name, which was profaned among the
heathen, which ye have profaned in the midst
of them; and the heathen shall know that I
am the Lord, saith the Lord God, when I
shall be sanctified in you before their eyes."
—Ezekiel 36: 21-23.

God did not hinder the Israelites in
walking in the way of demonism or religion which was practiced by the heathen or
nations round about them, but when they
repented for their wrong course and turned
again to God and cried unto him he received them, not for their sake, but because
he had put his name upon them. The Israelites were God's typical people, and they
foreshadowed particularly the people who,
during the period of time from the apostles to the second coming of Christ, have
claimed to be followers of Christ Jesus
and have appeared and carried on their
work under the name of "Christendom".
Most of such persons have practiced religion contrary to the Word of God, and God
has not prevented them from doing so, but
has continued to work with those who do
show faith and obedience to the end that

he might bring forth a faithful "people for his name". At the appearing of the Lord Jesus at the temple in 1918 he judged his people and separated the approved ones from the others and sent forth these approved ones as witnesses to the name of Jehovah "that they [might] offer unto the Lord an offering in righteousness", to wit, the praise of their lips.—Malachi 3: 1-3; Hebrews 13: 15.

"Other Sheep"

It is the will of God that Christ Jesus now gather unto himself his "other sheep", and these are designated in the Scriptures as "persons of good-will" or "Jonadabs". Having purchased them with his own precious blood, the Lord now sets before them his message of truth to the end that those who hear and believe and obey him may seek him and find the way to life. This he does not do because of the importance of the human creatures who are his "other sheep", but he gathers them to himself because the name of Jehovah God is involved and the name of Christ Jesus is linked directly with the name of his Father. Therefore what God is now doing toward those of good-will is for his name's sake. Those who are saved and brought through the great tribulation of Armageddon will be so favored, not because of their own merit, but because Jehovah's name is involved, and

they will be saved "for his name's sake,
that he might make his mighty power to
be known". — Psalm 106 : 8.

"For His Name"

It was some time after Pentecost and the
coming of the holy spirit that the apostles
of Jesus Christ began to understand and
appreciate why God had made salvation
possible for men who obeyed him, and that
without regard to nationality. Up to that
time God had dealt with the Jews alone,
and the Jews thought salvation was for
them alone; but in this they were wrong.
When the gospel of the Kingdom was first
taken to the non-Jews there was for a time
some difference of opinion amongst the apostles as to the propriety of such. They assembled at Jerusalem and considered the
matter, and the holy spirit directed them,
and Barnabas and Paul declared that God
had wrought miracles amongst the non-Jews,
of which they were witnesses. Then others
at that meeting spoke: "And after they had
held their peace, James answered, saying,
Men and brethren, hearken unto me: Simeon
hath declared how God at the first did visit
the Gentiles [non-Jews], to take out of them
a people for his name. And to this agree the
words of the prophets; as it is written, After
this I will return, and will build again the
tabernacle of David, which is fallen down;
and I will build again the ruins thereof, and

I will set it up; that the residue of men
might seek after the Lord, and all the Gentiles, upon whom my name is called, saith
the Lord, who doeth all these things." (Acts
15: 13-17) Thus the Lord God made them
understand that he was taking out from
among obedient men *a people for his name,*
and this he was doing without respect to persons or nationalities.

The people so taken out from the world
for the name of Jehovah are the ones who become Jehovah's witnesses to declare his purpose and to make known his name throughout the earth immediately preceding the time
when God shows his power against the organization of Satan, which he will do at
Armageddon. This is exactly in harmony
with his declaration made to Satan long
centuries ago. — Exodus 9: 16.

Those who are thus taken out as a people for Jehovah's name must bear testimony to his name and must carry the Lord's
message concerning his name and his kingdom to others who will hear. All such faithful ones are Jehovah's witnesses, and the
work in which they are engaged is God's
work, which he designates in his Scriptures
as "his strange work" because that work
exposes the fallacy of religion and seems
"strange" to religious men. It is the people
of good-will toward God who hear the message, and who give heed thereto, and who
flee to the Lord for refuge and protection,

which they see they must do before the expression of God's wrath at Armageddon. These people of good-will are the "other sheep" of the Lord, who from that time onward until Armageddon faithfully do the will of God and who, doing so, shall in due time become the "great multitude". These are saved and commissioned by the Lord God through Christ Jesus to do certain work, not for their sakes, but for his holy name's sake. All honor and praise are due to Jehovah God; therefore it is written in his Word: "Give unto the Lord the glory due unto his name; worship the Lord in the beauty of holiness."—Psalm 29:2.

SIMEON PETER VISITS FIRST GENTILES

All persons whom the Lord God has used to bear testimony he has used for his name's sake. When Jehovah sent Moses into Egypt to lead the Israelites out of that land where they were oppressed he did so for his own name's sake. He took the Israelites out of Egypt to be used to bear testimony to his name. "And what one nation in the earth is like thy people, even like Israel, whom God went to redeem for a people to himself, and to make him a name, and to do for you great things and terrible, for thy land, before thy people, which thou redeemedst to thee from Egypt, from the nations and their gods?" (2 Samuel 7:23; 1 Chronicles 17:21) Having chosen the Israelites to be used as witnesses to his name, God wrought with them thereafter for his own name's sake.

All the holy prophets selected and sent forth by Jehovah were used to bear witness to his name. Those men, together with other faithful men of old, God selected and used for his name's sake, and for that reason all of them were witnesses for Jehovah and properly called "Jehovah's witnesses". Jerusalem was the typical holy city, and God put his name on Jerusalem, and there he caused Solomon to build the temple, and that was for his name's sake.—1 Kings 9:3.

When Jesus was sent of God to the earth he came, not to magnify himself, but to magnify his Father's name and to bear testimony concerning his Father. (John 5:43) Jesus did testify to and glorify his Father's name while on the earth. (John 12:28) The capital organization of Jehovah, composed of Christ Jesus and the 144,000 members of his body and known as "Zion" or the official organization of Jehovah, is builded up for the sake of Jehovah's name. God gave to Jesus twelve apostles, all of whom were faithful except one. Of the faithful ones Jesus says to Jehovah: "I have manifested thy name unto the men which thou gavest me out of the world: thine they were, and thou gavest them me; and they have kept thy word."—John 17:6.

All the members of "the body of Christ" are selected to bear witness to the name and kingdom of Jehovah before others. When God's servants are in trouble he brings them out of trouble for his name's sake, even as he saved his typical people for his name's sake.—Psalm 143:11.

The great issue or question for determination, and which is before all creation, is the name of Jehovah, the Almighty God. Who is the supreme and almighty One? The Most High, the supreme and all-powerful, is Jehovah. This great truth Satan disputes, and therefore the name of Jehovah must be vindicated, and it will be vindicated completely by Jehovah in his due time. Jehovah God is the fountain of life, and everyone who calls upon Jehovah's name has the opportunity to be saved from death; but no others will be saved from death. (Romans 10: 13) Jehovah has put his name upon his official or capital organization, and through the Head of that organization he grants life to all who call upon and who remain faithful and true to his name. (Joel 2: 32; Acts 2: 21) Not one of these brings any profit to God, even as Jesus said: "When ye shall have done all those things which are commanded you, say, We are unprofitable servants: we have done that which was our duty to do."—Luke 17: 10.

God is under no obligation to save anyone, but he does save those who call upon his name and who render themselves willingly in obedience to him; and he receives them and saves them for his own name's sake and for the vindication of his name.

Why does Jehovah permit his servants to be persecuted? Because of Satan's challenge to God that no man will remain faithful to God when put to the severe test. (Job 2: 5) Jehovah does not compel anyone to obey him, but he sets before man life and death and he permits man to choose, and those who choose to serve God and who put forth their very best endeavors to do so God saves for his name's sake and the vindication of his name. It is the Devil, the chief of demons, and his agents that persecute the servants of God because they declare the name of the Most High. It will be found that in nearly every instance those who persecute the witnesses of the Lord are religionists and practice religion; and this is further proof of the fact that religion is the instrument of the Devil to blind men and then to use those blinded ones to persecute the servants of Jehovah and Christ Jesus. — 2 Corinthians 4: 3, 4.

God Forgotten

The nation of Israel were the typical covenant people of God and were used by him to foreshadow his covenant people under Christ, and hence the Israelites are known as a typical people. That which came to pass upon Israel applies particularly to the present time, because we are now at the end of the world, and God makes known these truths to his faithful servants that they may receive comfort and have their hope strengthened. — 1 Corinthians 10: 11; Romans 15: 4.

In the days of the apostles Christianity grew and many persons became followers of Christ Jesus. Shortly after the death of the apostles an organization was formed which was labeled "the Christian religion". Later other organizations similar were formed and they operated under the name "Christian religion". These religious organizations spread throughout the nations, and many of the nations of earth accepted that "Christian religion" and claimed to be "Christian nations", and hence such nations have been known and are known as "Christendom". Because the nation of Israel fell away from God, the Lord God called them "backsliders", and in that the Israelites foreshadowed "Christendom" as she exists now upon the earth. Although claiming to follow Christ and to obey God, the so-called "Christian religion" organizations have become backsliders and have joined hands with political and commercial organizations to govern the earth. By his prophet Ezekiel Jehovah long ago described "Christendom", foretelling her course of action and the end thereof, and that He would make all know that he is Jehovah when he vindicates his holy name. (See book *Vindication,* in three volumes.)

The nations that have called themselves "Christian" or "Christendom" have been before the Lord Jesus the great Judge for judgment since the coming of the Lord Jesus to the temple in 1918. The undisputed facts show that all such nations called "Christendom" are now properly labeled as "backsliders", because not one of those nations now advocates or supports the kingdom of Jehovah God under Christ the King. On the contrary, all nations are against God and his kingdom and propose to rule the world by selfish men. The founders of the United States of America fled from religious persecution in Europe and located in

America, where they might worship God without hindrance. Being so thoroughly convinced of the right of man to worship God according to his own conscience, those founders of the nation wrote into the fundamental law of the land that no human power shall interfere with any person in the worship of Almighty God according to the dictates of his own conscience. For 150 years, approximately, the nation and the states composing the nation have recognized the right of every man to worship God according to his own conscience and the courts have so held repeatedly. In more recent years there has been an organized movement to interfere with and to persecute those who worship God in spirit and in truth by declaring the name and kingdom of Jehovah.

This has been particularly made manifest since the coming of the Lord Jesus, and this is to be expected according to the prophecies written aforetime. Since then in particular the religious, political, and law-making and law-enforcement bodies of the nation put the state above God, and by rules or laws attempt to compel the people to serve God contrary to their own conscience and contrary to Jehovah's Word, and thus to indulge in religious ceremonies which are against God's Word. Therefore in these nations all the true followers of Christ Jesus who insist on announcing the name and kingdom of God under Christ are hated. And why are they hated?

The religious, political and commercial rulers of the nations of "Christendom" hate the true servants of Jehovah because they proclaim his name and his kingdom. They have forgotten God. Love for God and his kingdom is not among them. Selfishness rules in the hearts of such men. By their words they claim to serve God, but they have no love for or devotion to him whatsoever. The present-day condition now existing amongst the nations called "Christendom" was clearly foretold in the scripture, written under inspiration from God, and which therefore is prophetic, to wit: "This know also, that in the last days perilous times shall come. For men shall be lovers of their own selves, covetous, boasters, proud, blasphemers, disobedient to parents, unthankful, unholy, without natural affection, trucebreakers, false accusers, incontinent, fierce, despisers of those that are good, traitors, heady, highminded, lovers of pleasures more than lovers of God; having a form of godliness, but denying the power thereof; from such turn away."—2 Timothy 3:1-5.

God's Judgment

Today the religious organizations have and exhibit a form of godliness and perform ceremonies, claiming to honor God, but in fact they are against God and against his kingdom. The command of the Lord's Word to those who love righteousness is that they should turn away from such religious organizations, have nothing to do with them, and flee to Christ and to his kingdom. Many persons of good-will toward God, and who have been associated with such religious organizations, are now following the Scriptural advice and are shunning religion, fleeing therefrom, and diligently seeking the Lord. All persons of good-will toward God will now turn away from religion and flee to the kingdom under Christ, and this they will do and must do before Armageddon if they will be saved. Each one must choose for himself.

All those who have professed to serve God and Christ and who now oppose God and his kingdom under Christ are "wicked" within the meaning of the Scriptures. In the near future the wrath of Almighty God against all wickedness will be expressed at Armageddon in the most devastating tribulation the world will ever have known. (Matthew 24: 21) In that tribulation all the wicked shall go down to destruction. Mark, therefore, the judgment of ALMIGHTY GOD written against all nations and peoples that have forgotten God, to wit: "The wicked shall be turned back unto Sheol [hell, or, oblivion], even all the nations that forget God."— Psalm 9:17, *Am. Rev. Ver.*

God commands all of his covenant people, including those who are in an implied covenant with him, as follows: "Thou shalt have no other gods before me. Thou shalt not make unto thee any graven image, or any likeness of any thing that is in heaven above, or that is in the earth beneath, or that is in the water under the earth: thou shalt not bow down thyself to them, nor serve them: for I the Lord thy God am a jealous God, visiting the iniquity of the fathers upon the children unto the third and fourth generation of them that hate me."
—Exodus 20: 3-5.

The so-called "Christian nations" compel many to hail men and honor men, contrary to the Word of God and contrary to the fundamental law of the United States of America, and thus the state is placed above or superior to the law of Almighty God. Concerning such it is written: "If we have forgotten the name of our God, or stretched out our hands to a strange god; shall not God search this out? for he knoweth the secrets of the heart."—Psalm 44: 20, 21.

They cannot hide their wrongful acts from Almighty God, and in due time he will recompense them for their wrongdoing. "Because they regard not the works of the Lord, nor the operation of his hands, he shall destroy them, and not build them up."—Psalm 28: 5.

The nations of "Christendom" have forgotten what Jehovah did at the flood in Noah's day. Immediately following the flood God announced his "everlasting covenant" concerning the sanctity of human life. (Genesis 9:5, 6) All the nations of "Christendom", without exception, have forgotten God's everlasting covenant, and concerning this it is written: "The earth also is defiled under the inhabitants thereof, because they have transgressed the laws, changed the ordinance, broken the everlasting covenant. Therefore hath the curse devoured the earth, and they that dwell therein are desolate; therefore the inhabitants of the earth are burned, and few men left."—Isaiah 24:5, 6.

Today "Christendom", so called, sets a specific time in which prayers are offered for world peace and prosperity, while at the same time such nations indulge in the slaughter of many innocents. Inside the religious organizations men with their lips speak words appearing to honor God and yet at the same time indulge in persecuting every one who faithfully proclaims the name of God and his kingdom under Christ. Such persecutors have forgotten God, and therefore he says to them: "Wherefore the Lord said, Forasmuch as this people draw near me with their mouth, and with their lips do honour me, but have removed their heart far from me, and their fear toward me is taught by the precept of men: therefore, behold, I will proceed to do a marvellous work among this people, even a marvellous work and a wonder: for the wisdom of their wise men shall perish, and the understanding of their prudent men shall be hid. Woe unto them that seek deep to hide their counsel from the Lord, and their works are in the dark, and they say, Who seeth us? and who knoweth us? Surely your turning of things upside down [by putting the state and men above God, and man's law above God's law] shall be esteemed as the potter's clay: for shall the work say of him that made it, He made me not? or shall the thing framed say of him that framed it, He had no understanding?" (Isaiah 29: 13-16) "The way of a fool is right in his own eyes." (Proverbs 12: 15) "There is a way which seemeth right unto a man, but the end thereof are the ways of death."—Proverbs 14: 12.

The nations called "Christendom" now bitterly persecute the servants of Almighty God who declare his name and his kingdom, and these have forgotten that God has builded his own organization for his honor and vindication of his great name and that he has declared that he will avenge his people at Armageddon against those who have persecuted his servants.—Luke 18: 7, 8.

The nations that call themselves "Christian" or "Christendom" have forgotten Jehovah the Almighty God and his kingdom, and have made silver and gold, the work of men's hands, their gods, and have turned to idolatrous worship. "The idols of the nations are silver and gold, the work of men's hands." (Psalm 135: 15, *Rev. Ver.*) The public press furnishes the following information: "The United States Treasury has hidden away in secret strongholds $22,200,-000,000 in gold. . . . Students of men and events are wondering what good the hoarded gold will do to the United States." (San Diego *Sun,* March 5, 1941, edition)

God foreknew and foretold: "All hands shall be feeble, and all knees shall be weak as water. They shall also gird themselves with sackcloth, and horror shall cover them; and shame shall be upon all faces, and baldness upon all their heads. They shall cast their silver in the streets, and their gold shall be removed: their silver and their gold shall not be able to deliver them in the day of the wrath of the Lord: they shall not satisfy their souls, neither fill their bowels; because it is the stumblingblock of their iniquity." (Ezekiel 7: 17-19) Millions of persons who now have no gold are undernourished and are unable to get the necessities of life. Some religious institutions have hoarded a tremendous amount of silver and gold. It will do them no good.

The law which Jehovah first announced to his typical, covenant people, and which law never changes, now applies with even stronger force, if possible, to "Christendom", because the nations of "Christendom" have had the advantage of God's published Word, coupled with the experiences of the nations that have gone before and have perished. Concerning such Jehovah God's law is: "And it shall be, if thou do at all forget the Lord thy God, and walk after other gods, and serve them, and worship them, I testify against you this day that ye shall surely perish. As the nations which the Lord destroyeth before your face, so shall ye perish; because ye would not be obedient unto the voice of the Lord your God."— Deuteronomy 8: 19, 20.

"And the light of a candle shall shine no more at all in thee; and the voice of the bridegroom and of the bride shall be heard no more at all in thee; for thy merchants were the great men of the earth; for by thy sorceries [demonism] were all nations deceived."—Revelation 18: 23.

Never in all time has there been so much wickedness in the earth as at the present. It is even worse than in Noah's day. Wickedness has sprung up like the grass in the springtime. All nations of "Christendom" are against God and all servants of his kingdom they hate because such servants proclaim his holy name. Therefore says the Lord: "The great day of the Lord is near, it is near, and hasteth greatly, even the voice of the day of the Lord: the mighty man shall cry there bitterly." (Zephaniah 1: 14)

"When the wicked spring as the grass, and when all the workers of iniquity do flourish, it is that they shall be destroyed for ever." (Psalm 92:7) God will destroy them for ever, and "the name of the wicked shall rot".— Proverbs 10:7.

Vindication

The name of Jehovah shall endure forever. "His name shall endure for ever: his name shall be continued as long as the sun; and men shall be blessed in him: all nations [that survive] shall call him blessed." (Psalm 72:17) "Blessed is the nation whose God is Jehovah, the people whom he hath chosen for his own inheritance." (Psalm 33:12, *Am. Rev. Ver.*) There is but one nation embraced within that scripture, and that is God's "holy nation" which he has chosen for his name's sake.—1 Peter 2:9, 10.

Soon the "princes" and the "great multitude" will be associated with that holy nation in carrying out Jehovah's purpose. The THEOCRATIC GOVERNMENT is of greatest importance because that government will fully vindicate Jehovah's name. God ministers salvation to life through that government, and there is no other possible means of obtaining life everlasting. (Acts 4:12) Salvation is not for the wicked at any time. "Far from the lawless is salvation, for thy statutes have they not sought." — Psalm 119:155, *Rotherham.*

Those faithful men of old will soon be resurrected as perfect human creatures and shall be the "princes [or visible rulers] in all the earth". (Psalm 45:16) They have had their test and proved their faithfulness, and their coming forth to life everlasting will be a vindication of Jehovah's name.

The people of good-will toward God who are the "other sheep" of the Lord are now fleeing from religion and from every part of Satan's organization and taking their stand on the side of THE THEOCRACY and are joyfully proclaiming the name and kingdom of the Most High. Continuing faithful and maintaining their integrity, they will be carried through Armageddon in the antitypical ark, Christ Jesus, and will form the "great multitude" that shall receive life everlasting on the earth and carry out Jehovah's purposes concerning them. That "great multitude" will be a vindication of Jehovah's name. All these saved and blessed ones will be proof positive that Satan is the father of lies and that all his servants do his bidding and shall share his fate.

The Christ, the "princes" in the earth, and the "great multitude", all in due time forming "one fold", shall constitute the official servants of the Most High God and shall forever proclaim the glory of his name. All people that shall thereafter live shall sing the praises of the Most High.—Psalms 66:4; 89:15, 16.

The children that now hear the name of Jehovah and learn of his kingdom have set before them the greatest privilege that has ever come to children at any time. Many of these children are fleeing to the Lord's organization and taking their stand firmly on the side of his kingdom and are declaring his name, and the hope set before them is that they shall be members of the "great multitude" and dwell forever in righteousness upon the earth. Blessed is the child who is now a witness to the name of Jehovah and his kingdom. It was prophetically written concerning such children: "Out of the mouth of babes and sucklings hast thou ordained strength, because of thine enemies; that thou mightest still the enemy and the avenger."—Psalm 8:2.

Such children are now calling on the name of the Lord and are faithfully and effectively bearing testimony to his name and to his kingdom. Because Satan knows that such children will be a vindication of and forever a praise to Jehovah's name Satan desperately tries to keep the children away from God. He invents all kinds of ceremonies and schemes to turn them away from God. Parents that love God and love their children will now be diligent to instruct their children and lead them in the way of

God and his King, as the Scriptures direct
that they must do.

Contrast

God's prophetic Word draws a sharp con-
trast between the rule by selfish, ambitious
men and the rule of the world under The
THEOCRATIC GOVERNMENT: "When the righteous are in authority, the people rejoice; but
when the wicked beareth rule, the people
mourn."—Proverbs 29: 2.

The physical facts well known to all today make the understanding of the above
scripture quite easy. Every nation of earth
today is marked with great mourning. Many
of the nations are at war, and great sorrow
and suffering are upon all the people thereof. Other nations are fearful that they will
soon be plunged into war, and they are
mourning because of what they see coming upon the earth amongst them. In many
of the nations famine stalks through the
land and pestilence feeds upon the people.
The shroud of death is about all people,
and great is their sorrow and mourning. In
view of these facts let each one who thinks
soberly determine who rules the world today, "the wicked" or "the righteous"!
There is but one answer to that question.

Christ Jesus is the great and righteous
One, upon whose shoulder the government
of everlasting peace and righteousness shall
rest. (Isaiah 9: 6, 7) Under his rule there

will never be another war. (Isaiah 2:4)
Under the reign of the great THEOCRACY
death shall be destroyed and there shall be
no more crying or sorrow. (Revelation 21:4;
1 Corinthians 15:25, 26) The THEOCRATIC
GOVERNMENT will be ruled in righteousness
by its righteous King; and the earthly representatives thereof, or visible rulers, will
do justice to the people and carry out the
righteous judgments of Almighty God. (Isaiah 32:1) Under the rule of THE THEOCRACY,
therefore, all the people will rejoice, and
that righteous rule shall stand forever and
will be a monument to the supremacy and
righteousness of Jehovah and will be an everlasting vindication of his holy name. Those
who desire to live and who love righteousness will now give heed to the admonition
of the Lord and flee to that Kingdom.

Jehovah is now doing "his work", and he
is causing his name to be declared and is
making known the blessedness of his kingdom in order that all persons of good-will
toward him may choose to serve him and
live.

"My choice, Eunice dear, is to serve Jehovah and his THEOCRATIC GOVERNMENT, and
I now declare aloud that I make this my
choice. Will you choose to go with me?"

"Dear John, I would choose nothing else.
I delight to join with you now to speak aloud

and say, I too choose to serve Jehovah God and his kingdom under Christ. By His grace, we will serve him forever."

"Some sweet day, Eunice, we shall have some children and they will be greatly blessed. The prospect set before us is glorious. Seeing that God made the earth for righteous men, shall we in our next study learn if possible what Almighty God purposes toward beautifying the earth?"

CHAPTER 12

GLORIOUS EARTH

> "The earth abideth for ever."
> – Ecclesiastes 1:4.

THE ALMIGHTY GOD, whose name alone is JEHOVAH, created the earth by his Chief Officer, The Logos, who is Christ Jesus, the King of the THEOCRATIC GOVERNMENT. For his pleasure he created the earth, and in due time the earth and everything therein shall proclaim the praises of the great Creator: "Thou art worthy, O Lord, to receive glory and honour and power: for thou hast created all things, and for thy pleasure they are and were created."—Revelation 4:11.

Some persons, who have not understood the Scriptures, have said that the earth will be destroyed with fire. They have confused with the visible rule what the Scriptures say about the mundane sphere. That which God created, the literal earth, shall abide forever; and when his purpose concerning the earth is understood, then a keener appreciation can be had of his creation and of his purpose.

God created the earth to be the everlasting home of perfect men and women. The earth was created for righteous men and women, and God's creature Adam and his wife Eve were righteous when God placed them in Eden, the paradise of God on the earth. When man became a rebel, and therefore unrighteous, God put him out of Eden and said to him: "Cursed is the ground for thy sake." That did not mean a curse of the creation of earth. But it did mean that the ground where man must go and raise his living was in such condition that it would operate ultimately for his good. Since that time men have been required to fight thorns, weeds, thistles and suchlike, and their work has been laborious. That labor has been a blessing to man in this: that the Lord thus has provided employment for man's body and mind, and it was God's loving-kindness that provided for that employment.

Today many parents, including some who claim to be entirely devoted to Jehovah and his kingdom, bring up their children in idleness. They proceed upon the theory that the children should play and do no work. Such is contrary to God's law, and works a great injustice and injury to the children. An idle brain and idle hands lead to disaster. All parents who appreciate the goodness of God, and who love their children, will see to it that each child from the time it is able to walk and talk is assigned to some profitable work. Every day the child should perform its assigned task, and should be taught to love it. The parents should explain to the child why work is good for it. The child should be taught to be clean in mind and clean in body. Filthiness and idleness are abominable in the sight of God. The parents are responsible to teach their children that which the Lord has pointed out that they must do.–Ezekiel 16:49; 2 Corinthians 7:1; Ecclesiastes 10:18.

All creatures mentioned in the Bible with approval are those who have been workers. God and Christ work, and all of his approved creatures must avoid idleness and busy themselves in profitable matters. The child Jesus said: "I must be about my Father's business." (Luke 2:49) When some criticized him for working, the answer was: "My Father worketh hitherto, and I work." (John 5:17) All of God's approved creatures must work.

Men have asserted their claim of ownership of the earth, and, being selfish and ambitious, they have attempted and continue to attempt to control the earth and everything in it. No man or organization of men owns the earth or any part of it: "The earth is the Lord's, and the fulness thereof." (Psalm 24: 1) When men come to appreciate the fact that Almighty God made the earth for perfect men and that he is the owner of it and he provides it for those who love and serve him, then they will rejoice.

The "princes" and the "great multitude" and their children will proceed under the direction of the Lord to beautify the earth. That will be a task of joy, and all who have to do with that work will rejoice. It is the will and purpose of God that such work shall be done, and it will be a great privilege for righteous men and women to be permitted to have a part therein. The Almighty God says: "The heaven is my throne, and the earth is my footstool." (Isaiah 66: 1) All things are his.

And then Jehovah adds: "And I will make the place of my feet glorious." (Isaiah 60: 13) Everyone who believes the Lord, therefore, may be fully assured that in due time there will be complete harmony between everything in the universe, both heaven and earth, both invisible and visible rule, and that all creation shall together declare the praises of the Most High.

The capital organization of which Christ Jesus is the Head, and which is called "Zion", is the habitation of Jehovah God, which he has created, builded up and chosen for himself: "For the Lord hath chosen Zion; he hath desired it for his habitation." (Psalm 132:13) As the people of the earth carry on their work under the direction of the great THEOCRACY all the people will sing the praises of Jehovah and his King. (Psalm 48:1, 2) When the earth has been made a place of glory as the place of Jehovah's feet, then everything that hath breath shall praise Jehovah and all inanimate creation will in some manner join in that praise.—Psalm 150:6.

JESUS THE CARPENTER'S HELPER

Peace

There shall be no wars amongst the peoples of earth under the Theocratic rule. The people will dwell together in peace, and all work together to the honor of the Creator. All their tools and instruments will be used to beautify the earth and to produce that which is needed, and the great and righteous King will see to it that all the tools will be employed in peace and to the praise of the Most High: "And he shall judge among the nations, and shall rebuke many people; and they shall beat their swords into plowshares, and their spears into pruninghooks: nation shall not lift up sword against nation, neither shall they learn war any more."—Isaiah 2: 4.

The great King shall rule in righteousness, and peace shall have no opposition: "Of the increase of his government and peace there shall be no end, upon the throne of David, and upon his kingdom, to order it, and to establish it with judgment and with justice, from henceforth even for ever. The zeal of the Lord of hosts will perform this."—Isaiah 9: 7.

Righteousness

The rule of the world by the Lord Jesus Christ, him who is the King of the great THEOCRATIC GOVERNMENT, will be a rule of righteousness, and everything that continues to live must be in complete harmony with and obedient to the King. Where there is perpetual peace righteousness must rule. Says the prophecy of God: "Give the king thy judgments, O God, and thy righteousness unto the king's son."—Psalm 72:1.

Christ Jesus is the King, and the "princes" in the earth are the sons of the King. Throughout the reign of the King he will cause blessings to flow down upon the people. That will be a conclusive proof and demonstration that when the righteous rule the people rejoice: "He shall come down like rain upon the mown grass; as showers that water the earth. In his days shall the righteous flourish; and abundance of peace so long as the moon endureth. He shall have dominion also from sea to sea, and from the river unto the ends of the earth."—Psalm 72:6-8.

Righteousness, mercy, peace and truth will prevail throughout the earth and shall all work together in exact unison. Only those who love righteousness and do righteousness will live, and all these will live to the glory of God. The prophet therefore speaks for all such these words: "I will hear what God the Lord will speak: for he will speak peace unto his people, and to his saints: but let them not turn again to folly. Surely his salvation is nigh them that fear him; that glory may dwell in our land. Mercy and truth are met together; righteousness and peace have kissed each other. Truth shall spring out of the earth; and righteousness shall look down from heaven. Yea, the Lord shall give that which is good; and our land shall yield her increase. Righteousness shall go before him, and shall set us in the way of his steps.''—Psalm 85: 8-13.

Those who will form the "great multitude" cannot wait until after Armageddon to "seek righteousness", but all persons who will form that "great multitude" must begin now and continuously seek righteousness and do that which is right as they learn it. Such is the positive command of Jehovah to those who are of good-will who now have fled to the antitypical city of refuge. (Zephaniah 2: 1-3) The Jonadabs cannot content themselves by saying: "I will engage in the work of advertising Jehovah's name and his kingdom and I will go from place to place and do so, and that will be sufficient." In doing that they are only partially right. In neglecting other important things they are wrong. The Jonadabs must 'study to show themselves approved unto God' and learn what is contained in his Word, and therefore what is his will concerning them, and to seek righteousness, that they may know what is right and righteous, and then do that which is right. They must remember that now they are on trial, and they must comply with the rules of the "city of refuge", that is to say, the organization under Christ Jesus. The King is now gathering to himself those who will form the "great multitude", and such will be commissioned to fill the earth, and such persons must learn righteousness before Armageddon. "For the righteous Lord loveth righteousness; his countenance doth behold the upright."— Psalm 11: 7.

The eyes of Jehovah now are upon those who have sought refuge in his capital organization, and these must learn righteousness and do righteousness. Because Christ Jesus loves righteousness and hates iniquity God has blessed him and exalted him to the highest place. (Psalm 45: 7) It follows that all who are gathered into his fold and become his children must learn righteousness before being made any part of that fold. Complete righteousness comes when the Lord grants life with the right thereto, but before that the creature must do that which is right.

The "great multitude" will be the blessed people of the Lord on the earth, forming a part of his one great fold. (John 10: 16) They shall hear and obey the voice or command of the Lord. They must begin to learn obedience and righteousness from the very time that they turn away from religion and flee to the "city of refuge". Learning obedience and righteousness, they have the promise of being made a part of the "great multitude", and then they shall have opportunity to participate in beautifying the earth, to the glory of the Creator.

To hear the "joyful sound" or command of the Lord means to ascertain the will of

God and to obey his commandments. It is such that will receive the blessings of the Lord: "Blessed is the people that know the joyful sound: they shall walk, O Lord, in the light of thy countenance. In thy name shall they rejoice all the day: and in thy righteousness shall they be exalted."–Psalm 89: 15, 16.

Complete obedience will be required of the children born to those of the "great multitude", and all such will fear and obey the Lord with joyful hearts, if they are granted life everlasting: "But the mercy of the Lord is from everlasting to everlasting upon them that fear him, and his righteousness unto children's children; to such as keep his covenant, and to those that remember his commandments to do them. The Lord hath prepared his throne in the heavens; and his kingdom ruleth over all." (Psalm 103: 17-19) "Blessed are they that keep judgment, and he that doeth righteousness at all times." (Psalm 106: 3) It is easy to see that such creatures will rejoice in the beautifying of the earth as God brings it up to glory and beauty.

The Lord, foreseeing the blessings he will send to earth, commands all persons of good-will to walk now in the way of goodness and learn righteousness. "The righteous shall inherit the land, and dwell therein for ever." (Psalm 37: 29) "That thou mayest walk in the way of good men, and keep the paths of the righteous. For the upright shall dwell in the land, and the perfect shall remain in it." —Proverbs 2: 20, 21.

To those who will compose the "great multitude" this admonition is now given, and those who obey that admonition shall be recipients of the promised blessings: "Let the people praise thee, O God; let all the people praise thee. Then shall the earth yield her increase; and God, even our own God, shall bless us. God shall bless us; and all the ends of the earth shall fear him." (Psalm 67:5-7) The promise that the earth shall yield her increase is proof that work in the earth will be a great joy to those of the "great multitude", and they will greatly rejoice in having some part in beautifying the earth.

Paradise

Eden was a paradise, and in that paradise God placed his perfect man. Manifestly the earth shall become as Eden for the home of righteous and perfect human creatures. That being Jehovah's purpose, which is shown by what he prepared for perfect man in Eden, we may rest assured that his purpose will be carried out and that the habitation of man shall become the paradise of God made for righteous men. The earth was made for the pleasure of the Creator; and seeing that he takes pleasure only in that which is right, righteous and glorious, it follows that the earth shall be all to his honor and praise. This is "his footstool", and he will make it a place of glory forever. The following prophecy seems also to indicate as much: "And they shall say, This land that was desolate is become like the garden of Eden." —Ezekiel 36: 35.

Tree of Life

In Eden God caused "to grow every tree that is pleasant to the sight, and good for food; the tree of life also in the midst of the garden". (Genesis 2: 9) Every tree in that garden, with but one exception, was for perfect and righteous man. Man had permission from God to eat of the fruit, but with one exception, "the tree of the knowledge of good and evil." That being the only exception, it clearly appears that if Adam had remained true and obedient to God, and thereby proved his integrity to God, in Jehovah's due time Adam would have been permitted to partake of the tree of life and live forever.—Genesis 2: 16, 17.

It appears that the "tree of life" stands as a guarantee of life everlasting to all those who maintain their integrity toward God, and, when tried and approved by the Lord, such will be granted life everlasting. To those called to "the heavenly calling", and who maintain their integrity and receive the Lord's approval, the promise is that they shall partake of the tree of life. "To him that overcometh will I give to eat of the tree of life, which is in the midst of the paradise of God." (Revelation 2:7) "Blessed are they that do his commandments, that they may have right to the tree of life, and may enter in through the gates into the city." —Revelation 22:14.

Since the "great multitude" will be a part of the one fold or flock of which Christ Jesus is the good Shepherd, and since the members thereof must be righteous and shall be granted life everlasting on the earth, it must be that each one will, by the grace of the Lord, be permitted to eat or partake of the tree of life and live forever. That being God's express purpose for his perfect man in Eden, it must be for his perfect human creatures whom he will use to carry out his mandate to "fill the earth". Partaking or eating of the "tree of life" clearly means that such righteous human creatures will "live forever" on the earth in peace and joy to the vindication and honor of Jehovah's name. (Genesis 3:22; Revelation 22:14) "The tree of life," therefore, appears to stand as a symbol or guarantee of life everlasting to those who receive the final approval of Jehovah and to whom Christ Jesus administers life everlasting.

General Resurrection

The Scriptures use the words in the divine mandate, "multiply and fill the earth."

The original word which is translated "fill" is also translated "replenish" and may be applied either way. It does not appear that the "great multitude" will carry out that mandate to fill every nook and corner of the earth, but that they will, under the direction of the Lord, produce a population that will reasonably populate the earth. The people on the earth today are numbered by the millions, but there is room for many more. When all the earth is made glorious many more persons can well be on the earth than now are known to be there or ever have been. There appears to be no Scriptural authority for saying that the wicked will ever be resurrected. Hence the wicked, cleared out at Armageddon, will not come back, and that will be true with reference to the wicked in all times past. God knows who will be obedient to him, and he has in memory those who have a tendency for righteousness, and these shall be awakened out of death in his own due time.

All of the human race have been born unjust or unrighteous (Romans 5:12); and only those who while alive have proved their integrity to God have been counted by him as justified. Concerning the resurrection it is written: "There shall be a resurrection of the dead, both of the just and unjust." (Acts 24:15) "The unjust" here mentioned clearly means those persons who have lived and died but who have had no opportunity of learning of the ransom sacrifice, and therefore no opportunity of accepting the same. God knows the heart condition of each and every one, and those that are thus awakened out of death will come forth unjust or imperfect. Millions of such have died and are in the memory of God. They were not wicked, but manifestly persons of good-will. They could have no part in forming the "great multitude", because the Lord did not begin to gather his "other sheep", who will form the "great multitude", until after his coming to the temple in 1918.

God's Word announces that he has "appointed a day" in which the dead will be awakened out of death and given a full opportunity or trial for life. (Acts 17:31; John 5:29) Such is the general resurrection of the dead. None of those thus awakened out of death can have part in carrying out the divine mandate, because they will be unjust at the time of being awakened out of death, and the mandate can be carried out only by those who are righteous and possess the right to life. Those who are awakened in the general resurrection must learn of the ransom sacrifice, believe and accept the Lord Jesus Christ as the Redeemer, and then enter upon trial, and must prove their integrity and successfully pass the test which the Lord will impose, before receiving the right to live. At that time they will be justified, because being justified by the Lord means receiving the right to life. By the time that those of the general resurrection are justified the "great multitude" will have carried out the divine mandate concerning the filling or replenishing of the earth.

Concerning those that shall have part in the general resurrection of the dead and thus be given an opportunity for trial and receipt of life from the Lord, these words were uttered by him: "And Jesus answering said unto them, The children of this world marry, and are given in marriage: but they which shall be accounted worthy to obtain *that world,* and the resurrection from the dead, neither marry, nor are given in marriage; neither can they die any more: for they are equal unto the angels; and are the children of God, being the children of the resurrection."—Luke 20: 34-36.

In verse 35 above quoted, in the phrase "to obtain that world, and the resurrection from the dead", the word "world" manifestly means the "world without end" (Ephesians 3: 21), which world without end will be the paradise of God that shall result to the whole earth during the thousand-year reign of Christ. (Revelation 20: 4, 6) At that time there will be no further need to marry and bring forth children, because that work will have been accomplished. (For a more complete consideration see *Salvation,* page 354.)

It is only justified, righteous men and women that will carry out the divine mandate and have part in beautifying the earth. It seems clearly to appear from the Scriptures that it is the purpose of Jehovah to use the "great multitude" to carry out his mandate to replenish the earth and that this work will be done and completed during the Millennial reign of his King. It also appears that within that time God will make the earth a place of glory and beauty and a fit place for the everlasting dwelling of righteous human creatures, which creatures shall be forever to the glory and honor of the name of the Most High.

"Eunice, these studies together have been a great blessing from the Lord for us. Gratitude to God is in my heart, and my desire is to serve him and his King forever. We cannot stop here, but we must continue our studies of the Bible and thus diligently seek righteousness and meekness. Here are a number of books which have evidently been provided by the Lord to enable persons of good-will, such as we are, to learn where in the Bible we may find his marvelous truths. By his grace, we will avail ourselves of the privilege of learning more of his truth and how to serve him faithfully. And now I should like to walk out over the land and meditate upon some of the things that we have learned. It is a time for meditation, and I am sure you will be glad to join me.''

The two walked silently through the fields and stopped again by the great tree on the river bank where they had some time before discussed their future plans. Seated at this vantage point they had a general view of the landscape.

''John dear, look at that beautiful scene beyond the river and up the mountainside. I am reminded that several months have passed since we made our sacred agreement right here. It is now autumn season, the time of harvest, and which the Scriptures speak of as a time of joy. The trees and their foliage bespeak the glory of God. Mark the colors, yellow and brown, of the foliage of the maple and sweet gum, the chestnut and the other trees on that mountainside. This being the harvest time also suggests the ingathering, the time when the Lord is gathering unto himself those who shall be of his 'other sheep' and the 'great multitude'. Mark the evergreen amongst that beautiful foliage which adds color and beauty to the scene, and which evergreen symbolizes life everlasting. Now the Lord has graciously shown us that there is set before us the prospect of life everlasting upon the earth. And what a glorious prospect! The earth is now beautiful, but that beauty is nothing to compare with the glory and beauty that shall be upon the whole earth during the reign of Christ the King."

"How true are your words, Eunice. We have walked through these broad fields many times, during our childhood days. But to-day these fields mean much more to us than ever before. They belong to the Lord, and He will beautify them for his children. Armageddon is surely near, and during that time the Lord will clean off the earth everything that offends and is disagreeable. Then, by His grace, we shall begin our life with a greater vision and prolonged joy. Now we see by faith the great THEOCRACY, and we are wholly and unreservedly committed to that righteous government. From now on we shall have our heart devotion fixed on THE THEOCRACY, knowing that soon we shall journey for ever together in the earth. Our hope is that within a few years our marriage may be consummated and, by the Lord's grace, we shall have sweet children that will be an honor to the Lord. We can well defer our marriage until lasting peace comes to the earth. Now we must add nothing to our burdens, but be free and equipped to serve the Lord. When THE THEOCRACY is in full sway it will not be burdensome to have a family. Then we may often walk through these broad fields, amidst the beautiful forests and environments, and will walk with our beloved children by our side and tell them all we have learned from the Lord, and together we shall all be quick to obey our Leader and our King, Christ Jesus."

"I recall, John dear, that your father will be asking you now for your decision as to the future and what you shall do."

"Eunice, my decision is made. I shall shun politics, religion, and commerce, and I shall avoid the cities and the enticements thereof. We are both committed for ever to THE THEOCRACY. Our present duty is plain. We must now be witnesses to the name of Jehovah and to his kingdom. Our place of residence we can continue with our parents as long as it is God's will to have it so, and we shall engage in the service of the Lord by carrying his message of his name and kingdom to others who are hungering for righteousness. We shall, by God's grace, be forever the children of the great King, and our children shall be forever with us, subjects of the Kingdom. We have found refuge in Christ, and we shall abide here until the blessed time when we may have part in fulfilling the divine mandate. We shall not see each other very often for a time, but we can have like thoughts every day of the glorious prospect that is set before us. I suggest that our first thought on awakening each morning be expressed by repeating these words of the psalmist: 'Bless the Lord, O my soul: and all that is within me, bless his holy name. Bless the Lord, O

my soul, and forget not all his benefits.'
—Psalm 103:1, 2.''

To this young man and young woman all
the environments now appeared more beautiful. The birds in the trees seemed to be
singing the praises of Jehovah and His
King. So, hand in hand, they joined their
voices with them in song and gave thanks
to God for His manifold blessings bestowed
upon them.

INDEX

NOTE: Numbers refer to pages; Roman numerals, to paragraphs.

369

bride of Christ, 282, I
built upon the Rock, Christ
Jesus, 133, II-136, I
one body, 136, III
Cities of Refuge, execution for
not abiding within,
307, II-309, I
God's provision and law
concerning, 196, II
not to be left till high priest's
death, 307, II; 308, I
represented God's
organization, 197, I; 199, I
City, Abraham looked for
God-built, 79, I; 163, I, II
prepared for the faithful
of old, 174, I; 175, I
symbolizes governing
organization, 76, I
Coming of Christ, faithful
remain dead until,
142, I, II; 149, II
marks beginning of reign,
127, II
to temple, 146, I, II; 151, I;
186, II; 187, I
Companionship of parents with
children, 275, I-276, I
Consecration, John and Eunice
decide on, 215, I-216, II
stand taken for Kingdom
by, 203, I
step of obedience, 216, III
Covenant, between Logos
and God, 102, II
Jesus by baptism
symbolized his, 92, I
Jesus faithfully completed
his, 107, II; 108, I
made with disciples for
Kingdom, 124, I
made with Jesus for
Kingdom, 124, I
parental teaching of
children included in,
265, II; 267, I-270, II
Creation, The Logos,
God's first, 53, I
of God is perfect, 110, I
of perfect man for the
earth, 55, II
Cross, Jesus' tree not a,
98, I, II
taken up to follow Christ,
128, I
Curse upon ground for man's
sake, 287, I; 349, I

D

David, faith and faithfulness
of, 170, II
not in heaven, 176, II
Day that Adam died, 59, I
Dead, judged at Christ's
appearing, 149, I, II
resurrection of Christian,

140, II; 141, I
until Christ's coming,
142, I, II
Where are they? 70, I-74, II
Death, baptism into Christ's,
130, I
Devil retains power of,
62, I; 70, III
disobedience brought,
51, I, II; 50, I-50, I
everlasting to forsakers
of God, 307, II; 309, I
inherited, 62, I; 69, I;
70, I; 110, I
no more of children under
divine mandate,
315, I; 316, I
of high priest typical,
196, II; 199, I; 307, II; 308, I
to be no more, 76, I; 153, I;
154, I; 345, III
Deborah, 168, II
Demonism, 67, II; 341, I
Demons, active today as in
Noah's day, 252, II, III;
303, I, II
men yielded to, 66, I
origin of the, 64, I
Denial of self to follow
Christ, 128, I
Destiny, 62, I
Destruction, for the wicked,
121, III; 241, II; 341, II
of the Devil, 195, II
why the delay of Satan's,
59, I-60, I; 218, I-220, II
Devil, blinds unbelievers,
157, III; 158, I
brings woes upon people,
150, I-III; 195, I, II
brought reproaches upon
faithful of old, 243, I
meaning, 55, I; 242, I
men deny existence of,
157, III; 158, I
murderer, 62, I; 70, III; 160, I
not immortal, 70, III
slanders, reproaches God's
name, 242, I
Devil's Organization, Babylon,
67, II; 211, I
Divine Mandate, Adam
disqualified to carry out,
289, II-290, I
canceled toward Adam and
Eve, 289, II; 291, II
carried out after
Armageddon, 310, II-312, I
carried out only by righteous
persons, 287, III; 290, I;
297, I; 299, II; 311, I
carried out under righteous
overlord, 288, I; 297, I;
298, II; 306, I
does not apply to spiritual
class, 298, I, II

INDEX   ·   375

organization, 206, II
which is above, 158, II
Jesus, angel announces
  birth of, 88, II
as child at temple, 91, I
baptism of, 92, I; 114, II
begins preaching
  Kingdom, 92, II
birth of; by virgin,
  90, I; 111, I
by blood purchased
  mankind, 116, II-120, I
charged with treason,
  97, I; 98, I
covenants to do God's
  will, 92, I
finished assigned work on
  earth, 96, II; 102, II
laid aside spirit life for
  human, 108, I; 111, I-112, II
made lower than angels,
  108, I; 111, I
magnified Jehovah's
  name, 329, III
nailed to tree, why? 98, I, II
now spirit unseen,
  179, II; 231, I, II
presented purchase price
  in heaven, 114, II-119, I
previously spirit in
  heaven, 96, II; 97, I
resurrected as spirit,
  114, II; 119, I
testimony to birth and
  human life of, 33, II, III
John, pictured God's people
  banished, 187, II
Revelation given to
  apostle, 152, I-153, I
John Alden, at home and
  school, 9, I; 10, I-13, III
decides on Bible study
  with Eunice, 21, 1-23, I
discusses course in life
  with Eunice, 13, III-20, II
finally decides on God's
  service, 367, I, II
John Baptist, less than least
  in Kingdom, 177, I
witness for Jehovah, 223, IV
Jonadab, 200, I, II
Jonadabs, must now seek
  righteousness, 355, I
people of good-will, 200, I
Joshua, 166, I
Joy, of John and Eunice at
  truths, 318, III; 319, I
set before the Lord,
  104, I; 105, I
Joyful Sound, 238, II; 356, III
Justification, by faith,
  129, I; 130, I; 162, II, III
of "other sheep" after
  Armageddon, 308, I-310, II
of those in general
  resurrection, 362, I

to life, 120, I
to those maintaining
  integrity, 361, I

K

King, Christ Jesus the
  anointed, 42, I; 92, II;
  97, I; 98, I; 180, I
Kingdom, a spirit
  organization, 122, I
begins to function,
  148, V-153, I
completed before
  perfecting faithful
  of old, 175, III; 176, I
covenant for the, 124, I
emphasized as above all,
  93, I-96, I
Jehovah's organization, 122, I
like hidden treasure, pearl
  of price, 104, I-109, I
membership of, 101, I
most prominent in the
  Bible, 42, I; 75, I; 77, I; 99, I
not of this world, 97, I
of God is among you, 92, II
of paramount importance,
  99, I; 103, I-108, II
of priests, 112, IV-114, I
prepared for, inherited
  by sheep, 187, I
selection of associates
  for, 127, II
Knowledge, beginning of,
  261, I-263, I
of God and Christ, unto
  life, 124, II; 125, I; 261, I
pure, in Bible, 27, I
way to life, 27, II

L

Last Days, 221, II; 335, I
Law, covenant with Israel,
  82, I-83, II
given to safeguard from
  religion, 83, I
Law of God, is truth,
  26, I; 33, III; 39, I
recorded in Bible, 21, I; 29, II
Life, everlasting covenant re,
  196, II; 197, I; 338, I
power given to Christ
  Jesus to administer, 301, I
Life Everlasting, by obedience,
  60, I
fixed rules for entering
  way to, 124, II-128, I
gift of God by Christ,
  74, II; 119, II-121, I
God provides means for,
  70, I; 74, III; 110, I; 121, II
on earth to those
  consecrating now, 205, I
order of granting creatures,
  176, I-178, II; 301, I; 302, I

pictured Christ Jesus and
body, 293, II; 294, I; 297, I
sons of, could not fulfill
mandate, 299, II
survived Flood,
67, I; 78, I; 161, I
warned of God's
purpose, 235, I
Nurture, 257, I; 274, I, II; 280, II

O

Obedience, essential to
life everlasting, 203, I
learned by suffering,
139, II; 140, I
parents should teach
children, 280, II
proves love, 139, I; 270, II
required (of children)
for life everlasting,
280, I, II; 357, I
required of great
multitude, 356, I
Obedient, salvation for, 202, II
**One Hundred Forty-four
Thousand,** and One King-
dom members, 101, I; 301, I
members of Christ's
body, 136, III; 140, II; 189, I
Ordained Minister, 226, I, II
Ordination of God to preach,
37, I; 225, II-226, II
"Other Sheep," become part
of universal organization,
316, II-318, I
do good to witnesses, 147, I
gathered after 1918, 305, II
must gather into ark,
301, I-302, II; 304, I; 310, I
must now seek, abide in
refuge city, 307, I-308, I
not of little flock,
148, I, II; 184, I-185, I
parents and children of, 275, I
place on earth provided for,
186, I; 187, I; 205, I; 281, I
protected during Armaged-
don, 280, II; 294, I, II; 302, I
Overlord of Earth, Satan since
Eden, 157, I, II; 218, I; 241, II
the righteous, invisible,
241, II; 306, I; 307, I

P

Parables, of hid treasure and
pearl of price, 104, I-109, I
why Jesus spoke in, 103, II
Paradise, God's purpose to
have all earth a,
287, I, II; 358, II
of Eden, 285, I; 287, I
Parents, blessed by teaching
children, 266, I
diligent to obey God
respecting children,

279, I; 280, II
exemplary, win
children's respect, 276, I
first inform selves to
teach children, 265, I, II
in the Lord, to be
obeyed, 256, II-258, I
obligated to teach children,
257, I; 258, I; 264, II
punished by State for teaching God's law, 272, I-273, II
teach children to be
witnesses, 277, I-278, I
under covenant
to teach children,
267, I-272, II; 274, I, II
Peace, amid strife and
turmoil, 195, I, II
of Christ's government
without end, 153, I;
156, I; 345, III; 353, I
righteousness with
rule of, 353, II-354, II
Pearl of price, 105, I-109, I
People for His Name, become
Jehovah's witnesses,
326, I-327, II
separated from religion, 324, I
Perfect, faithful of old
made, 175, II-178, II
Jehovah's work is, 287, II, III
Permission of wickedness,
59, II; 60, I; 320, I; 321, I
Persecution, flight from
religious, 9, I; 333, I
God will avenge, 339, I
in all nations, 249, I-250, I
in United States,
250, II; 252, I
not by Christians,
but by religionists,
244, I-250, II; 331, II
Peter, identifies Jesus as
Rock or Stone, 134, II
not pope nor church's
foundation, 136, I
Poor in spirit, 93, I-94, II
Praise to Jehovah by all
creation, 351, III; 368, I
Prayer, Bible guides to
proper, 25, I; 95, I, II
for Kingdom, 42, I
for peace, 338, II
Preach, anointing to,
37, I; 209, III; 225, II
Prince, chief ruler
among men, 180, I
of this world, Satan, 157, II
Princes, get life after
completion of capital
organization, 301, I
in all the earth, 181, I; 182, I
resurrected as perfect, 343, I
shall rule in justice,
156, I; 182, II; 345, III
sons of King, 353, II; 354, I

John and Eunice Decided to Subscribe for

As John said, on page 214 herein, THE WATCHTOWER is published TWICE A MONTH, on the 1st and 15th. The excerpt therefrom which he read, on pages 208-213, will manifest to you why John and Eunice wanted this 16-PAGE MAGAZINE as a regular visitor and companion—to aid them in studying the Bible and to see the unfolding of its prophecy in modern events and to be led in the way that leads through this dark valley of the shadow of death and unto life as children of God's kingdom.

The subscription rate is $1.00 a year ($1.50 in foreign countries), for 24 issues. Mail your subscription to

WATCHTOWER, 117 Adams St., Brooklyn, N. Y.